DATE DUE

The Minister's Desk Book

The Minister's Desk Book

Lowell Russell Ditzen, D.D.

PARKER PUBLISHING COMPANY, INC.

West Nyack, N.Y.

PRINTED IN THE UNITED STATES OF AMERICA

B & P

Dedication

To Eleanor Davies Ditzen
with appreciation, admiration and love

Introduction

What may be of merit in this book will be due to the thinking and experience of a wide circle of America's most competent clergymen in churches large and small. I have made of course many of my own suggestions, but when I think of the quantity of materials received from hundreds of churches and the counsel I have had from many of our country's finest church administrators, I sometimes feel I've been little more than an editor.

A few years ago a publisher convinced me that my varied experience in the ministry, from small rural churches to large urban churches, had fitted me to discuss some of the varied problems faced by the modern clergyman. That book, on church administration, plus a subsequent one written for Prentice-Hall, Inc., entitled, *Handbook for the Church Secretary,* have led to many associations with religious leaders concerned about competent church administration.

My present work as director of the National Presbyterian Center in Washington, D.C., has, in more recent years, given me contact with far-flung churches throughout our country. Also some teaching at Wesley Seminary, and American University in Washington, D.C., has widened contacts with both theological students and mature church administrators, who are concerned with making their ministry effective. Through these relationships I have become increasingly aware of the modern pastor's need for guidance in the area of church administration.

The claims on the twentieth century minister are so diverse and demanding that his resources may be nearly exhausted when he comes to the mechanics of preparing an agenda for his Official Board, or dealing with a staff problem or a committee meeting. Any tools that will increase his efficiency in the deportment of modern church administration, I know, from long experience, can be helpful.

The limitations of space in this volume prohibit full discussion of the minister's role as a preacher, prophet, or priest. Few will deny that these are of higher worth to the cause of Christ than whether or not the Sunday morning bulletin happens to be free from typographical errors, or the files of correspondence in the church office are arranged for efficient use. On the other hand, one of the roles of the "minister" is that of "ad-minister," and if there is inattention to the prosaic details of church management, the major ends of the Christian ministry may be undercut. The horse, rider, battle, and then finally the kingdom were lost "all for the want of a horseshoe nail!"

Many of the materials offered as illustration in this volume are given to stimulate the reader rather than as final guides for a specific church. Our congregational situations vary so greatly that no one detailed plan on any specific item may be suitable for all. Both broad ideas and specifically detailed suggestions are to be adapted for local use.

My debt is great to some two hundred and fifty clergymen, carefully selected for their known skills as administrators and vital religious leaders. I asked them to give me programs and procedures that had been found useful in the building of their congregations. They did so with generosity and enthusiastic responsiveness. In each instance I asked permission to use the material which they shared, but without specific recognition of them or their church. Again, there was whole-hearted assent, with the realization that we ministers need to help each other. If in any instance I have used material from any source where such approval has not been granted, it is completely unintentional.

In instances where a title of a church is used I have written: "Christ Church." In speaking of the official governing body of the local church, the title "Official Board" has been used. In certain instances where our denominations will have more than one board overseeing the local congregational life, such as with the Presbyterian Church, I have designated "Session," "Board of Deacons," and "Board of Trustees." However, because the materials are intended for every denomination and for the whole gamut of our churches, whether large or small, inter-city, suburban or rural, I have refrained as much as possible from using denominational terms such as "vestry," "consistory" or a number of others.

If a reader feels that some illustrative material used in this volume must come from city churches with large congregations and budgets, and therefore does not apply to a smaller situation, I can attest that I have tried to be sensitive to every church situation. That illustration has been selected from ten to more than a hundred possibilities, and can be adapted in many ways to a particular church.

The first church I served had a membership of fifty souls. It was a great step forward when we obtained a duplicating machine, which I operated myself. Yet I recall that some of the most constructive programs instituted in that smaller church came from studying the emphases and literature of a larger church in the area. In almost all instances there was an adaptation of the idea or the program to our immediate situation. Creativity is not limited to our more established churches. Some of the most sensible and creative answers to administrative problems, I've found in the newer and the mission churches which are seeking to be relevant. Many such are included in this volume.

If this book saves one consecrated clergyman a bit of time or offers suggestions which may assist him and other church officers in a more effective ministry to the people under their care, and above all, for the cause of Christ, I, and many others whose heart and hand are contained herein, will feel rewarded.

LOWELL RUSSELL DITZEN, D.D.

Contents

CHAPTER   PAGE

1. THE MINISTER AS AN EFFECTIVE ADMINISTRATOR 1

The Necessity for Administrative Competence in the Twentieth
    Century Church   1
Ways to Develop Administrative Skills   2
Importance of bylaws of the church.

2. THE OFFICIAL BOARD 11

How to Select Church Officers   11
    Qualifications and duties of official board members. Inform-
    ing congregation of its duties. Functions of board of deacons
    and members. Installation and ordination of officers.
Organizing the Board   19
    Importance of more detailed organizational charts. Roster
    of committee members and committee functions. Admin-
    istrative manuals.
Preparing for Board or Committee Meetings   35
Conducting the Meetings   37
    Types of pastoral reports. Financial reports.
Agenda and Minutes   41
    Necessity for agenda and meeting minutes. Types of agenda.
    Meeting minutes—forms and types.
How to Make Committees Function Effectively   49
    Helpful outlines of functions of committees. When specific
    committee duties are assigned. Form of letter for greeters

2. THE OFFICIAL BOARD (*continued*)

*committee personnel. Special types of communications to
committee personnel.*
Developing the Vital Church 55
*Long-range planning committee techniques. Evaluation re-
ports. The benefits of retreats. Special problems for committee study. A commentary on the function of such a staff-
personnel committee.*

3. ADMINISTRATION OF THE CHURCH STAFF 67

How to Determine the Need for Additional Staff Personnel 67
A specific form of recommendation for the staff.
The New Staff Member 72
*The job description should be adequate. Duties of church
administrator. Checking of references. Interviewing techniques for new personnel. Informing applicant of details of
employment conditions. How to introduce the new staff member to his work. Relationship of the personnel committee
to the staff member. Personnel committee counseling with
staff members. Periodic review of individual performance
standards.*
Supervision of the Staff 83
*Staff meetings, worship, social affairs. Paper on staff rela-
tionships. Staff meeting agendas. Organization of the annual
staff conference. Typical office work schedule. Relationship
of the staff members to the congregation. Office hours and
general deportment of staff members. Statement of employment regulations and policies. Weekly schedule of events.*
Examples of Job Descriptions of Principal Staff Positions 96
*The minister and assistant ministers. A simplified outline.
Organist, choirmaster. Director of Christian education. Administrative assistant. Business and office manager. Secretaries. Sextons. Housekeeper and kitchen personnel.*
Volunteer Staff Members 105

4. THE CHURCH PROPERTY 107

House and Grounds Committee 107
Periodic Inventory and Appraisal 108
Annual Maintenance Inspection 108
Principles of Effective Property Management 108
Established rules for care of church property.
Types of Insurance Protection 110
Care of Furnishings and Equipment 110
Snow plows and lawn mowers. The organ. Heating system. Church kitchen. Woodwork. Stained-glass windows. Rugs, carpets, hangings. Choir robes. Vestments. Communion service.
The Minister's Study and Office 114
Equipment and furnishings of the study. Files for the minister.
The Church Office 116
Lighting and ventilation. Proper desks and equipment. Types of machines. Handling of the mail. Correspondence. Files for the church office. Various forms and supplies. Telephones. Problems between staff members. Supply closet. Machine room.

5. THE SANCTUARY AND CHANCEL 127

Preparation for public use. Uses for holy rites. Information sheet for weddings. Baptisms—General procedure. Funerals. Pastoral guideline leaflets for general distribution. A helpful form for accumulating funeral information. The Lord's Supper. Functions and procedures of chancel committee. Procedure for communicants at chancel rail. The head usher. Good ushering means a richer spiritual experience for worshipers. Ushers' meetings. Ushering assignment follow-up. The atmosphere for worship.
Special Rooms and Equipment 161
Care of Memorials and Special Gifts 171
Rules Regarding the Use of Church Property 171

6. NEW BUILDING PROJECTS 173

Initial Studies   173
The Building Committee   174
The Architect   175
The Builder   176
The Fund Raising   176
Ceremonies and Dedications   177

7. CHURCH FINANCES 180

The Annual Budget   180
The Every Member Canvass   185
What to do after EMC Sunday.   Specific instructions for district EMC captains.
Expressing Appreciation for Pledges   192
Education in Stewardship   194
Educating the congregation on stewardship.   Education with pastor's leadership.   Forms re stewardship for new members. Education in self-giving for the congregation.
Dedication of Gifts and Pledges   199
Church Office Financial Records   200
Monthly Report to the Official Board   200
The Annual Audit   203
Principles of Budget Control   204
Special Gifts and Memorials   204

8. THE MUSIC DEPARTMENT 206

The Music Committee   206
Organization and functions of "Council of Music."   Prime purposes of music committee.
The Organist and Choirmaster—Job Descriptions   208
Care of Organ   210
Soloists and Multiple Choirs   211
The Choir Guilds   214
Summer Choirs   214
Hymns and Congregational Singing   215

9. PUBLICITY AND PUBLIC RELATIONS 217

The Public Relations Committee   217
Local Facilities   217
Pastoral Letters   218
Bulletin Boards and Signs   218
Letterheads, Postcards and Other Types of Correspondence
      Material   219
Church Publications   220
      *The Sunday bulletin. A church magazine. The annual direc-
      tory. Annual reports. Sermons. Departmental publications
      and notices. Special leaflets and brochures.*

10. THE MAINTENANCE OF CHRISTIAN EDUCATION 227

The Christian Education Committee   227
Recruitment and Training of Teachers   228
Records That Are Meaningful   231
Teaching Materials   234

11. THE INDIVIDUAL CHURCH MEMBER 237

The Outreach Program of the Church   237
      Contacting new members moving into community.
Inviting and Receiving New Members   240
Integrating the New Member into the Church Life   242
The Pastoral Relationship to Each Member   243
The Older Church Member   244
The Sick and Hospitalized Member   245
Congregational Programs   246
      Basic principles for congregational programs.

INDEX 249

1

The Minister as an
Effective Administrator

Our churches, whether they are located in rural or urban areas, no matter what size their membership, all have property that must be maintained, budgets to be raised, bills to be paid, some form of church organization that needs to be run efficiently, a congregation with widely varied interests that should be met effectively in the name and spirit of Christ.

In meeting these needs, the minister cannot evade the role of the chief administrator of his church, related to every aspect of the congregational life. The administrator is "the manager"—one who is capable of organizing and executing a program. He is to discover needs, propose ways of meeting them and then direct the effort so that the opportunity may be met. As you look up the word "administrator" you will find the dictionary suggesting that such a one engages in "regulation." The good administrator is one who sees that interpersonal relationships go along smoothly and that there are regulatory procedures for the governing and guidance of the common life of the congregation.

With vast social questions and portentous opportunities confronting

1

mankind, and with complex and changing conditions in almost every community where we seek to minister, the need for intelligent administration is at high premium.

WAYS TO DEVELOP ADMINISTRATIVE SKILLS

Skill in any activity calls for practice, attention and study. Those qualities are needed to become a good administrator. The young man starting in the ministry will do well to become friends with mature ministers of effective churches in his district, diocese or presbytery. As suggestions: get information from churches which are doing an effective job: confer with senior men whose judgment and life work you admire. As a young man do not be afraid to ask for an interview, and lay before your senior friend your problem or need! One of the privileges of the ministry is to counsel with younger men. Prepare for the interview so you will ask the right questions. Take notes of the conference. If there are serious problems in your parish that demand discretion and ability, get the judgment of two or three respected clergymen before you take action.

One of the most effective ways I've found of developing administrative competence is through the judgment of able laymen. In almost all of our churches there are individuals who are in positions of great trust and responsibility. They have arrived at those positions through their ability to deal effectively with people, with ideas, and with situations. Listen to the counsel of such able laymen. Be humble before demonstrated executive and administrative ability.

A small executive committee, with which your ideas can be tested before they are presented to the Official Board, may be much in order. Errors in judgment can be averted. A close camaraderie between able men may be developed and many secrets of practical wisdom regarding administration can be passed on between men in an intimate committee, where loving mutual respect is established.

Then, no one becomes competent as an administrator without developing the techniques of research and "getting the facts." Ruminate on the facts that you do get. What is their significance? What trends do they indicate? What, from an evaluation of the past and the present, can one foresee and project into the future? An example concerns one church that wanted to discover whether it could develop a more effective method for its Every Member Canvass. A survey was made concerning the per capita giving of the people of that parish. A résumé of the study is as follows:

CHRIST CHURCH
A SIX-YEAR STUDY OF GROWTH

	1958	1959	1960	1961	1962	1963
1. Membership (Communicants)	1,394	1,464	1,489	1,450	1,491	1,489
	$	$	$	$	$	$
2. Total Receipts (Cong'l current)	57,906	63,601	67,081	71,873	75,763	79,901
3. General Mission incl. Youth Budget & Benevolences	9,635	10,060	10,924	11,565	11,902	12,900
4. Spec. Offerings	915	1,487	1,240	1,744	1,907	2,054
5. Spec. Receipts (Capital Funds)	6,797	20,649	14,567	12,230	10,291	11,261
A. Per Capita Giving	$ 59.00	$ 70.22	$ 72.37	$ 75.67	$ 74.47	$ 80.28
B. National Average per Capita Giving	$ 78.14	$ 82.10	$ 84.31	$ 87.90	$ 88.08	$ 90.46

A special church-wide committee, studying the foregoing statistics that indicated a lack of growth over the last four years, not alone proposed a revision of the methods for the Every Member Canvass, but developed directives and enthusiasms for evangelism, mission, and youth activities that put the church on a completely new level of service for Christ. The pastor, as ex-officio member, was an amalgam to list past weaknesses and errors, but most importantly to help define the goals for the future.

The most competent administrators I have known have been able to "take" duress. They have achieved an ability to remain calm in the face of pressured or excited situations.

Remember Robert Louis Stevenson's marvelous sentence, "Quiet minds cannot be perplexed or frightened, but go on in fortune or misfortune at their own private pace, like a clock during a thunderstorm." That kind of competent administrative attitude comes through self-discipline and the enforcement of mental control at the time of excitement or emotional disturbance. The clergyman can develop this skill in many ways. Having full information is basic. Visualizing and being prepared for times of adversity is essential. Remember Joseph's preparation for the lean years? Then the good administrator will continually, in prayer and meditation, seek to be close to Jesus, who, at the time of the great storm, arose from His sleep to ask, "Why are ye fearful?" The closeness of Christ's calm can make the church leader have a similar strength to quiet potential parish storms.

The competent administrator in the local church will know the constitution, laws, and bylaws of the church and will continually seek to inform his church officers of those laws and regulations. He will see that the church is conducted in keeping with required ecclesiastical procedures.

Importance of Bylaws of the Church

Most of our ecclesiastical constitutions deal in broad principles and generalities. Many a local congregation finds it desirable to elaborate beyond those laws and principles and devise specific bylaws for the conduct of the affairs of the local church. If needed, the good ministerial administrator will see that such bylaws are proposed and developed. This usually is done through a strong, small committee that will give adequate study and time to the whole matter. The proposed bylaws and regulations should be submitted for study to all the officers of the church, and sufficient time should be given for individual evaluation before they are considered for discussion and action. The pastor, of course, should be an active ex-officio member of this and all committees of the Official Board. An example of such local bylaws, identified with a particular denomination, is the following, which is presented as a guide for varied adaptation in any church, subject to its particular ecclesiastical association:

BYLAWS OF CHRIST CHURCH

AS APPROVED BY THE OFFICIAL BOARD. (Considered and amended at the Congregational-Corporation meeting of October 17, 1964, and adopted at the Annual Congregational-Corporation meeting, January 17, 1965.)

BYLAWS OF THE CONGREGATION

1. Christ Church, being a particular congregation of the United Presbyterian Church in the United States of America, recognizes that the Constitution of said Church is, in all its provisions, obligatory upon it and its members.
2. There shall be two annual meetings of the congregation in

the church edifice. One meeting shall be held during the third week in January for the transaction of any business properly coming before such meeting. The second annual meeting shall be held during the third week in October for the transaction of any business properly coming before such meeting and for the purpose of electing the ecclesiastical officers who, after attending the Church Officer's Training Classes conducted by the pastor, will be ordained and installed in time to take office on January 1 of the following year.

3. Special meetings may be called by the Board or the Presbytery. Such calls shall state clearly the purpose of such special meeting, and no other matter, save that specified in the call, may be considered.

4. Public notice of the time, place, and purpose of all meetings of the congregation shall be given at least two weeks prior to the appointed time.

5. The senior minister shall preside. If the senior minister is ill or otherwise unable to be present, the substitute presiding chairman should be cleared through the Ministerial Relations Committee of the local Presbytery.

6. The Clerk of the Session shall be secretary of the meeting of the congregation. In his inability to attend, the Board shall designate a secretary in his stead.

7. All communicant members in good and regular standing shall be entitled to vote at congregational meetings.

8. Voting by proxy is not allowed.

9. Meetings shall be conducted in accordance with the General Rules for Judicatories adopted by the General Assembly of the United Presbyterian Church in the United States of America, so far as they apply. When they do not apply, procedures shall be conducted according to the usual legislative rules of order.

10. All meetings shall be opened and closed with prayer.

11. A quorum shall consist of the moderator, secretary, and a minimum of thirty-five eligible voters.

12. There shall be eighteen members of the Official Board, divided into three equal classes, one class of which shall be elected each year at the annual meeting in October for a three-year term. An elder having been elected to the board for consecutive terms aggregating six years shall be ineligible to serve thereon for a further term until at least one year has elapsed from the expiration of the last term for which he was elected.

13. There shall be eighteen deacons, divided into three equal

classes, designated as the Board of Deacons, one class of which shall be elected each year at the annual meeting in October for a three-year term. A person having been elected to the Board of Deacons for consecutive terms aggregating six years shall be ineligible to serve thereon for a further term until at least one year has elapsed from the expiration of the last term for which he was elected.

14. Vacancies on the Official Board or the Board of Deacons may be filled at a special meeting of the congregation or at the annual meeting, as the Official Board shall determine. When a vacancy occurs due to a resignation, the officer resigning shall make his request in writing to the clerk of the board. The unexpired term may be filled at the next annual meeting of the congregation.

15. There shall be a representative Nominating Committee, as directed by the Form of Government, Chapter XVII, Section 1, Item 2, chosen in accordance with the further specifications of the Form of Government. Two members of this committee shall be designated by and from the Official Board, one of whom shall be named as chairman. One member shall be designated by and from the Board of Deacons, and one by and from the Board of Trustees. Other members of the committee (none of whom may be in active service on the Official Board, the Board of Deacons, or the Board of Trustees), in sufficient number to constitute a majority thereof (exclusive of the pastor), shall be chosen by the congregation at its annual meeting in October. In addition, the pastor shall be a member of this committee, ex-officio and without vote.

The Nominating Committee shall be chosen annually. The committee shall discourage nominations to any of the three boards of the church of more than one member of any particular family to serve during the same period of time. The Nominating Committee is privileged to nominate members at large from the congregation for the Nominating Committee to succeed it.

The Nominating Committee shall bring to the annual meeting nominations of one eligible person only for each office to be filled. Additional nominations of qualified persons may be made from the floor by any eligible voter who has obtained consent of the nominee to place his name in nomination, and who received from the nominee the assurance that he will serve faithfully if elected.

16. Amendments may be made by an affirmative vote of a

majority of qualified voting members present at any regular or special meeting of the congregation in which a quorum is present; provided that written notice of the proposed amendment or amendments shall have been given to all members of the congregation by mail not less than ten days prior to the date of the meeting. All amendments made must be in accordance with the provisions of the Constitution of the United Presbyterian Church in the United States of America.

BYLAWS OF THE CORPORATION

This Corporation is organized for the purpose of supporting worship of Almighty God and instruction in the Christian religion, according to the Constitution of the United Presbyterian Church in the United States of America.

1. The Bylaws of the Corporation of Christ Church as a corporation shall always be subject to the Constitution and Laws of the particular State, and also to the Constitution of the United Presbyterian Church in the United States of America.
2. There shall be two annual meetings of the Corporation. The first shall be held during the third week of January for the transaction of any business properly coming before such meeting. The second meeting shall be held during the third week in October for the transaction of any business properly coming before such meeting and for the purpose of electing new officers to the Board of Trustees.
3. Special meetings may be called by the Board of Trustees or at the request of the Official Board. Presbytery may call a special meeting or direct the trustees so to do. All such calls shall state clearly the purpose of such meeting, and no other matter save that specified in the call may be considered.
4. Public notice of the time, place, and purpose of all meetings of the Corporation as prepared by the trustees (or Presbytery) shall be publicly announced on the two successive Sundays preceding the day of such meeting.
5. The president of the Board of Trustees shall convene meetings of the Corporation and shall preside, unless by majority vote the Corporation shall elect another of its membership in his place.
6. The secretary of the Board of Trustees shall be the secretary of the meeting of the Corporation. In his inability to serve, the Board of Trustees shall designate a substitute.
7. Only communicant members of the church, in good standing,

shall be entitled to vote on matters brought before the meeting (unless otherwise specified by the laws of the particular State governing incorporation).

8. Voting by proxy is not allowed.

9. All meetings shall be opened and closed with prayer.

10. A quorum shall consist of a minimum of thirty-five eligible voters.

11. There shall be twelve members on the Board of Trustees, divided into three equal classes. One class shall be elected each year at the annual meeting in October for a three-year term. A person having been elected to the Board of Trustees for consecutive terms aggregating six years shall be ineligible to serve for a further term until at least one year has elapsed from the expiration of the last term for which he was elected.

12. All nominees must be communicant members in good standing in the church.

13. Vacancies on the Board of Trustees by reason of death or resignation shall be filled at the next annual meeting of the Corporation unless a special meeting is called for that purpose. If for any reason a trustee must resign before fulfilling his term, the request should be made in writing to the secretary of the Board of Trustees.

14. Trustees shall be nominated, one only for each vacancy, by the Nominating Committee. Additional nominations may be made from the floor by an eligible voter at the Corporation meeting, but only when assurance can be given that the nominee has consented to having his name placed in nomination and has further agreed to serve faithfully if elected.

15. The duties of the trustees shall be only those delegated to them by the laws of the particular State, the Constitution of the United Presbyterian Church in the United States of America, the Official Board of the church, any congregation by-laws, and by formal action of the meetings of this Corporation.

16. The trustees shall report annually in January to the Corporation:

    (a) The receipts and payments for the previous fiscal year.

    (b) An estimate of expenses and income for the year ahead.

    (c) An exhibit of real property, trust funds, and other resources of the congregation.

    (d) New business necessary to be undertaken for the welfare of the congregation with regard to the three items above.

17. The accounts of the trustees shall be open to the inspection

of members of the Corporation on request, but the Official Board shall at all times have access thereto.

18. These bylaws may be amended subject to the charter of the Corporation, the laws of the particular State, the Constitution of the United Presbyterian Church in the United States of America, and any bylaws of the congregation at any annual meeting, or at any special meeting, by a two-thirds vote of the voters present, provided that written notice of the proposed amendment or amendments shall have been given to all members of the congregation by mail not less than two weeks prior to the date of the meeting.

BYLAWS GOVERNING THE CHURCH TREASURER

1. The Church Treasurer shall be elected annually in October at the congregational meeting.
2. The Nominating Committee shall present one name only for this office. Additional nominations of qualified persons may be made from the floor by any eligible voter who has obtained from the nominee his agreement to serve faithfully if elected.
3. The Church Treasurer shall receive and distribute all monies of the church, including current, special, and benevolence funds. He shall prepare a complete report of all receipts and disbursements to be presented by the Board of Trustees at the January annual meeting of the congregation and Corporation. He shall cooperate with the appointed auditor in providing all information needed to prepare the annual audit.
4. The Church Treasurer shall make a complete report of the church finances each month to the Board of Trustees at its stated monthly meeting. The Church Treasurer may be an elected member of the Board of Trustees. However if he is not a member of the Board of Trustees serving a designated term of office, he shall act as an ex-officio member of that board but without vote.
5. If the treasurer is not a member of the Official Board he may ask to appear before the board to present any financial matters pertaining to the welfare of the church. He shall be present only during the period of time of the presentation and discussion of the financial matters relating to his office.

When a local church may be considering the making of bylaws it is advisable for the committee appointed to get a number of such established bylaws from other local churches. Also the pastor, with the officers, will wisely consult a wide number of officers and members in the church for the most effective methods for procedure in that particular congregation.

The minister who develops his role as administrator will be both "the servant" and "the leader." The officers and laymen of the church will look to him for ideas and will consider with care the recommendations he will make for the development of the congregation. He will seek to be wise as the serpent and as harmless as the dove. He will "listen" as much as he will speak. Having a conviction about democratic processes and the importance of each individual's outlook and experience, he will consider with respect the thoughts and evaluations of others.

He will be free from pique and hurt feelings when proposals he makes may not be accepted.

He will learn to enlist others when a matter of major importance is to be presented to the Official Board, so that prior evaluation can be given to the matter and support have been gained when the matter is presented for group consideration.

The good administrator will see that all those who are related to a project or a program are adequately informed.

The good administrator involves as many people as possible in the cause and the programs which he supervises. He will be aware that all individuals are sensitive, and that every man wants to feel important. Therefore, he will give continuous encouragement and prompt and warm expression of appreciation for able work done in the service of the church.

Perhaps the key to the great administrator is found in the frequency with which he seeks to unlock the doors to the presence of God and the guiding spirit of Jesus Christ. As he does this his heart and mind are strengthened with the humility and wisdom that exposure to such perspective and grace alone can give. Cultivating those graces, he will be one to radiate breadth and harmony and joy. His spirit will cause others to be free from "littleness" and narrow self-interest. Objectivity and the excitement that come in working for a cause that is greater than one's self begin to permeate the Official Board and the entire parish. There then come high direction and blessing to all.

2

The Official Board

Those who rule the church with the pastor are key instrumentalities to the church's effective administration in matters both spiritual and material.

1. HOW TO SELECT CHURCH OFFICERS

In answer to the question "How are church officers to be selected?" the first item is that the entire congregation be informed as to the qualifications for a church officer.

One congregation clarified certain principles regarding the church officer for its Nominating Committee in the following terms and items:

NOMINATING COMMITTEE
CHRIST CHURCH

How to Select Church Officers—General Principles and Suggestions

1. No one should be chosen or elected as a church officer to do him honor. He should be known for his Christian character and devotion to the church, but he should be chosen for his willingness and ability to fulfill the responsibility of the office.
2. Selection should be made from those who attend service and show an interest in the church's activities.
3. Care should be taken to select individuals who can regularly attend meetings.

4. Caution should also be taken not to overload one person, or one family.
5. Effort should be made to sustain a balance between those who have had long relationship with the church and those who are younger in their church association.
6. Nominees will be briefed in training sessions about the meaning, duties, and responsibilities of the various offices.
7. The Nominating Committee, throughout the year, should let the congregation know that it is seeking suggestions for vacancies on the Official Board.
8. The Nominating Committee should meet in privacy. Discussions of potential nominees should not be repeated beyond the bounds of the committee meeting.
9. Consideration should be given to special qualifications that may be needed by the Official Board, as for example:

Training and experience in the maintenance of property.
Skill in fund-raising; public relations.
Knowledge in the fields of investments or music, or other specific abilities that may enhance the effective service of the board.

Our various church constitutions may require that more than one name be submitted for each office. In my judgment, where there is an option, only one name should be proposed by the Nominating Committee for each vacancy, thus eliminating the possibility of disappointment or public embarrassment for the individuals not winning election.

Qualifications and Duties of
Official Board Members

The minister or chairman of the Nominating Committee should seek the approval of the agreed-upon individual before the time of his election. It should be made clear to the potential church officer what the qualifications and duties are.

Such duties may be outlined simply:

DUTIES OF MEMBERS OF THE OFFICIAL BOARD

I. LEGAL QUALIFICATIONS
   1. Member in good standing.
   2. Willingness to serve.
   3. Acceptance of the Scriptures.

4. Adoption of Confession of Faith as "containing the system of doctrine taught in the Holy Scriptures."
5. Approval of system of government.
6. In the performance of their duties, officers are to observe "in all cases, the rules contained in the Word of God."

II. DUTIES

1. Attendance at meetings.
2. Loyalty to the board of which he is a member.
3. Helpfulness to the pastor in fulfilling his parish duties.
4. Regularity in church attendance.
5. Exhibition of exemplary conduct.
6. Diligence in concern for the welfare of the congregation.
7. Sympathy with the children and young people, recognizing that they are the future church.
8. Generous in financial support to the church, setting an example for others.

Informing Congregation of
Its Duties

It may be helpful to inform the entire congregation of its duties, as well as officers, through the publication of a special statement to be distributed to each member.

One congregation included such items in a leaflet entitled:

"WHAT IT MEANS . . ."

I. WHEN I BECAME A CHRISTIAN, I promised to try:
To live, act, and talk, with the help of God's Spirit, in such a way that I will show my consecration to Jesus Christ.
To use the Means of Grace (prayer, Bible study, worship) to keep my spirit open to God's presence.
To read and study Christian writings to improve my knowledge and the quality of my service to Christ and the church.
To express my stewardship by giving a definite portion of my working hours, talents and money to God's service, realizing that what I am and have belongs to Him.

II. WHEN I BECAME A MEMBER OF CHRIST CHURCH, I promised to try:
To regularly attend worship services and partake of the Sacraments of the Lord's Supper.
To seek to lead a consistent Christian life.

To support the stewardship budget of the church and participate in its activities of service and study.

To pray for and encourage my pastor in his ministry.

To improve myself in the service to Christ and His Church.

III. WHEN I BECOME AN OFFICER OF CHRIST CHURCH, I shall:

Attend the meetings of the official group of which I am a member.

Serve faithfully any committee to which I accept appointment.

Become personally informed about the various activities and services of the church locally and nationally.

A. *If I am called to be an Elder,* I shall:

Seek to find God's will for my church in the decisions which I as a member of the Board will confront.

Attend at least one meeting of the Presbytery or the Synod during my term of service.

Assist the pastor in taking the Sacrament of the Lord's Supper to the ill and invalided.

Help contact the members of the parish before each communion, distributing communion cards, keeping in touch with the members, discovering and correcting any instance where there appears a lessening interest in the church.

Be genuinely concerned about the people of my parish for whom I am responsible.

Fulfill assignments given to me to call on newcomers, prospects, those who are sick or shut-ins, and at the time of the Every Member Canvass.

Report to the pastor concerning needs of individual parishioners.

B. *If I am called to be a Deacon,* I shall:

Search for ways in which I and the Board of Deacons may help others in the name of Jesus Christ.

Serve my assignment as usher faithfully.

Assist the Elders of the parish in their duties.

C. *If I am called to be a Trustee,* I shall:

Be alert to the needs involved in the care of the church property.

Act responsibly in any committee appointments.

Seek to administer the funds of the church as a good steward.

Oversee with care any special funds and endowments.

Seek to deepen the stewardship commitments of all members.

Functions of Board of Deacons

Once the new officer is elected, the pastor should provide him with basic materials that will assist him in fulfilling his duties. A personal conference is more desirable than telephone or written communications. At such a conference the prospective new officer should be given full details of the committees and activities of his board. One church has prepared a simple statement of the functions of its Board of Deacons:

FUNCTIONS OF THE BOARD OF DEACONS

TRADITIONAL

1. Members to attend all regular and special meetings of the Board.
2. Care of the poor, sick, and distressed.
3. Study the peace, unity and purity of the church.
4. Promote brotherhood, fellowship and loyalty among members of the congregation.
5. Discover new areas in which Christian encouragement, support and service may be rendered.

COMMITTEES AND SPECIAL SERVICE (Duties)

A. *Evangelism and New Life Committee*
   1. Be alert to prospective new members.
   2. Advise the church office of emergencies requiring the attention of the pastor or other officials.
   3. Assign an active family in the church to each new member for one year. The assigned family should be friends of the new member, live nearby, be of the same age group or have common interests.

B. *Flower Committee*
   1. Make necessary arrangements for each usher to have a boutonniere at worship services.
   2. See that all flowers from the chancel go to such sick or distressed persons as are suggested by the church office.
   3. Provide flowers for decoration for the annual congregation dinner.

    4. Send floral tribute in special cases as directed by the Board.

C. *Activities Committee*

    1. Make all arrangements and assume responsibility for the following traditional events:
        a. Father and Son Meeting.
        b. Men's Retreat.
        c. Church Picnic.
        d. Men's Thanksgiving Breakfast.
        e. New Members Reception.
    2. Assume responsibility for further special congregational events as ordered by the Board.

D. *Ushering Committee*

    1. Assume responsibility for the selection, training and maintenance of a full staff of ushers to function at each regular church service and at special services as designated. A full staff is to be considered four teams composed of ten men each.
    Changes in procedures are carried out in consultation with the Worship Committee of the Official Board.

E. *Youth Service Committee*

    1. Promote and provide supervision for young people engaged in Church League basketball and baseball. Assist in obtaining equipment, furnish coaching staff.
    2. Assist in the Sunday evening supper for youth program.

F. *Church Guide Committee*

    1. Select, train and maintain a staff of church guides. These guides to be available to conduct interested persons on a tour of the church plant.

G. *Welfare and Visitation Committee*

    1. Make personal calls on the sick or distressed.
    2. Advise the Board if material assistance is advisable.

H. *Parking Lot Committee*

    1. Assume responsibility for the selection, training, and maintenance of a staff for proper handling of parking at each regular church service and at special services as designated.

Here, as in each instance, the needs of the local church, its parochial program, its parish objectives, will determine the designation of committees and the specific assignment of responsibility.

Installation and Ordination
of Officers

The installation and ordination of the new officer should be handled with care and dignity.

So that the newly elected officer will feel at ease about the occasion of his ordination, an outline of the procedure should be put in his hands. A suggested form is as follows:

CHRIST CHURCH

PROCEDURES FOR THE SERVICE OF ORDINATION AND INSTALLATION OF NEWLY ELECTED ELDERS AND DEACONS

To: *All Newly Elected Elders and Deacons*

1) The orientation with the pastor is scheduled for (*hour, place, date*).
2) *The Service of Ordination and Installation* is scheduled for *Sunday* (*date*).
   a. Elders are to be ordained and installed at the _____ service.
   b. Deacons are to be ordained and installed at the _____ service.
3) On the appointed Sunday please sit toward the front of the church. As your name is called, come into the chancel and stand facing the minister. Let an equal number be on each side of the Communion table and spaced about two feet apart, so that when you kneel you will not be crowded.
4) Six questions are addressed to the ordinands. The answers are as follows:
   Questions 1 and 2: "I do so believe."
   Question 3: "I do so receive it."
   Questions 4, 5 and 6: "I do."
5) After a question to the congregation is answered the minister says, "Let us pray." Ordinands kneel, and during this prayer the minister observes the apostolic tradition of the laying on of hands.
6) Rise after the prayer, to receive the charge of the minister, followed by his charge to the congregation which

concludes with the words, "and follow them so far as you see them follow Christ."

7) At this point, turn to receive the hands of other officers who will say, "We give you the right hand of fellowship to take part in this office with us."

8) After the minister pronounces the benediction, return to your seat in the congregation.

In a word, the church officer should be one devoted to Jesus Christ and His Church, an individual known for his

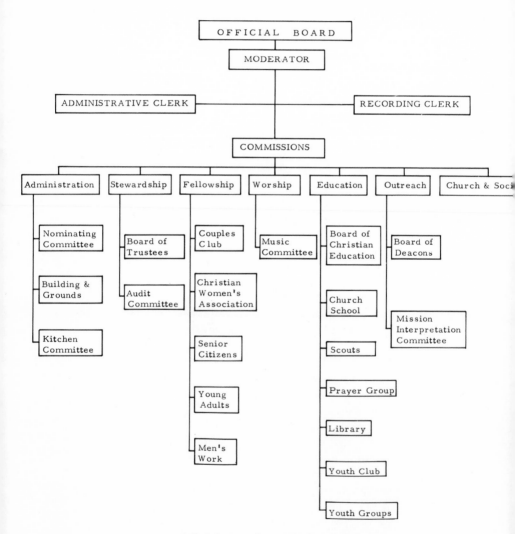

Official Board—Organizational Chart

BOARD OF TRUSTEES

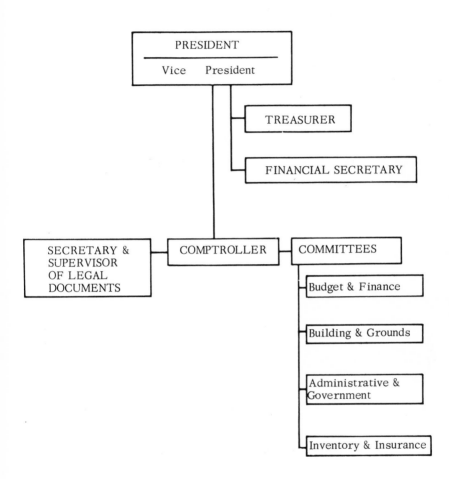

Board of Trustees—Organizational Chart

integrity and character. One who has the time and ability to contribute to the Christian cause, who has good judgment, discretion, and who can provide loyal support to the clergymen and the church staff.

2. Organizing the Board

There should be a clear organizational chart available to board members so that each officer may understand his relationship and

BOARD OF DEACONS

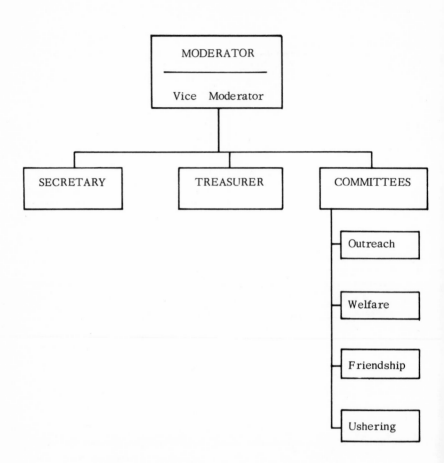

Board of Deacons—Organizational Chart

that of his board, to the staff, to other boards and to committees in the church.

Various types of organizational arrangements, as noted in the four examples, can be helpful in giving each officer a sense of the organization of his church and what is expected of him in relation to the whole congregation. The four organizational charts presented are self-explanatory and can be adapted for any church organization regardless of size.

A Detailed Church Organization Chart

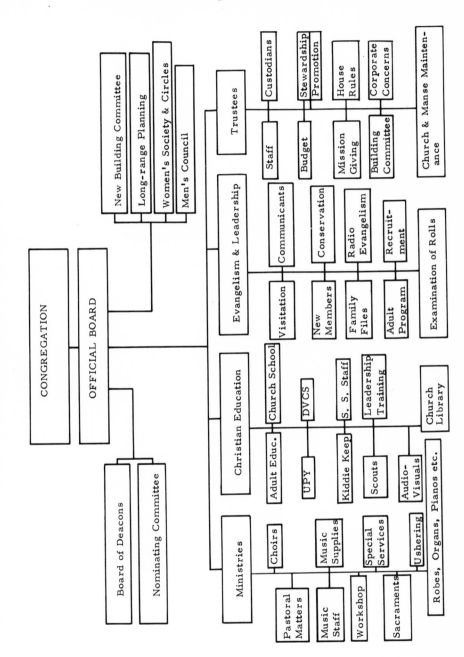

ORGANIZATIONAL CHART FOR CHRIST CHURCH

Importance of More Detailed
Organizational Charts

Beyond outlined suggestions made earlier, a more detailed statement of the duties and expectations of divisions and committees can
be important in organizing the board and in seeing that efforts and
energies are conserved and properly directed. Whenever the church
begins a new year, or new members come into divisions or committees, the chairman of each would do well to remind members of the
duties and objectives of that particular segment of the organization.

This end may be accomplished by a detailed chart and prepared
statement that will be put into the hands of each officer.

Following is a detailed presentation of duties and expectations of
church officers and administration:

THE OFFICIAL BOARD

The Official Board of Christ Church shall fulfill the responsibilities and obligations designated to it by the Constitution of the
National Church. The Official Board shall be responsible for the
spiritual growth of the congregation, the involvement of the congregation in its mission and ministry to the community and the
world, and be responsible for the church facilities, finances, and
administration.

The Official Board shall meet the second Wednesday of each
month at 8 P.M. (except July and August) at the call of the pastor
or by other methods as designated in the Constitution of the National Church.

The Official Board shall be composed of three divisions: I.
The Division of Mission and Ministry; II. The Division of Nurture; and III. The Division of Administration.

The role of each division is advisory and consultative. The
division shall discuss the work and responsibility of the church
as assigned to it and make recommendations to the Official Board,
other committees, the church staff and appropriate church organizations.

Membership of the division shall consist of the pastor as ex-
officio, an assigned staff person, members of the Official Board,
and other persons with like responsibilities in various church organizations (i.e., the World Service Chairman of the Women's
Association shall be a member of the Division of Mission and
Ministry).

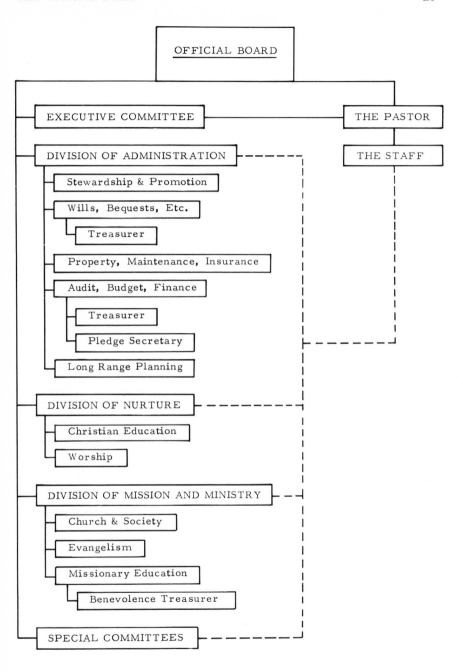

The divisions of the Official Board shall meet at least four times a year.

The presiding chairman of the division shall be appointed by the pastor and with the approval of the Official Board.

Each division shall have a secretary who will keep accurate records of the proceedings and submit them to the Official Board through its chairman.

I. THE DIVISION OF MISSION AND MINISTRY

   A. The responsibility of the Division of Mission and Ministry and its Committees is to relate the congregation to the ministry of Jesus Christ through service in the community and world and through study and discipleship.

   B. *The Church and Society Committee* will provide information for the church on social issues confronting the community, state, nation and world. The committee will provide opportunities for the congregation and community to learn the nature of these issues and the response of faith to them through speakers and discussion groups. The committee will also recommend policy and strategy to the church through the Official Board with reference to these issues.

   C. *The Evangelism Committee* will provide for the visitation of prospective members, the visitation of church members both active and inactive, provide for the visitation of the sick and needy, and administer the programs of charity. The committee will make arrangements for the transportation of people, where needed, to and from church. The committee will maintain close contact with service personnel and college students. The committee will supervise the church roll and maintain contact with those people who have moved, encouraging them to become active members of a church in their new community. The committee will also supervise the Parish Zone System of the congregation.

   D. *The Missionary Education Committee* will provide instruction on the mission of the church at home and abroad and provide liaison relationship with other churches in the community in areas of mutual concern. The committee shall encourage young people to enter summer work camps, etc. The committee will supervise the work of the Benevolence Treasurer, who shall report to the Official Board through this committee.

II. THE DIVISION OF NURTURE

A. The responsibility of the Division of Nurture and its committees shall be to provide for the spiritual enrichment of the congregation in faith and knowledge, that individuals and groups may be equipped for their work of ministry.

B. *The Committee of Christian Education* will supervise the Christian Education program for all ages and in all areas of the church's life; initiate new programs for the understanding and implementation of the Christian faith; provide leadership training; training of new members; supervise the church library and the distribution of pamphlets and audio visuals. The committee will recommend applications for the Scholarship Fund.

C. *The Worship Committee* will give guidance to individuals, families and groups within the church in the nature of public and private worship. The committee will make arrangements for the observance of the Sacraments and special services of worship. The committee will assist in the ministry of the choirs and fulfill any need and opportunity for the musical enrichment of the congregation.

III. THE DIVISION OF ADMINISTRATION

A. The responsibility of the Division of Administration is to encourage stewardship of all members in the support of the church, and adequately finance the overall mission of the church.

B. *The Stewardship and Promotion Committee* shall provide complete interpretation, through all news media including the Parish News of the congregation, concerning the mission of the church. The committee will maintain a continuing stewardship educational program. The committee will initiate and supervise the Every Member Canvass and the Youth Budget Program. The committee will provide special consultations and seminars on stewardship.

C. *The Wills, Bequests, Memorials and Endowments Committee* will publicize the needs of the church to which people can make special contributions. The committee will work with the National Foundation of its denomination. The committee will determine the manner of investments of all funds entrusted to it, and maintain the historical records of the church, the Memorial Fund Book, as well as the Memorial, Endowment and Scholarship accounts.

D. *The Property, Maintenance and Insurance Committee* will supervise the property, repairs and purchases of the church. The committee will supervise the maintenance of the physical church plant, including office supplies, equipment, and the manses of the church. The committee will supervise the work of the custodians and shall control the use of all church property by all groups.

E. *The Audit, Budget and Finance Committee* shall maintain a continuing supervision of the church budget in light of pledges, current income and disbursements. The committee will supervise the income of all treasurers of the church and church organizations. The committee shall supervise the payment of the church indebtedness and receive the reports of the church Treasurer and Pledge Secretary.

F. *The Long-Range Planning Committee* will study the future growth of the community and the church, make recommendations concerning possible future needs of the people, future programs, physical changes and buildings to meet future needs. The committee will make recommendations as to the proper time for any special fund campaign in the light of the total stewardship program.

THE EXECUTIVE COMMITTEE

The Executive Committee shall meet at the call of the pastor or the Official Board, and have the responsibility for the general administration and coordination of the church program. The Executive Committee shall be charged with salary review of the staff and salary recommendations to the Official Board.

THE PARISH ZONE

The congregation shall be divided into geographical areas, with one member of the Official Board assigned to each zone. The officer shall call on those in need in his zone and assist the pastors in calling on prospective members in his parish zone.

The parish zone may be used in conducting the Every Member Canvass, Study Groups, etc., by the Official Board or organizations of the church.

THE OFFICERS OF THE OFFICIAL BOARD

1. The *Moderator* shall be the pastor of Christ Church.
2. The *Vice Moderator(s)* shall be an elected member (or

members) of the Official Board. The Vice Moderator shall preside at the meetings of the Official Board at the request of the Moderator, or in his absence.

3. *The Clerk of the Official Board* shall be elected by the Official Board for a term of one year. He shall serve as the parliamentarian of the Official Board and keep accurate records of all meetings. He shall have responsibility for maintaining the church rolls.

4. *The Benevolence Treasurer* shall be elected each year by the Official Board and will administer the benevolence receipts under the supervision of the board in cooperation with the Missionary Education Committee.

5. *The Church Treasurer* shall be elected each year by the Official Board and will administer the current expense and capital funds of the church. He shall be under the supervision of the Official Board through the Audit, Budget and Finance Committee.

6. *The Memorial Fund Treasurer* shall administer the receipts and disbursements from the Wills, Bequests, Memorial and Endowments Funds. He shall be responsible to the Official Board through the Wills, Bequests, Memorial and Endowments Committee.

7. *The Pledge Secretary* shall be elected each year by the Official Board and keep a record of the giving of individual members and families of the church through the envelope system. The Pledge Secretary will be responsible to the board through the Audit, Budget and Finance Committee.

THE STAFF

The pastor shall be responsible to the Official Board and his ecclesiastical superior for the administration of Christ Church. All members of the staff shall be responsible to the Official Board of the church through committees assigned to their responsibility and through the pastor, who will be responsible for the job descriptions of staff members.

The Pastor shall have oversight of the program administration of the church, fulfilling the Constitutional requirements of his office. He shall appoint staff personnel to specific tasks and be responsible for the supervision of their work.

The Assistant Pastor for Mission and Ministry shall be assigned responsibility for working with the Division of Mission and Ministry and its committees. He shall assist in all other aspects of the church's life at the request of the pastor.

The Assistant Pastor for Nurture shall have responsibility for working with the Division of Nurture. He shall assist in all other aspects of the church's life at the request of the pastor.

Simplicity, clarity, and brevity are the three principles to guide the pastor and other officers in the preparation of an outline of the duties of the church officer and the board on which he will serve. An example of the outline of the committees of a church having a Board of Trustees is as follows:

BOARD OF TRUSTEES
COMMITTEES AND THEIR FUNCTIONS

I. BUILDING COMMITTEE

This committee shall:

1. Have responsibility for the physical maintenance and safeguarding of the real estate owned by the church, and physical equipment therein.
2. Consider any and all orders, recommendations, or suggestions in respect to the physical properties and equipment of the church which may be received from public officials or members of the congregation.
3. Cause to be made, on authorization of its chairman and without prior reference to the Board of Trustees, any urgently needed repairs involving aggregate cost of not more than $100 in any one month, subject to eventual approval by the Board of Trustees.
4. Recommend to the Board of Trustees such alterations and improvements to physical properties and equipment of the church, as from time to time it may deem necessary and desirable.
5. Supervise the performance of all maintenance, alterations, and improvements upon physical properties and equipment of the church.

II. INVESTMENT AND INSURANCE COMMITTEE

This committee shall:

1. Have primary responsibility for supervision of the church's investments and insurance coverage.
2. Review the investment portfolio from time to time and make recommendations to the Board of Trustees with respect thereto.
3. Review the church's insurance coverage from time to time and make recommendations to the Board of Trustees in respect to changes deemed desirable to provide adequate protection at reasonable cost.

III. Personnel Committee

This committee shall:

1. Have primary responsibility, in cooperation with the pastor, for supervision of the secretarial and custodial staff of the church.
2. Confer with the pastor and make recommendations to the Board of Trustees in respect to compensation, working conditions, employment and separation, of members of the secretarial and custodial staff of the church.
3. Act as liaison between the secretarial and custodial staff of the church and the Board of Trustees.

IV. Every Member Canvass Committee

This committee shall:

Have primary responsibility, in cooperation with the Stewardship and Service Committee of the Session, for the planning and conducting of the annual Every Member Canvass, and any supplemental fund-raising activities which may be approved by the Board of Trustees.

V. Finance and Budget Committee

This committee shall:

1. Keep informed about the general financial position of the church. The chairman shall make a regular report and forecast to the Board of Trustees on the financial condition of the church's operation.
2. Together with such other persons as shall be selected, this committee will develop the proposed Annual Budget prior to the Every Member Canvass, and shall submit this budget for approval to the Corporation and congregation before the Every Member Canvass is initiated.

VI. Legal Committee

This committee shall:

Have responsibility for supervision and handling of all legal problems affecting the church, and for advising the Board of Trustees respecting such problems.

VII. Planning Committee (Joint Boards)

This committee shall:

1. Study the present situation and needs of the church.
2. Study and plan for future development and growth.
3. Submit to the boards proposals for attaining long-range objectives in program, property, plant, etc.

One church outlined the responsibilities of committees for its Board of Deacons as follows:

RESPONSIBILITIES OF THE COMMITTEES
OF THE BOARD OF DEACONS
CHRIST CHURCH

1. USHERING

   It shall be the responsibility of the Ushering Committee to supervise the ushering and the receiving of offerings at all worship services in the church or in the chapel where ushers are needed. The chairman or co-chairman will assign the ushers to their particular posts. All deacons will be eligible to serve as ushers. Other members of the congregation may be asked to share in this responsibility. The ministers will contact the chairman when extra services are to take place and ushers will be needed. Generally ten to fourteen ushers are needed for the Sunday service at 11 A.M.

2. AUDITING

   It shall be the responsibility of this committee to supervise the counting of the money after each service where an offering is received, and make a complete record of checks and pledges that are received. This committee works in the room at the front of the chapel. A schedule is made up with a captain and five or six workers assigned to serve two months of each year. A letter is sent from the church office to the captain when his assignment comes up, and a postcard reminder is sent to each worker.

3. VISITATION

   This committee will have the responsibility of making calls on the sick, shut-in, and bereaved members of the congregation. It shall also visit prospective new members and visitors at Sunday morning service. Names will be assigned from the church office.

4. ORIENTATION

   The responsibility of this committee is to help new members become acquainted and oriented into the life of the total church program. A sponsor will be assigned by this committee to each new member at the time he or she joins the church, and will help the new member get acquainted. Where a couple is joining the church it is helpful to assign a couple of about the same age and living within a reasonable distance to be their sponsor. The sponsor should meet the new member at the Preparatory Service before he or she joins the church, and try to keep a friendly interest and contact for at least six months.

5. WELFARE

This committee will have the responsibility of giving financial assistance and other help to members of the church and others who appeal to the church for aid. Cases of need that come to the attention of the ministers may be turned over to the Welfare Committee for investigation. This committee will work with appropriate agencies in the city to meet special needs of individuals and families.

6. FINANCE

This committee will be responsible for the financial matters relating to the Board of Deacons. A budget will be prepared at the beginning of each year and submitted to the Board of Deacons for approval. Special requests for money outside of the budget should be made to the Finance Committee.

7. RECEPTIONS

This committee will be in charge of greeting all members of the congregation at services of the church on Sunday mornings or any other occasion where services are held in the church. They will open the outer doors for the people coming in to the services. The members of this committee must try to get the names and addresses of visitors and strangers attending services. Visitors should be encouraged to sign the guest register, or fill in cards which can be given to the ministers as soon as possible. This committee represents the first impression of the church to newcomers. Their greetings should therefore be warm, representing the concern for Christ. The committee will assign a couple to greet those attending church dinners and special functions in the dining room or church hall.

*Roster of Committee Members
and Committee Functions*

One church, seeking to keep the duties of committees with current officers up to date, annually prepares a paper showing the names of committee members, with a brief statement of the duties and function of the committee:

1968 COMMITTEES OF OFFICIAL BOARD
CHRIST CHURCH

I—Prayer Life
Roy Stewart Jr., chairman
Wayne Holden
Mark Sayer
Howard McNeese
Fred Schwartz

To plan for and supervise the prayer groups. To promote the use of the monthly devotional booklet and to encourage participation in classes and other study, and devotional programs. The chairman selects those to open and close the Official Board meetings with prayer, and selects the officer who gives the devotional thought at the monthly Official Board meeting.

II—Missionary & Stewardship
Harvey Brown, chairman
Abe Solomon
Lee Price
Howard Porter
Joseph Hunt
Linda Galbraith
Susan Paulsonn
Lloyd Boyd

To encourage and supervise the promotion and teaching of missions and stewardship in the church. It shall be the duty of the committee to correspond regularly with the adopted missionaries of the church throughout the year. This committee will see that the Church School classes that have been assigned a relationship with the missionaries of the church shall keep in contact with them and remember them at Christmas and at other times.

III—Church Service & Communion
Forrest Jones, chairman
Douglas Larson
Richard Lang
Clive Johnson
William Jackson
Philip Hunter
Dick Jones
George Kauffman

To be responsible for complete arrangements for each Communion Service. (Other officers may be called upon by the committee to assist.) This committee shall have charge of all worship services for the regular church services and shall assist with all special services in the church.

IV—Christian Education
William Brady, chairman
Mrs. James Roberts
Mrs. Robert Matthews
Marilouise Gutsch

To direct all educational activities of the parish, including Bible School, Communicant Classes, Young People's Societies, Boy Scouts, Church Library and Vacation Bible School.

George Evans

Robert Eyler

This committee shall supervise the Director of Christian Education and shall counsel with him concerning its work.

Director of Christian Education (ex-officio)

Minister (ex-officio)

Administrative Manuals

It is important to give all officers a sense of the total program of the church. This can be effectively done through the preparation of a manual showing the entire administrative program. Officers will be listed; the outline of the duties of all committees will be included. An annual calendar showing all events for the church year may helpfully form a part of the booklet. A detailed outline of specifics for the committees may well be included.

One church, known for the care of its administrative procedures, developed such a manual. It gave specific guidelines based on the denominational requirements, and then included instructions for each area of the local church work.

One department, that of Evangelism and Pastoral Care, was detailed in manual form as follows:

EVANGELISM AND PASTORAL CARE

Primary Objective:

To lead the church in bringing men and women to faith in God and membership in the church, and to strengthen the bonds of concern and affection which should bind people together as members of the body of Christ.

Specific Functions:

To aid the pastor in his work; to maintain liaison with the Board of Deacons; to establish and supervise a zone program for the care of the congregation; to prepare for and oversee the every home visitation in preparation for World-Wide Communion; to supervise programs of calling on prospective members, newly received members, inactive members, the sick and shut-ins; to review the membership roll and make recommendations to the Official Board for the suspension of inactive members.

To assist the Board of Deacons in providing greeters and ushers for worship services, including Official Board greeters at the close of worship service, coffee-hour fellowships and at receptions of new members; to foster the warmth of Christian fellowship in all meetings of the church; to develop informal social activity as an aid to the evangelism program; to encourage regular church attendance; to stimulate and guide the members of the church in the life of prayer.

Constitutional Provisions:

"The church, with its ordinances, officers, and judicatories, is the agency which Christ has ordained for the edification and government of His people, for the propagation of the faith, and the evangelization of the world." (Form of Government, V-9)

Provisions for Nonresident Church Members:

When a church member shall remove his residence beyond the bounds of the congregation of which he is a member, so that he can no longer regularly attend its services, it shall be his duty to transfer his membership by presenting a certificate of dismission from the church of which he is a member, to the church with which he wishes to unite.

When a church member shall remove his residence beyond the bounds of the church of which he is a member into the bounds of another, it shall be the duty of the Official Board of the church of which he is a member to continue pastoral oversight of him and to inform him that according to the teaching of the Constitution of the church it is his duty to transfer his membership as soon as practicable to the church in whose bounds he is living. It shall also be the duty of the Official Board of the church from whose bounds the member moved to notify the Official Board of the church into whose bounds he has moved and request them to take pastoral oversight of the member, with a view of having him transfer his membership.

When the member has been informed of his duty to transfer and the Official Board of the church into whose bounds he has moved has been requested to take pastoral oversight, his name shall then be placed on a separate roll for nonresident members.

A person whose name has been on the roll of the nonresident church for a period of one year, but who has not requested a letter of transfer, shall be advised again at his last known address by the Official Board of the church of which he is a member, to apply for a regular certificate of dismission. Failing to do so, he may, without further notice, be suspended from the communion of the church until he shall satisfy the Official Board of the propriety of his restoration. (Book of Discipline VII-3. See also VII-2; Form of Government, X-7; XI-6; Bylaws IV-4b.)

A number of Protestant churches develop a Board of Women, sometimes called "deaconesses," to assist in the work of the church. One congregation utilizes such a board, outlining its responsibilities in the following terms:

DUTIES OF THE BOARD OF DEACONESSES

1) Serve as receptionists in the narthex before and after all worship services. Two receptionists are needed on duty at each service.
2) Prepare and arrange the communion elements, and cleanse and care for the communion ware and linens after each observance of the Sacrament.
3) Call on families with new babies.
4) Arrange for flowers in the chancel each Sunday.
5) Call on the sick and shut-ins and distribute the chancel flowers as directed.
6) Send cards to the sick and bereaved.
7) Serve as receptionists for new members at the social hour following Official Board meetings when new members are received.
8) Serve in every practical way families at the time of bereavement.

Deaconesses are ordained and installed, and have a high standing in the church. With the deacons they compose the Diaconate. With the Official Board the Diaconate is a spiritual office and one held in honor and respect. The deaconesses will attend all joint board meetings and will have all privileges accorded ordained officers in the church.

3. PREPARING FOR BOARD OR COMMITTEE
   MEETINGS

The church officers should know in advance the date of each board meeting. A card should be mailed at the beginning of the church year reminding the officer of every future date and suggesting that the dates be placed on the officer's calendar for the year. Committees with specific assignments should be reminded when their reports are due at a particular board meeting.

The place of meeting is important and should be established with the approval of all. The board meetings preferably should be held in the same place, in a room well lighted and ventilated. The agenda and other mimeographed reports should be at each seat. An adequate table should be provided for the clerk for the taking of minutes.

Materials concerning major matters for discussion should be mailed to the board members at least a week prior to the meeting. The minister and moderator should be prepared with supporting material available on matters that may involve complicated issues. Extra copies of the minutes of the past meeting and other papers from past meetings should be available for members who may have been absent from earlier meetings.

Committees, if properly prepared and meeting regularly, can greatly facilitate the board meetings. One church provides suggestions to new committee chairmen which is helpful in preparing them to organize the committee, holding it to its task, and so assisting the board, by the following memo:

MEMO TO NEW COMMITTEE CHAIRMEN

We are delighted that you will serve Christ and His church as a committee chairman. To aid you in your new responsibility the following suggestions may be of some merit:

1) Read carefully the written purpose of your committee.

2) Secure from the previous chairman the committee file of past minutes and papers. Learn what the committee has done and what it hoped to do. Plan to keep an ordered file of the business of the committee under your chairmanship to pass on to the next chairman.

3) Make an appointment with the pastor who has been designated as "resource minister" for your committee and review the needs, problems and hopes of the committee with him.

4) If it is your responsibility, suggest additional names for your committee and submit them for approval to the Official Board before the next meeting of that body.

5) Get your committee together as soon as possible. Always seek God's guidance in prayer at the opening and at the end of each meeting.

6) Explain the purpose of the committee to your fellow members.

7) Set specific goals for action. Place them in order of priority, and set target dates for each. Keep this overall planning before your committee.

8) As each goal is clarified and action projected, bring specific recommendations to the Official Board meeting in writing for approval.

9) Each month review the responsibilities and goals of your committee to evaluate the degree of progress.

10) Set dates for the committee meeting covering the span of one year.

11) As chairman of the committee, keep discussion centered on the immediate topic.

4. CONDUCTING THE MEETINGS

The chairman or moderator should prepare an agenda, a copy of which is available for each participant. The meeting should start on time and be adjourned at an appointed hour. If there is unfinished business at the agreed-upon hour for adjournment, the meeting should be extended only by a majority vote.

Discussion should be to the point. An item needing committee study should be referred to the proper committee for recommendation, rather than having it discussed at length by the entire board.

Some boards and committees, composed of men with heavy responsibilities, may meet effectively at noon or at a convenient hour in the late afternoon.

The spiritual aspect should never be neglected. Every meeting should open and close with prayer. The reading of a passage of the Bible or some inspirational thought is in order at the opening.

Types of Pastoral Reports

The chairman will demand concentration on the item at hand, will discourage discursive comments, and will provide an atmosphere of geniality and good will. It may be wise for the pastor and assistant pastors to give a regular report to the board. If this is an agreed item on the agenda, the minister may helpfully present a mimeographed statement in a similar form for each occasion when the report is expected. Two types of reports are as follows:

I.

DR. SMITH'S QUARTERLY REPORT TO THE OFFICIAL BOARD
January 1, 19___–March 31, 19___

I. WORSHIP SERVICES	TYPES OF ACTIVITY
22	Sunday mornings in the Sanctuary
4	Sunday mornings with Sunday School

2   Holy Communion services
14   Funerals conducted
3   Lenten Bible study classes
1   Preached at Lenten Service, Christ Church
3   Holy Communion services for shut-ins at their homes
1   Infant baptism
31   Sermons delivered

II. RELIGIOUS TRAINING AND EDUCATION

2   Communicant classes for adults
1   Communicant class for young people
3   Youth groups attended
10   Adult groups attended

III. ADMINISTRATIVE, COUNSELING AND PASTORAL WORK

41   Calls on new members
48   Calls on general membership
134   Calls on sick in hospitals
122   Calls on sick and shut-ins at home
11   Calls on bereaved

356   Total calls made
69   Personal consultations
3   Staff meetings
8   Board meetings
37   Consultations with staff members
5   Official Board committee meetings
1   Annual Corporation-congregational meeting

IV. DENOMINATIONAL RESPONSIBILITIES

6   Denominational Council and committee meetings
1   Commission for installation of new pastor
2   Synod Committee on Interpretation and Stewardship meetings
3   Denominational trustees meetings
1   Addressed Fairview Men's Council
1   Addressed Spencer Church Women's Association

V. CIVIC AND COMMUNITY ACTIVITIES

2   Addresses at Spencer High School convocations
2   Board of Directors meetings—Cancer Society
1   Opening prayer at State Senate

1	Judged oratorical contest at Hartford County Junior High
1	Williams College Development Board meeting
1	Williams College Alumni Council meeting

II.

REPORT OF THE REVEREND JONES, ASSISTANT MINISTER

I. *Worship Service Participation*
  a. Assisted 11
  b. Sermons 2
  c. Chapel services 6

II. *Judicatory meetings*
  a. Official Board 4
  b. Denominational 3
  c. Cong. meetings 1

III. *Christian Ed. Dept. meetings*
  a. C. E. Committee 3
  b. Youth Work Comm. . 3
  c. Adult Work Comm. ... 2
  d. Nursery Dept. 2
  e. Kindergarten Dept. .. 1
  f. Primary 2
  g. Junior 2
  h. Children's W. Comm. . 3
  i. Church School
     Administration Staff . 1
  j. VCS Committee 1

VI. *Pastoral calls* 30

VII. *Person consultations* 15

IV. *Youth Fellowship meetings*
  a. Senior High 12
  b. Junior High 12
  c. Senior High advisors .. 2
  d. Junior High advisors .. 1

V. *Related activities*
  a. Circle Bible Study 3
  b. God & Country Award
     mtg. 6
  c. Troop & Pack meetings 1
  d. Blue & Gold banquet .. 1
  e. Communicant Class ... 3
  f. Lenten Bible study 3
  g. Adult study group 2

For this past quarter, the general trend of attendance at church school has been down from what it was for the same period in 1966. This continues the same downward trend that has been going on since about 1961.

The response and attendance to the Youth Fellowship Program has been good. The Junior High Fellowship is growing. In order to correct the problem in the Senior High group, new officers were elected and installed—Marc Jones, moderator; Katy Rossman, vice moderator; Barbara Rothman, secretary; and Dave Johnson, treasurer. Two new couples are beginning as advisers on April 1, the Bill Allports for Junior High Fellowship, and the Garry Blooms for the Senior High Fellowship. They are replacing the Jim Myers and the Dave Comptons, whose term of service ends March 31.

Promotion Sunday will be June 27. The presentation of Bibles to the third graders will be made at that time. The summer schedule of classes has been determined. Steps are being taken to firm up the Vacation School staff and obtain the 1967-68 teaching staff before June 13.

The Church School office will be without the services of Mrs. Fred Rosebrock after July 1. She has served as secretary for the past five years. A replacement has not yet been found.

The change in the Sunday Service schedule has not had a great effect on the attendance figures as yet, although we can say that the 9:30 service attendance is nearer equal to the 11 o'clock service, with the latter still the greater.

I feel the need for more time to do calling, but with the great number of meetings which I must attend under the present setup, it is physically impossible for me to do any more. I am planning to take a close look at the whole structure of the C.E. Department this summer, with the idea of developing a plan that will provide more time for calling.

Respectfully submitted,

Financial Reports

Accurate financial reports should be mimeographed and on hand for each officer at the board meeting. One type that readily gives the officer the financial picture of the church is the following:

CHRIST CHURCH

CASH RECEIPTS - GENERAL FUND

March 31, 1967

	Estimated 1967	March 1967	3 Months 1967	3 Months 1966
Current Pledges	$143,185.00	$12,334.95	$38,197.10	$37,847.32
Prior Pledges	2,500.00	226.00	3,666.56	3,622.66
Loose Offerings	6,500.00	506.99	1,434.63	1,974.38
Special Offerings	1,800.00	7.00	213.56	854.14
Presbyterian Life	400.00	43.75	226.80	190.75
Youth Budget	1,200.00	100.00	300.00	300.00
Miscellaneous	1,500.00	68.00	453.00	535.00
Totals	$157,085.00	$13,286.69	$44,491.65	$45,324.25

Disbursements		11,494.43	38,137.01	36,360.16
Excess		1,792.26	6,354.64	8,964.09
Beginning Balance		4,354.64		
			6,354.64	$ 8,964.09
		$ 6,354.64	$	

SPECIAL FUNDS

	Balance 2-28-67	Receipts	Disburse- ments	Balance 3-31-67
Youth Budget	$ 1,658.04	$ 978.14	$ 645.63	$ 1,990.55
Choir	1,145.92	--	--	1,145.92
Trustees Spec. Fund	58,425.69	--	--	58,425.69 *
Parish Fellowship Fund	$ 29.55	$ --	$ --	$ 29.55
Organ Fund	286.00	--	--	286.00
Library Fund	53.65	--	--	53.65
Reserve Choirroom	156.67	--	--	156.67
Fifty Million Fund	1,940.61	2.00	--	1,942.61
Fund for Freedom	204.13	25.00	229.13	--
One Great Hr. of Sharing	--	2,592.15	--	2,595.15
Totals	$63,900.26	$3,600.29	$ 874.76	$66,625.79

5. AGENDA AND MINUTES

Necessity for Agenda and Meeting Minutes

The Official Board meeting should have a carefully prepared agenda. Without it, time can be wasted, important items will not receive the attention which is warranted, and frustration results. One church, which had interminable and often disorganized trustees meetings, came to the conclusion that a more ordered and clear-cut procedure was necessary. The chairman sent the following letter to board members. A much more intelligent meeting was forthcoming, and a happier and more effective board resulted.

June 8, 19__

Dear Fellow Trustee:

At the last long meeting of our board, a suggestion was made that we operate with an "agenda" at future meetings. There was a favorable reaction among the members to the suggestion.

I would like to suggest that we initiate the agenda at our June meeting. This procedure is in no way designed to curtail relevant discussion, but seeks, among other things, to make our discussion more relevant. Its main purpose is to aid us in having more organized meetings, give members an opportunity to be more intelligently informed, and cut the length of the meetings.

Following are the basic ground rules that will be required to make an agenda workable:

1. The secretary will prepare the minutes of each meeting and mail them within two weeks to each member. This will save time at the next meeting, as it will eliminate reading of the minutes except where there are questions or corrections.

2. Any member desiring to present a subject to the board will contact me prior to the meeting (at least one week) so that the subject can be put on the agenda.

3. The agenda will be prepared by me and mailed to each member at least three days before the meeting.

4. Items not on the agenda will be considered only when they are of an emergency nature.

I urge your cooperation with this proposal. I believe it will help us do a more effective job for our church. If you have any questions or comments, please contact me.

Sincerely,
Charles H. Hanson
Chairman

It will be found that church officers will respond to an agenda that shows respect for their time and which is a vehicle for the orderly conduct of church business.

Types of Agenda

Three types of agenda follow:

(*Example No. 1*)

CHRIST CHURCH
OFFICIAL BOARD MEETING
DOCKET

December 2, 19___
7:30 P.M.

1. The Convening of the Board with Worship. Matthew 3:11
2. The Taking of the Roll and Excuses for Absence.

3. Adoption of the Docket.
4. Approval of the Minutes of the Last Meeting.
5. Communication with the Board of Trustees—Mr. John Walter.
6. Report of the Clerk—Mr. Edward Way.
7. Report of the Benevolence Secretary—Mr. Thomas James.
8. Report of the Assistant Pastor—Reverend Tucker.
9. Report of the Pastor:
   A. Stewardship Advance Meetings—Completed.
   B. Bible Study—December 8 and 22—Book of Exodus
   C. Men's Council Meeting—Dr. Paul Warfield
   D. The Meeting of the Congregation—Sunday, December 13
   E. The Church School Christmas Pageant—Sunday, December 13, 3:30 P.M.
   F. Candlelight Service on Christmas Sunday, 8 P.M.
   G. Christ Eve Service, 8 P.M.
   H. New Year's Eve Service, 8 P.M.
   I. Conference on Multiple Staff—January 4-7
   J. Annual Meeting of the Congregation—Wednesday, January 27, 6:30 P.M.
   K. Race Relations Sunday—February 14
   L. Wedding Receptions: "No Smoking" Regulations
10. Reports of Permanent Committees:
    A. Christian Education—Elder Dodd
    B. Church Finance—Elder Spivey
    C. Church and Society—Elder Russell
    D. Evangelism—Elder Pickett
    E. Mission—Elder Danser
    F. Stewardship—Elder Archard
    G. Worship—Elder Linck
11. Dismissal of Members:
    Letters of Transfer:
        Mr. and Mrs. Kenneth C. Lundeen, New Cumberland, Pa., to United Church, Boston, Mass., 11/22/67
        Mrs. Scott Pike, Wood Ridge, N. J., to Trinity Church, Reistertown, Md., 11/10/67
12. Discipline of Members:
    Suspension: Mr. Robert R. Winter
    Erasure: Mr. John D. Hart, who was received into membership of First Church of Christ, Aberdeen, on November 8, 1967
13. The Meeting of the Denomination on Saturday, December 12, 9:30 A.M. in Christ Church.

14. Other Business
15. Adjournment with Prayer.
      For Clerk of Board Records:
      Marriage: Dennis S. Long and
                    Diane Jones, November 21, 19__

(*Example No. 2*)

AGENDA
BOARD OF TRUSTEES
CHRIST CHURCH

February 26, 19__
5 P.M.
Meeting in the Board Room—First National Bank
James Rush, Presiding

INVOCATION
MINUTES OF THE PREVIOUS MEETING
CORRESPONDENCE
TREASURER'S REPORT—Snyder Hardy
   1. Income Account
   2. Accounts Payable
FINANCE COMMITTEE REPORT—George Ekley
PROPERTY COMMITTEE REPORT—John Ludlum
SPECIAL ITEMS
   1. Annual Meeting
   2. Long-Range Improvement Plans—Lyle Wikstrom
   3. Election of Officers
NEW BUSINESS
ADJOURNMENT WITH PRAYER

(*Example No. 3*)

CHRIST CHURCH
OFFICIAL BOARD AGENDA

April 14, 19__
8 P.M.

DEVOTIONS   Larry E. Grace
ABSENTEE EXCUSES
APPROVAL OF MINUTES
COMMUNICATIONS
ITEMS OF OLD BUSINESS

COMMITTEE REPORTS:

Christian Education	John Waters
Committee on Committees	W. W. McKay
Finance	W. W. McKay
Minister's Advisory Committee	James Tucker
Parish Work	Gerry Mack
Spiritual Life and Worship	Robert Morris

OTHER BUSINESS AND REPORTS

Dedication of First Christian Church	
Steering Committee on 75th Anniversary	William Pickett
Denominational Action on the Reg Hillier Fund	

CALENDAR

April 13	Maundy Thursday Communion
April 14	Community Good Friday Service
April 16	Easter Services
April 17	Men's Prayer Breakfast
April 23	Sacrament of Baptism
April 24	Men's Prayer Breakfast
April 24	Ushers' Banquet
April 26	Adult Church School Leaders
April 30	New Members
May 1	Men's Prayer Breakfast
May 3	Pastors' Prayer Fellowship
May 3	Deacons' Meeting
May 7	Mothers' Day and Christian Family Sunday
May 10	Women's Association
May 10	Official Board Meeting

ITEMS OF NEW BUSINESS
DATE OF NEXT MEETING
ADJOURNMENT WITH PRAYER

Minutes will be carefully kept by the secretary and mailed to the members of the board, ideally within a week of the meeting. One secretary found the following mimeographed sheet helpful in the keeping of the minutes of the meeting:

*Meeting Minutes—Forms
and Types*

MINUTES—BOARD OF DEACONS

The regular meeting of the Board of Deacons was held on _____ at _____ in the lounge.

The meeting was opened with prayer by _____.

DEACONS PRESENT: (last names)

DEACONS EXCUSED:

DEACONS ABSENT:

COMMITTEE REPORTS:

OLD BUSINESS:

NEW BUSINESS:

DATE OF NEXT MEETING:

OTHER:

The meeting adjourned with prayer at _____ by
_____.

_____
Secretary

Minutes should be brief, but should contain all pertinent information. The following are various types of minutes, use of which is optional for efficiently informing the church executives.

(*Example No. 1*)

MINUTES OF THE ADJOURNED MEETING
OF THE OFFICIAL BOARD
CHRIST CHURCH

Sunday, May 21, 19___

An adjourned meeting of the Official Board, set over from the regular meeting on May 2, was convened in the lounge following the church service at 12:30 by Dr. Jackson, who presided as moderator and gave the constituting prayer.

The following members were *present:* Adams, Aker, Allen, Boyer, Colestock, Curtis, Finley, Frear, Harris, Hawley, Johnson, Kier, McQuiddy, E. Moore, Noonan, Rossman, Tyson, Woodward, and Young.

Absent with excuses: Barnes, Reynolds, and Wakefield.

Absent without excuses: Hegwood, Stouffer, and Warfield.

Also present were Mr. Richardson and Mr. Wenger.

The principal matter on the agenda was the consideration of a special report by the Christian Education Commission relative to a possible rearrangement of the Sunday School schedule.

Mr. Boyer, chairman of the commission, reported that a request had been received from the senior high school group asking that they be included in the membership of the commission. On his recommendation it was moved and carried that two high school members be named to the Christian Education Commission with full voting rights.

Mr. Boyer further stated that the commission was concerned at the large number of refusals of persons asked to teach in the church school. The reason most frequently given was a lack of confidence in the ability to teach.

Mr. Woodward spoke of the need for a re-formation in our church. He suggested that some churches had a greater involvement of adults in study, but that in general our church needed to have the adults worship and the children study.

The commission proposed a "Sunday morning family study-worship experience." Study courses with relevant material were shown to the board.

Mr. Kier moved that the Official Board approve a program of

study and worship involving combinations of families, adults and young people. The motion was seconded and carried.

Mr. Noonan raised a question about the possible effect of a change on the various choirs and other programs. Dr. Jackson suggested that the Worship Commission might well work with the Christian Education Commission in developing an experimental program along lines suggested by Mr. Kier, and that a detailed proposal of such be made to the next regular meeting of the board.

Following the closing prayer by Mr. Tyson, the meeting adjourned at 1:18 P.M.

Respectfully submitted,

John R. Aker, clerk of Official Board

(*Example No. 2*)

MINUTES OF THE MEETING OF BOARD
OF DEACONS—CHRIST CHURCH
September 22, 19__

Present: Donald Becker, John Boccalini, William Brewer, David Collins, Dave Crompton, Raymond Faczan, Tracy Hewitt, William Hohe, Stanley Rubinsky, Steve Satir, Thomas Schwartz, Warren Vose, and Dr. Jackson

Absent: Allen Sanborn, James Smith, Edward Southworth, and William Young

The meeting was called to order at 8:03 P.M. by Warren Vose, vice chairman, who presided until the arrival of the chairman, William Brewer.

Opening prayer was offered by Dave Crompton.

Minutes of the past meeting were approved.

Treasurer's Report

Commercial Checking Account . . . . Balance 9-22-67 . . . $124.56
Reserve Savings Account . . . . Balance 6-23-67 . . . 500.00
Scholarship Savings Account . . . . . Balance 9-22-67 . . . 372.33
Special Funds . . . . Balance 9-22-67 . . .   75.38
Unsecured Notes . . . . Balance 9-22-67 . . . 534.00

Deacon's Discretionary Fund balance reported to be $35.05 as of 9-22-67.

A Motion made by Mr. Becker, directing the treasurer to remit $500 to Lewis and Clark College covering the two $250 scholarships for Ann Clark and Carol Kennedy, was passed.

Donald Becker reported for the Scholarship Committee, presenting the components of a good scholarship program based upon need. It was suggested that the program should include:

1) Five scholarships of $300 each.

2) Christ Church freshmen to have first consideration, but the program should not be limited to communicant members.

3) Acceptance by a college is required.

4) Final choice of recipients is to rest with the Board of Deacons.

5) Funds for the scholarships ($1,500) should come from the general budget.

6) Funds to be paid directly to the college.

7) A third party is to rate the financial ability of applicants.

After considerable discussion it was moved, seconded and passed that these be the guidelines for the scholarship program.

The Scholarship Committee was asked to present these ideas to the Christian Education Committee for its approval and cooperation in administering the program.

Thomas Schwartz made an appeal on behalf of the Official Board for volunteers to work through the speakers bureau in presenting the 1968 stewardship program to the various church groups. This year's theme will be, "Not yours, but you!" Six Deacons volunteered.

Dr. Jackson reported that the following men are being considered for the new class of deacons: Charles Miller, Kenneth Todd, Philip Wescott, and Douglas Wright.

No old or new business.

Meeting adjourned with prayer at 9:02 p.m.

Submitted by Steve Satir
Secretary

6. How to Make Committees Function Effectively

In the majority of our churches, basic research, thinking and evaluation come through properly appointed committees. Even though a committee has been defined by a "wag" as a group of people who individually can do nothing, and collectively decide that nothing can be done—committees can do valuable work for the church *if properly informed of their function and then stimulated and guided to do it.*

Helpful Outlines of Functions
of Committees

It may be helpful to give each member of each committee a brief outline on the functioning of committees. The following is an example:

CHRIST CHURCH
OUTLINE
ON THE FUNCTIONING OF COMMITTEES

A significant part of the work of the church is done through board committees. They serve as an instrumentality to study specific areas of the church life, become informed, engage in direction and oversight which would be impossible by the board as a whole, and make recommendations to the board.

(1) The committee chairman has the responsibility for calling committee meetings and, directing the secretary of the committee, will see that all members receive a written reminder of the meeting date, place and hour.

(2) Each committee needs to meet regularly at a stated time and place. Chairmen and their committees are asked to schedule meetings well in advance. The meeting date, time and place must be cleared with the church office and be placed on the full church calendar.

(3) A docket or agenda should be prepared for each meeting. One person, who may be designated as secretary, is charged with keeping a typed record of meetings, including all recommendations and decisions. Such records, along with all other papers bearing on the responsibility of the group, become a part of the permanent records of the committee. They may be kept at the church office if desired, and are passed on to succeeding chairmen.

(4) Written or typed committee reports, particularly any recommendations, are to be made available in board meetings to the clerk of the board. Committee chairmen should not bring before the board any item of business which should be worked out within the committee.

(5) Additions may be made to committees. Church members may be co-opted, but only after the chairman checks with the board president and the pastor.

(6) The office staff is glad to assist committees in the fulfillment of their tasks. Cooperation is given on two conditions: first, that the church office is called in advance

to determine whether the time is convenient; second, typing or mimeographing to be done by the office staff should be in the office three days before it is needed.

IN GENERAL

(1) Minutes of the prior meeting and an agenda of the coming meeting should be mailed to all committee members a week preceding the next meeting.

(2) All committee members are expected to attend monthly meetings, and if unavoidably prevented from coming, are to notify the chairman or secretary in advance.

(3) Church officers and all committee members will find it helpful to their work to obtain one or all of the following paperbooks, available in a new edition each year through the church office at $1 a copy: "The Constitution of the National Church," "National Church Law Relating to the Local Church," and "The Handbook for Church Boards and Committee Members." These books describe the work of the whole denomination, the many decisions and guidelines for the conduct of the local church.

When Specific Committee Duties Are Assigned

When specific duties are assigned to a committee, specific details regarding that assignment should be prepared, duplicated, and put into each member's hands. One committee was assigned the duty of serving as host at a coffee hour, held between church services. Assignments for the year were made in detail as follows:

HOSPITALITY COMMITTEE

Christ Church   February 10, 19—

Dear Member of the Hospitality Committee:

Below is a schedule of dates on which each of you will be responsible for coffee hour service between the first and second services. It is recognized that there will be times when coffee will not be served because of special occasions, summer vacations, etc. To help remind you, *The Spire* will publish each week the names of the deacons assigned for that Sunday, as well as notice when there will be no coffee hour.

If you cannot attend on the Sunday assigned to you, please arrange a substitute. Wives of deacons are expected to assist whenever possible.

Please plan to be present about ten minutes before the end of the first service in order to check the table, especially the one set up for juice for children.

Thanks for your cooperation.

Carl F. Carroll, Chairman
Coffee Hour

Coffee Hour
Date Schedule

Bartell Klein	Shell Donovan	Deming Marco	Coal Johnson	Brice Vincent	Podell Harris
Feb. 14	Feb. 21	Feb. 28	Mar. 7	Mar. 14	Mar. 21
Apr. 4	Apr. 11	Apr. 18	Apr. 25	May 2	May 9
May 23	May 30	Jun. 6	Jun. 13	Jun. 20	Jun. 27
Jul. 11	Jul. 18	Jul. 25	Aug. 1	Aug. 8	Aug. 15
Aug. 29	Sep. 5	Sep. 12	Sep. 19	Sep. 26	Oct. 3
Oct. 17	Oct. 24	Oct. 31	Nov. 7	Nov. 14	Nov. 28
Dec. 5	Dec. 12	Dec. 19	Dec. 26	Jan. 2	Jan. 9
Jan. 23	Jan. 30	Feb. 6	Feb. 13	Feb. 20	Feb. 27

Myers Peterson
Mar. 28
May 16
Jun. 16
Jul. 4
Aug. 22
Oct. 10
Nov. 28
Jan. 16

Note: Such a precise outline is helpful in getting the individual member to fulfill his assignment.

Even though clear assignments are made, there should be a reminder sent shortly before the duty is to be fulfilled. Some such mimeographed card or letter as the following can save many an occasion of "forgetfulness" and so ineffectiveness in the work of the committee:

Form of Letter for Greeters
Committee Personnel

CHRIST CHURCH
GREETERS COMMITTEE

Dear Friend and Fellow Committee Member:

The Committee of Greeters welcomes you as a greeter for the Sunday morning services of Christ Church during the month of _____. You will greet at the _____ service and will be stationed in the vestibule by the guest book or opposite it on the other side of the door.

Your duties will consist of shaking hands with the worshipers as they arrive and greeting them with a friendly "Good morning." Greeting is an important function of the church service, and when done sincerely will have a part in making each worshiper, whether an old member or a stranger, feel at home and better prepared for the experience of worship.

Be attentive and helpful, as there are particular needs of individuals. Know where rest-room facilities, the church office, and other physical areas of the building may be reached.

There is a wheelchair in the closet to the left of the literature desk. Also in this closet there is a first-aid kit on the top shelf.

Please be present on Sunday morning at least fifteen minutes before the service begins. If you do not come as agreed, it will mean a lack in the overall intent to make Sunday worship an occasion when we gather before the Lord in love and concern for Christ *and for each other*. IF FOR ANY REASON YOU ARE UNABLE TO ATTEND please notify _____, so that a replacement can be obtained as soon as possible.

Thank you for accepting this responsibility, and we are looking forward to seeing you on Sunday morning.

Sincerely yours,

THE COMMITTEE OF GREETERS

Special Types of Communications
to Committee Personnel

Our churches increasingly concern themselves with important social problems. These can be dealt with effectively only as adequate information is provided, and with thorough discussion to devise a plan of constructive action. Following is an example of some of the material sent to the committee by one of the members, appointed for the purpose, on the problem of alcoholism:

INFORMATION REPORT TO
CHRIST CHURCH SOCIAL ACTION COMMITTEE
January 6, 19—

"An initial report on Alcoholism in Our Area—How to Help."

There are 35,000 alcoholics in Salinus-Queens County. Each one affects from three to five persons directly (himself, family, employer, community). There are only approximately 10 percent of these persons on "Skid Row"; the remaining 90 percent are able to carry on in home, business, industry, professions,—but this work is not what it could be, due to alcoholic excess.

PROBLEM

Due to the lack of information and misunderstanding:

—Most alcoholics go undetected until their illness is deeply serious.

—Most families, friends and co-workers inadvertently assist them in staying hidden at the brink of excess, because they do not understand the true nature of the problem and are uninformed on how to help.

RESOURCES—SPECIALIZED HELP

One cannot learn in "three easy steps" how to help an alcoholic. The problem is too complex. Specialized help is available to assist the alcoholic directly or guide him to other sources. They are:

—SALINUS COMMITTEE ON ALCOHOLISM .... MA 3-8380
—ALCOHOLICS ANONYMOUS .... MA 3-3909
  (On call twenty-four hours a day)
—UNITED PASTORAL COUNSELING SERVICE .. LA 4-3700

PERSONAL RELATIONSHIPS

Until an alcoholic will accept specialized help, a personal relationship can be of the utmost importance. The following will help an individual in aiding him:

—Do all possible to avoid making an alcoholic resent or distrust his desired helper.

—To maintain his belief that he has a friend is important.

One can help by:

—Encouraging all beneficial activities and cooperating in making them possible. Most important, try to put him more and more in an environment where there is no drinking.

—Don't lecture, moralize, scold, blame, threaten, argue, lose your temper, or cover up the consequences of drinking.

—Pray that the alcoholic may recognize his problem and be willing to accept specialized help.

Our committee can increasingly prepare itself to guide the alcoholic to specialized help and aid him in becoming a part of our Christian fellowship in the church.

Committees will function effectively if they are carefully appointed, if it is clear what they are to do and informed when their reports are to be made, if they are provided with tools for their working, and are given periodic reminders and stimuli.

7. DEVELOPING THE VITAL CHURCH

In our changing world, the church must be sensitive to the changes and meet them in a fresh, creative way. John Watson (Ian MacLaren) put the essence of it well: "Christianity is not a school of morals, nor a system of speculation; it is an enthusiasm. This religion is Spring in the spiritual world, with the irresistible charm of the quickening wind and the bursting bud. It is a birth, as Jesus would say, a breath of God that makes all things new." [1]

This is true. One of the ways such creative vitality is developed in the local church is by thoughtful and forward-looking proposals from the minister.

Following are two examples of proposals made by clergymen to their Official Boards:

(Example No. 1)

MY DREAMS FOR CHRIST CHURCH FOR THE NEXT FIVE YEARS
Claude E. Smiley, D.D.

1. Set up small discussion group of twelve persons to train twelve each in the next year.
2. Promote the church as a spiritual counseling center.
3. Hold group therapy classes on Tuesday, Wednesday, Thursday nights.

---

[1] John Watson, D.D. (Ian MacLaren), *The Mind of the Master* (New York: Dodd, Mead and Co., 1896), pp. 179-180.

4. Enrich the Wednesday night program with Bible Discussion units and a three-term School of Religion each year.
5. Develop a Volunteer Social Service Desk manned by volunteers daily 10-4 p.m.
6. Develop the public relations program of the church.
7. Create two annual distinguished lectureships:
   a. In Pastoral Psychology;
   b. In Pastoral Preaching.
8. Develop a Benevolence Plan of individuals who will meet with and consult with potential beneficiaries of the church.
9. Establish small group meetings in homes.
10. Schedule art and other exhibitions of religious works.
11. Develop several church-wide social and fellowship events of the highest caliber.
12. Start a weekday nursery school.
13. Start a Protestant Information Center and a book rack of pertinent religious literature.
14. Develop an ushers association of fifty men.
15. Start a noon weekday service once a week.
16. Explore the possibility of a spiritual healing ministry by professionals and laymen.
17. Start a "Books and Coffee" discussion group of twenty to twenty-five persons.
18. Revise the outreach program to obtain qualified new members for the congregation.
19. Develop a "Spiritual Adventurers" group to meet Sundays and take assignments for special personal contact.
20. Revise the format of *Voice* Magazine.
21. Deepen the congregation's sense of mission and social consciousness.
22. Do long-range planning to continue the fine work of property improvement.

(*Example No. 2*)

A DETAILED PLAN FOR EFFECTIVE MINISTRY
CHRIST CHURCH—ROGER SMITH, PASTOR

This "paper" is presented to the Official Board for information, approval or whatever action may seem wise and for the well-being of Christ Church.

In previous years, the "emphasis" on "parish calling" has been *extensive*. Each of the 1,200 homes of Christ Church members received a call from one of the ministers. This has not been without real satisfaction and has had many positive results. It has had some apparent weaknesses—notably, no one at home, men rarely present, considerable time wasted.

The staff proposes for the Official Board's consideration the following program of an "intensive" parish ministry to be administered by the parish minister. It might be more dramatically described as "A Ministry to the Crises of Life." However, it sets a definite and detailed series of steps in a program, and progress can be reviewed as often as desired.

THE HOME

1. A program of pre-marital counseling.
2. A post-marital ministry to include:
   a. A call in the home shortly after the honeymooners return.
   b. A call some six months to a year later for a period of post-marital counseling.
3. The new home
   a. Call to dedicate it with a prayer.
   b. If removed to a new home outside the church's area—an attempt to introduce the family to a church in that city.
   c. Newcomers
      (1) Introductory call by a member of the staff.
      (2) A follow-up call to introduce the newcomer to Christ Church with specific information for the specific family.
      (3) Further follow-up by sponsoring family or invitation by two specific organizations.
      (4) Follow-up call six months after membership by one of the ministers.

BIRTH

1. Flowers to hospital and letter.
2. Call in home after mother and baby return—materials to be used.
3. If not possible before, a follow-up call six months later to familiarize parents with the purposes and meaning of the sacrament of infant baptism.

SICKNESS

1. Twice weekly calls in hospitals.
2. In case of surgery, a pre-surgery call.
3. Call upon return home, if there is a period of recuperation.
4. Shut-in calls regularly.

VOCATION

1. Counseling session with each high school junior during second semester regarding vocational future.
2. College students
    a. College Sunday
    b. Christ Church News
    c. Summer and/or vacation staff counseling
    d. Special programs at holidays
3. Armed forces personnel
    a. New Testament
    b. Christ Church News
    c. Christmas season greetings
4. Change of position—letter and such news clippings as are available.

PROGRAM CENTER CALLING

1. Minister of Education calling at homes of church school staff.
2. Minister of Music calling at homes of choir members and potential choir members.
3. Recruiting for program and educational units of the church.

PERSONAL PROBLEMS

1. Announce and emphasize repeatedly the fact that the staff is always available for counseling at the request of individuals and families, and that such arrangements can best be made by appointment.

DEATH

1. Call at time of death.
2. Periodic calls during period of adjustment.
3. A call on the first anniversary of the sorrow.

EXTENSIVE PARISH PROGRAM by district meetings—all to be held in the church with the minister as co-host with the deaconesses. This makes it possible to meet the men of the church as well as their wives.

RETIREMENT

1. Call in the home.

INACTIVE MEMBERSHIP VISITATION

1. By staff and officers of the church.

Such recommendations can stimulate thought and enthusiasm among the church officers and the entire church. Until we come to the kingdom of heaven here on earth, the local church must constantly seek to improve. Wasn't it Matthew Arnold who said:

"There is nothing so revolutionary, because there is nothing so unnatural and convulsive, as the strain to keep things fixed when all the world is, by the very law of its creation, in eternal progress; and the course of all the evils in the world may be traced to that natural but most deadly evil of human indolence and corruption that it is our duty to preserve and not to improve."

The ability to break out of the old "wineskins" of custom to meet the current needs calls not alone for vision on the part of the pastor, but for the study and the evaluation of the officers of the church.

Long-Range Planning
Committee Techniques

A "long-range planning committee" is much in order for many of our churches that are located in changing communities.

The following indicates activation, identification, and functions of such a committee:

LONG-RANGE PLANNING COMMITTEE, CHRIST CHURCH, 1967–1972

The Official Board of the church passed the motion to form a Long-Range Planning Committee at the regular meeting on April 9, 1967. The following "Purpose of the Long-Range Planning Committee" was approved:

"The purpose of the Long-Range Planning Committee is to study our congregation and its needs together with the anticipated needs of our community and to make recommendations to the Official Board that may serve as guides for the future development of a vital church. These recommendations should be based on the spirit and teachings of Jesus Christ, enable our church to serve Him more effectively by meeting the spiritual needs of the individual and the requirements of a Christian community and strengthen the world for Christ, recognizing that our church and people are involved with mankind."

With this "purpose" as a guide, the Long-Range Planning Committee is directed to present to the Official Board a written report or reports of the recommendations it feels should be emphasized or incorporated into the church program during the next five years.

This committee is to study all phases of the church program. To facilitate the study and the reporting of its recommendations, the committee divided the church program into the following groups:

Adult Program and Church Organization

Youth Program

Community, National and World Program

Physical Facilities, Finance and Personnel Programs

The essential question for this important committee, and for the Official Board which it represents, is this: "How can Christ Church, in the spirit of Him whose name it bears, minister best today and tomorrow, to the men and women, boys and girls who are in its fold?"

Evaluation Reports

The church may find it advisable to appoint a special committee to evaluate its immediate program and to propose ideas for improvements.

A report of one local church on this matter is contained in the following form:

INITIAL PROGRAM EVALUATION REPORT

"HOW WE CAN IMPROVE CHRIST CHURCH"

May, 1968

The following comments and suggestions were abstracted from the reports of the various committees and divisions of the church as submitted to the Special Evaluation Committee, pursuant to the resolution adopted by the Official Board at its February meeting:

"Moved, seconded and carried that the moderator appoint a special Program Evaluation Committee to consider all aspects of our current program and report back to the board with its findings and recommendations. It is understood that the committee will enlist the cooperation of all committees and divisions of the church, asking all to make prayerful and thoughtful suggestions to the question, "How can the faith and work programs of Christ Church be improved?"

PUBLIC WORSHIP

1. Official Board members should meet regularly at 10:40 or 12:15 each Sunday.
2. Popular hymns should be selected for the public worship services.
3. Count attendance at Sunday worship service. Keep a record to show monthly and yearly averages.

MUSIC

1. Investigate possibility of working with other institutions to develop a more extensive program.
2. Develop youth and children's choirs.

CHILDREN AND YOUTH

1. Develop junior high and senior high fellowship groups and/or clubs with emphasis on the relationship of our faith to community and world problems.

ADULT EDUCATION

1. Establish a discussion forum on timely subjects.
2. Establish a subject-oriented study/lecture class.

EVANGELISM

1. A program to generate interest and active support of a greater percentage of members from the boards.
2. A speakers forum—a "flying squadron" consisting of qualified men to speak to outside groups.
3. Major guest speakers on evangelism.
4. Consideration of retreats for selected groups to develop understanding of our faith and a deeper commitment to it.

MISSIONS

1. The Christian Education and Mission programs should be more coordinated.
2. The Church Vocations subcommittee should make further efforts through the written word and by presenting the cause of Christ by addresses to our young people.

STEWARDSHIP AND SERVICE

1. The stewardship program should include a program of education throughout the year.
2. More members should be encouraged to serve on boards, committees and in service projects.
3. Records should be maintained to show the vocations, avo-

cations, abilities and other interests of each member. This file would be available to the Nominating Committee and the boards as they seek for adequate leadership in specialized tasks.

SOCIAL AND CONGREGATIONAL

1. A subcommittee should be established to welcome and help initiate new members into a full church life.

PUBLIC RELATIONS AND INTERPRETATION

1. Such a committee should be established to assist all agencies of the church in adequately publicizing their programs, be alert to negative reactions and areas of weaknesses, assisting the pastors and boards in helping new members become acquainted with the church program and integrated into it.

LONG-RANGE PLANNING

1. Consider improvements to the Christian Education building.
2. Study the need for a counseling clinic.
3. Evaluate the need for a kindergarten and a church-supported school.

EXECUTIVE

1. Elected leaders of every church organization for whose program the church is responsible should meet semi-annually with the executive committee of the board. (This should not include groups such as the nursery school, for whose program the church is not responsible.)
2. The group should study the significance of gains or losses in membership and attendance, develop methods of cooperation between the various church organizations, and study the overall, as well as particular, interests and concerns within the membership of its congregation.

The committee expresses its gratification at the fine cooperation of the various church groups which responded.

In addition to receiving the above, the following actions were voted by the Official Board at its regular May, 1967 meeting:

1. Authorize study and planning by the Long-Range Planning Committee for a more adequate church parish house, including improved educational facilities.
2. Funds should be sought by the Stewardship and Service Committee in the 1968 budget to provide an increase in the staff for pastoral counseling.

Carl J. Hardy, moderator

David R. Davidson, clerk

The Benefits of Retreats

To keep the church vital, the officers themselves may be called for periods of study and evaluation. "A retreat" for one to two days away from the church premises may be helpful in evaluating the church program and in bringing forth suggestions for the improvements of the church life.

A condensed report of one such "retreat" is the following:

REPORT ON OFFICIAL BOARD RETREAT
April 17, 18, 19__

A number of proposals were discussed. The following seemed worthy of further consideration. One suggestion was that these ideas be reviewed by the Coordinating Committee and referred by it to appropriate commissions for study and implementation.

1. *Programs for Improvement of Church Leadership*
   1. Periodic retreats of the church officers (two times a year suggested).
   2. Program of reading for all officers.
   3. Part of each Official Board meeting devoted to leadership training and improvement.
   4. Regular reports to the Official Board of denominational activities.
   5. Formulation of a sharper Statement of Purpose and Objectives for the guidance of church officers, committees, etc.

2. *Programs for Improvement of General Membership*
   1. Every member visitation to improve interest—this by means of a special mobilization of officers.
   2. Increased effort to assimilate new members and to develop the interest of nonparticipating members in the worship and service activities of the church.
   3. A study of the possibility of special programs and activities for men, such as a Sunday morning study class, etc.
   4. Inclusion of a résumé of Official Board meetings in the church magazine.

3. *Programs Involving the Community*
   1. Study special "publics" which might be reached more effectively, such as college students, elderly, and single people living near the church.

2. Broaden the basis of membership, with community-wide representation and a welcome for all.

Compiled by Haynes and Potter

Special Problems for Committee Study

When there is a specific problem that arises in the church, it may be advisable to appoint a special committee to study the matter and to make proposals for suitable action. One church, troubled by personnel problems and without a permanent personnel committee, referred the matter, on approval by the Official Board, to a Special Coordinating Committee appointed by the chairman of the board.

Its report, which proved to be helpful to that particular church, was set out in the following form and terms:

A RECOMMENDATION TO THE OFFICIAL BOARD OF CHRIST CHURCH

FROM: SPECIAL COORDINATING COMMITTEE

It is recommended that the Official Board approve the appointment of a permanent standing committee to be known as the Staff-Personnel Committee, and that its composition, means of appointment, and areas of responsibility shall be as follows:

COMPOSITION AND TERMS OF OFFICE

The committee shall be composed of not less than six (6) members with each member serving for a term of three (3) years, with the membership rotating so that one-third of the committee is replaced each year. At least three (3) of the members of the committee shall be members of the Official Board, with the balance of the committee chosen from the congregation at large.

APPOINTMENT OF THE COMMITTEE

The committee shall be appointed by the moderator and confirmed by the Official Board.

AREAS OF RESPONSIBILITY

The committee shall be responsible to the Official Board for the following:

1. Recommend short- and long-range personnel policies.

2. Develop job descriptions for church staff positions.
3. Make an annual review of all staff salaries.
4. Serve as a confidential consultative body available to all professional and non-professional staff in all personnel matters.
5. Investigate the feasibility of a pastoral study leave program.
6. Supervise the church's retirement program.
7. Act as consultant to the Pastor Seeking Committee that may be appointed to fill vacancies in our professional staff, and be the liaison between our church and the Denominational Ministerial Relations Committee in the matter of calling ordained ministers to our church.

A Commentary on the
Function of Such a
Staff-Personnel Committee

This committee would be at the disposal of the various commissions of the Official Board for consultation in the area of personnel needs, job analysis, salary review, and preparation of the annual budget as it relates to the staff.

The studies on job analysis should include the ministerial staff and its composition, the organization of the administrative office staff, the definition of all job responsibilities. The present and future requirements of Christian education, music, and senior adults should be immediate areas of study.

The creation of this committee by the Official Board will help to give continuity of communication between the Official Board and staff members. Items that probably will receive attention are: the feelings and concerns of the individual staff members about their job, evaluation of staff member's efficiency, guidance in correcting deficiencies, review of long-range and immediate vocational goals, and review of salary and other forms of compensation.

This committee would replace the annually appointed Salary Review Committee and such staff and program study committees as have been appointed from time to time.

This permanent committee would give valuable assistance to future Ministerial Replacement Committees that may be appointed.

The Staff-Personnel Committee would assist the moderator in selecting new members for the committee as may be needed. It is suggested that membership include people with broad personnel experience, and that the women of the church be appointed on it.

The committee should report regularly to the Official Board, particularly when it has concluded a study in a particular matter, or when it has a recommendation to make.

The pastor and the Official Board should be fearless in restudying and re-evaluating the church program and the administrative setup of the boards, and most particularly in facing the spiritual, economic, political, and social questions which concern the members of the parish. Seeking to relate Christianity to the urgent questions and needs of our time will help make the church truly relevant to men and women, boys and girls.

3

Administration
of the Church Staff

No matter how small the church may be, there are likely to be other individuals, either paid or volunteer, in addition to the clergyman, who assume some portion of responsibility for the maintenance and operation of the church. Usually there is someone called the sexton or janitor, who has responsibility for seeing that the church is heated and clean. (In Norway, the office called "church servant" is looked on with great respect.) Other positions probably will involve those of choir director, pianist, organist, superintendent of the church school, and someone to look after the records, files, and correspondence of the church. This last may be the elected secretary of the Official Board.

As the church grows in complexity, program, and number of members, it may be necessary to have additional staff members who are employed and paid by the church, either full time or part time.

1. How to Determine the Need for Additional Staff Personnel

The primary objectives by the church staff will be to conduct the affairs of the church and administer its programs in the spirit of Christ and for the enrichment of the entire parish. It may be found that these objectives may be achieved more efficiently through trained and paid personnel, who free the minister to concentrate more on the primary spiritual objectives.

Most of our churches will profit by having a personnel committee appointed by the Official Board and responsible to it in an advisory capacity. The minister will be an ex-officio member of this committee. The committee will constantly study the program of the church and will rely on the minister to report to it needs that are not being met or opportunities that could be fulfilled with additional staff assistance.

If the time comes for the church to employ a part-time church secretary or any other worker, the reasons for such employment should be carefully documented. The matter should be carefully surveyed by the personnel committee and a recommendation be made by it to the Official Board.

*A Specific Form of Recommendation
for the Staff*

An example of a study with specific recommendations, made by one minister in a growing community, and then presented to the personnel committee, is contained in the following memorandum:

April 10, 19___

MEMORANDUM FOR: PERSONNEL COMMITTEE AND
                  THE OFFICIAL BOARD CONCERN-
                  ING THE STAFF

FROM: John D. Calhoun, Pastor

I

Having been your pastor now a year and a half, I have had opportunity to evaluate our present staff, the needs of our membership and our opportunities in the community. Several factors are clear:

1. The present system of membership records and addressograph plates is in need of improvement and revision.
2. The church had no active prospect list prior to September 1. That list has received what attention I and other members of the staff of the Committee on Evangelism could give to it. We now have some 500 names of individuals of Protestant background who are living in this community and are without active church affiliation.
3. An improved phase in our public relations in greeting new

people who move into the community is only in its incipient stages. I have done what I could, but the work has been extremely limited in terms of the need and opportunity.

4. In this period, we have instituted several programs that put a heavier strain on our existing staff. Among these are the following:

   a. Regular monthly publication of the church magazine mailed to all members and constituents.
   b. A program of contact, through mail, with students away at school and members of the church serving in the armed forces.
   c. A sermon publication program which entails the mailing of sermons to our membership and other specified individuals.
   d. The beginning of a wider publicity program including not alone the local papers but those of surrounding towns.
   e. Increased activities in the church house which will be augmented further in the Fall. Among groups that have been or will be started in the immediate future are the following:

      (1) Children's Choir.
      (2) Activation of the Young Adult Group, meeting each Sunday afternoon.
      (3) A study class for young homemakers.
      (4) A day nursery school which is planned for opening in the Fall of 1969.
      (5) Family nights for parents of Church School children and the children themselves. (The first to be held this Spring and thereafter two or three each year.)
      (6) A youth program for junior high school-age young people.
      (7) Regular adult religious classes.
      (8) Evening services.
      (9) These, with added attendance at the Women's Society, Couples' Club, and other existing organized groups in the church, have put an added obligation on our present staff. (One hundred and fifty new members have been received in the past year.)
      (10) Also in the picture is the possibility of the organization of a permanent dramatic group in the church.

(11) Also the need for an active men's program is clear. There should be one evening a month for men of the church.

THESE AND OTHER INCREASED PROGRAM ACTIVITIES NECESSITATE ATTENTION FROM ALL MEMBERS OF THE STAFF. The features outlined above may all be put in the category of "new obligations."

II

There is need for the addition to our staff of one further individual at the earliest opportunity.

1 To carry through the above program the present staff is working overtime. They have all shown a most excellent and cooperative spirit, but we are asking too much of them.

2. My recommendation would be that the staff responsibilities be roughly delegated as follows:

a. Miss Anderson to be executive secretary, office receptionist, overseer of the church property, with the sextons under her immediate supervision, representing the Building and Grounds Committee.

b. Mrs. Clausen, as minister's secretary, would be freed from publicity, printing, and general mailing responsibilities (except for special or rush mailings when the whole staff cooperates), to give primary attention to correspondence, assistance in administrative responsibilities, sermon publication, etc., directly related to the minister's study.

c. Mrs. Langley could be in charge of the financial aspect in its entirety under the supervision of Miss Anderson. Mrs. Langley also to be the staff member in charge of all publicity. Also to have charge of the publication of the Sunday morning bulletin and materials for the church magazine.

d. The sextons' duties are well clarified and need no comment, except that consideration might be given the matter of compensation for extra demands placed upon these staff members.

e. *ONE ADDED STAFF MEMBER IS NEEDED.* The primary responsibility of this individual would be to be in charge of the church membership lists, records, addressograph files, etc. This staff member would spearhead a program to find the addresses of the 400-odd church members we have at present listed as "inactive members." A further duty would be to be in charge of the prospect list and the public relations outreach to new people as they move into the community. (As an example of the ramifications of this position, note the attached instructions which we attempt to follow now with the staff for new members who have just joined.)

This additional staff member, as he or she has time, could call in the afternoon on prospective members and new people who move into the community.

While in some ways it might seem desirable to wait until the fall to engage such a person, the work at hand is already very great. To prepare a good membership file and to bring all records up-to-date might well be a full summer's job.

III

The problem of proper work space is a very real one. The best suggestion I have is to put the new staff member with temporary office facilities on the stage of the Assembly Hall. Dr. Jones should have an office somewhere—exactly where, I do not know. The suggestions of the Official Board and the Operations and Maintenance Committee would be very much appreciated. In this connection, added telephone extensions should be considered.

I have consulted with the chairman of the Finance Committee, and while we have no item for salary for such an individual during the current church year, it would appear that from the items of "Contingencies" and "Compensation for Special Work," we can obtain approximately $500 in 1967.

Such a presentation, with its careful and clear documentation of the facts, provides an instrument that fulfills some of the basic items in determining the need for staff personnel. These are:

1. Has the problem been clearly stated?
2. Is there analysis of all the factors and facts, which also are made very clear?
3. Has the proposal taken into account the program of the present staff?
4. Has the documentation shown why the present staff cannot meet the need?
5. Why can't the need be met by committees or volunteers in the church membership?
6. Have appropriate committees been consulted?
7. Has the recommendation been distributed to the Personnel Committee or to the board sufficiently ahead of time so each member may consider the matter before the meeting?

8. Does the proposal to add a new staff member take into account the feelings and responsibilities of the present staff?
9. Has there been adequate preparatory conference with other staff members? Has their judgment and recommendation been sought?
10. How about budget and financing? Can this be done without undue strain on the budget or weakening other aspects of the church program?

J.D.C.

2. THE NEW STAFF MEMBER

The Job Description Should Be Adequate

The pastor and Personnel Committee should clearly define what kind of person they are seeking for the specific job. Age, experience, family responsibilities, temperament, knowledge of and past relationship to the church, and many other items may be on the list to guide the committee in selecting the best person for the position.

But equally important is an outline of the duties of the new employee. This job description should be detailed and should be made clear to the prospective employee. Such a job description should be reviewed and updated at least once a year. One congregation with several staff members outlined the responsibilities as follows:

DUTIES OF THE STAFF

CHRIST CHURCH

(Annual Review)

January, 19___

As Christ Church has grown, the staff responsibilities have changed: 1) to meet the parish needs, and 2) to make fullest use of the individual gifts and abilities of the staff. Each staff member is asked to make notations of any change on his job description made during the year. Such will be noted in the modified job description to be made in January, 19___.

I. *The Pastor* is the chief executive officer of the church and its staff, the moderator of the board and the congregation meetings. As such he is ex-officio member of all boards, councils, and committees in Christ Church.

Besides working directly with the board as a whole, he is specifically requested to work closely with the Advisory, Steering, and Worship Committees of the board.

He is also the staff member assigned to a relationship with the Board of Trustees, the executive board of the Women's Association, and the Men's Club.

The pulpit preaching is his first responsibility, and secondly, such individual counseling as he may be called upon to do. His pastoral calling shall be related to the Pastoral Care Council. His teaching of special groups will be related to the Council of Christian Education.

One area of responsibility is specifically spelled out in the Constitution of the denomination: "There are certain responsibilities which belong to the minister as pastor which are not subject to the authority of the board, but which must be exercised by him subject only to the constitutional authority of the denomination, namely: the selection of the hymns or psalms to be sung at each service, the selection of the passage or passages of Scripture to be read at each service, the leading of the people in prayer, and the preparation and preaching of the sermon." (Form of Government, Ch. VIII, Sec. 4). In the discharge of these responsibilities, he may have the help of the associate pastors and other persons especially trained.

II. *The Associate Pastor* is responsible for the details of the administration of the church's program, and as such is invited to meet regularly with the board and is an ex-officio member of such councils and committees as he may be assigned by the senior pastor.

He is charged specifically with meeting and working with the Board of Deacons, the Council of Pastoral Care, and the Council of Christian Education.

In the Council of Pastoral Care, he is the staff member assigned to work with the Committee on Outreach, concerned specifically with the program of evangelism and orientation.

In the Council of Christian Education he is responsible for implementing its program, and is to supervise other staff persons who are engaged to help in this work.

He is also assigned as the liaison person between the Official Board and the board of the Christ Church Day School, and the Council of Christian Education.

III. *The Assistant Pastor* is responsible for the Youth Program of the church, and as such is invited to meet regularly with the Official Board and is an ex-officio member of the committees directly related to his area of responsibility.

He is assigned to work under the guidance of the Youth Committee of the Committee of Christian Education in the program for young people, junior high through college age.

He also is to work with the pastor in calling and with the Council of Pastoral Care in the fulfillment of other pastoral duties to parishioners.

IV. *The Minister of Music* is called by the Official Board to assist, and be responsible to, the pastor for organizing and directing the activities of the music program, relating them to the total program of the church. He shall work under the guidance of the Council of Church Music in developing choirs, in using the organs and carillon, in directing and supervising the paid and volunteer staff persons in music, and shall participate in the services of worship as needed.

V. *The Business Manager* is called by the Board of Trustees, responsible to it and the pastor for organizing and keeping the financial records, scheduling the use of the building and its facilities, and maintaining the property of the church, relating these responsibilities to the total program of the church. He shall work under the guidance of the Board of Trustees and its various committees in directing and supervising the paid and volunteer staff in the office and building. In addition to the pastor, he is also under the supervision of the chairman of the Maintenance and Operations Committee.

VI. *The Church Hostess* is employed by the Board of Trustees, cleared through and with the approval of the general board of the Women's Association. Her work is under the business manager and with the Women's Kitchen Committee, developing and implementing all social activities of the congregation.

Note: Each employee should be reminded, as assignments or duties are modified, to make the changes in his or her job description for ultimate modification by the personnel committee.

Such job description—as with every paper, memorandum, agenda, minutes—should be dated. If the date is always put in the same place, such as the upper right hand corner, it will be helpful for present and future use.

Duties of Church Administrator

The following outline of the position of Church Administrator suggests only broad areas of responsibility. Actually, the individual who filled this position, however, under each item was given a sizable number of detailed responsibilities and activities.

DUTIES OF CHURCH ADMINISTRATOR
CHRIST CHURCH

I. OFFICE

Supervise, schedule and give direction to the office staff. Prepare and implement such special projects as are assigned by the Official Board. These include the membership directory, annual report, and stewardship visitation.

II. BUILDING AND GROUNDS

Supervision of the work of the custodian and assistants. Schedule and oversee the daily, weekly, and seasonal cleaning and repair of buildings and equipment. Attend trustees meetings and carry out the specific tasks assigned by them (i.e. obtain bids, supervise outside workmen, authorize payment of bills when work completed, etc.).

III. STRATEGY COMMITTEE

Work with Strategy Committee in surveying the future program of the church. Study what other churches are doing and assist the committee in preparing a program to meet projected needs.

IV. USE OF BUILDINGS

Receive requests for use of church property from organizations within and outside the church and clear with the Church Use Committee. Schedule the use for the church calendar and for the office and maintenance staff. See that all groups operate within accepted church procedures.

V. WORK WITH OFFICIAL BOARDS

The Church Administrator is responsible directly to the Board of Trustees and the Personnel Committee of the Official Board. He is to assist other committees of the church (i.e. Stewardship, Budget, etc.) as they request his assistance.

VI. PURCHASE AND INVENTORY

Control all purchases and maintain an inventory of church property.

Checking of References

Every prospective employee should be asked to give references, which, in turn, should be carefully checked.

Wherever it is possible, there should be a personal interview with the individual which the prospective employee gave as a reference.

If such direct conversation is impossible, the individual should be asked in writing to give an honest evaluation of the prospective employee and should be told that any information given would be held in the strictest confidence.

People do not like to say unkind or damaging things about others. So the wise minister and Personnel Committee may be saved mistakes in the hiring of the new employee, or can receive valuable insight into the character of the proposed staff member, by carefully checking with previous employers and acquaintances of the candidate. All such references, whether in notation from direct conference or correspondence, should be placed in a "confidential file."

Interviewing Techniques for
New Personnel

Usually the Personnel Committee will ask the minister, or some other staff member, to do the initial screening of prospective employees. This initial interview is one of extreme informality. The minister, if he is to do the screening, will use all means to put the prospect at ease. If there are several prospects, it may be wise to have a mimeographed paper that requests name, address, telephone number, educational background, interest, hobbies, former work history, together with a list of references. If there is no such form, then the interviewer will make full notes on these facts. Other notations that should be made will include the following: general appearance, attitude, age, etc.

The interviewer should be seeking to determine whether the individual is interested in the position, and should listen attentively and make mental notes, if not on paper, regarding any impression of the prospect.

The second interview will probably be with the minister and one, or more, members of the Personnel Committee.

It should be recognized that the prospect may be in a stress situation and everything must be done to create an atmosphere of ease and conviviality. The factor of possible nervousness on the part of the prospect should be taken into account in the final evaluation.

The merit in having more than one individual's judgment is obvious. The staff member in the church will be related to many people and will become a part of the church family. Several minds and hearts can bring better judgment to bear as to the worth of the prospective individual than the single interviewer.

The interview should be kept on a high plane. It may be appropriate for the minister to open or close the interview with a word of prayer. Certainly it is most appropriate for the minister or the chairman of the Personnel Committee to make a brief statement as to the spiritual aims and objectives of the church and to indicate that the employee will be a very real part in fulfilling that primary end of the congregational life.

Following the interview the minister and those who have spoken with the prospective employee should have a frank and prompt conference of evaluation. If the corporate judgment is that the particular individual is suitable for the position, the recommendation, going through the Personnel Committee, will be approved by the Official Board, which already will have given assent to the Personnel Committee to seek the new staff member.

There is value in keeping, in a confidential file, the notations and application forms of those who have applied for the position, even though all may not have been hired. This material may be helpful for future reference when a new employee may be needed through unexpected changes in the staff or in the program of the church.

Informing Applicant of Details of Employment Conditions

During the interview the employee should be informed as to hours, salary, and all other details regarding the position. When the decision is reached to extend an invitation to the employee to join the staff, all such details should be spelled out in a formal letter to the prospective employee. It is a good idea to make two copies of the letter and ask the employee to sign one in acknowledgment and acceptance and return it for the office files.

If there are several employees in the church, it may be desirable to prepare a personnel policy and duplicate it so that each employee and certainly every new employee will have a copy. An example of such is the following:

PERSONNEL POLICIES CHRIST CHURCH

May 19___

I. EMPLOYMENT

The minister and others specifically designated are employed by an official call in accordance with Presbyterian

Law. All other personnel are employed on the recommendation of:

A. The minister

B. The pertinent operating committee

C. The Personnel Committee

Recommendations must be approved by the Official Board and/or the trustees, or the congregation, whichever is requisite, prior to employment.

II. SALARIES

Initial salaries will be established by those recommending and approving employment. Salaries will be reviewed annually and recommended changes submitted to the Budget Committee. Salaries are normally paid bi-monthly on the fifteenth and last day of each month.

III. DEDUCTIONS

Deductions, where applicable, are made for the following:

A. All federal and state employment and income taxes

B. Hospitalization insurance payments

C. Group insurance

IV. HOSPITALIZATION AND MEDICAL PLAN

All employees have the option to participate in the Group Blue Cross-Blue Shield hospitalization and medical plan available. Participation is strictly on a voluntary basis. The policy of Christ Church is to pay one-third of the annual premium. The employee, if participation is elected, is to pay two-thirds of the premium, which will be deducted from the employee's salary.

V. VACATIONS

The minister is entitled to one month, plus two extra Sundays, vacation per year.

The director of Christian Education, and other personnel employed by an official call, shall be entitled to one month's vacation per annum.

All other full-time employees shall be entitled to vacations as follows:

A. After one year's full employment—two weeks

B. After five years' full employment—three weeks

C. After ten years' full employment—four weeks

Earned vacations shall be with full pay at the employee's normal rate of pay. Vacations are not cumulative from one year to the next. On the item of vacations, the church treasurer, choir director, and organist are considered full-time employees.

Part-time employees, such as Youth Choir directors and Youth organist, and Youth worker, are not eligible for vacations.

Present employees who have earned, by a previous policy, vacation in excess of those stated above, will continue under the old plan.

VI. TIME OFF, OTHER THAN VACATIONS

A reasonable time off, with pay, will be allowed for illness. In the case of an extended illness, the church will use as a guide the general practices of local industries in dealing with each individual case.

Time off, other than for illness, requested by the employee will be without pay. Such time off must have the approval of the minister and the pertinent operating committee, and must be requested far enough in advance so that the services of a qualified substitute may be obtained.

VII. RETIREMENT

The church does not have a retirement plan for all employees. Payments are made to the denominational retirement fund and considered part of total compensation for certain employees.

Note: The details of employment are subject to annual review. The personnel committee should periodically study the work program, salaries, and other items pertaining to the staff. The minister will be in the most sensitive position to make recommendations for change in personnel policy and is the key person to give the Personnel Committee an evaluation of each employee's attitude and work.

How to Introduce the
New Staff Member to
His Work

Every effort should be made to see that the new employee begins his work under the most favorable circumstances. He should be warmly introduced to all members of the staff. It may be beneficial to retain the outgoing staff member to work with the new employee for several days, guiding, coaching, and making him familiar with details of his new work. This is largely dependent on the attitude of the retiring employee and the reasons for his resignation. In some instances it may be wiser for the new staff member to begin his work without any relationship to the past employee.

It should be clearly understood who is "the boss." If the church has a business manager in charge of the office, and the new employee is a secretary, it should be clear that the office manager will oversee and supervise the work of the employee and is the one to be consulted regarding any questions of procedure. It should, however, be understood that the minister is the chief administrative officer and the church manager has his authority by delegation. The minister should be available as a friend and counselor to all members of the staff.

The chief administrative officer does well at the beginning of an employee's term to convey the idea: "Your work is very important. You are now a member of a small team, where there is a desire to serve all the congregation and where we have a deep commitment to cooperate with each other in the service of Christ."

The minister will be generous in commendation for work well-done and will be exacting in expecting the highest quality of work.

Felicitous introductions of the new staff member should be made to key people of the Official Board. This is particularly important when there may be responsibilities on the employee's part to committees and leaders of the Official Board. It must be made clear what the relationship of the Personnel Committee is to the employee. This should be stated to the employee in the presence of the chairman of the Personnel Committee and possibly other committee members.

Relationship of the Personnel
Committee to the Staff Member

The staff members should understand the function of the Personnel Committee. For most churches, the Personnel Committee is the liaison instrument between the employee and the Official Board.

In introducing the Personnel Committee to the new employee, the minister may fitly indicate that the committee seeks to serve the best interests of the congregation but also is the instrumentality of the board as a friend and supporter of the employee. In this connection the Personnel Committee will give thoughtful concern to the working conditions, salary, sick leave, vacations, and all other items that have to do with the welfare of the staff member.

The chairman of the Personnel Committee, in his turn, should make it clear to the staff member where the "staff responsibility" of the employee lies and will indicate that the committee expects observance of all office rules and procedures and the fullest cooperation with the minister of the church.

As the minister is an ex-officio member of the Personnel Committee, he is usually the agent to bring requests of employees to the committee. However, it may be appropriate for the chairman of the committee to say that if there are unusual personal problems, the individual staff member is to feel free to come directly to the chairman of the committee. Here is an area requiring the highest discretion and clarity. There cannot be two "heads" and the employee must be made to feel that the chief responsibility is to the pastor. The wise employee does not "go over the chief administrator's head."

Personnel Committee Counseling with Staff Members

In the event tension develops between the minister and the staff member, the personnel chairman or another member of the committee may be helpful in resolving the situation by counseling with each of the parties. The Personnel Committee may find it desirable to have an annual or biennial conference with the employee.

One church has developed the following points for the committee's guidance at such a conference:

CHRIST CHURCH

PERSONNEL COMMITTEE

INTERVIEW GUIDE WITH STAFF PERSONNEL

Suggestions on points to be covered by the Personnel Committee during interview with employees. Interviews held once or twice a year can prove very valuable.

1. The opening of the interview should always point up the purposes, such as:
   a. Better acquaintance between the staff and church officers.
   b. Improvement of communications between the employees, church officers and church members.

2. Discussion of the assignment of the employee:
   a. Does he like the type of work he is doing?
   b. What part of overall duties are most difficult to perform or tolerate?
   c. If any point of this nature is mentioned by the employee, what can be done to improve the situation?
      (1) What should the employee do about it?
      (2) What does the employee feel the Personnel Committee could do about it?
3. Does the physical setup in connection with his job—location, equipment, etc.—contribute to the efficiency of the employee's job performance or otherwise?
4. Is there a general feeling of friendliness and harmony among all employees?
5. What, in the employee's opinion, can he do to make himself more valuable in his assignment?
6. A discussion may helpfully proceed to those areas in which others—ministers, Official Board members, trustees—feel opportunity exists for improvement in the employee's job performance.
7. Are there any other matters or suggestions the employee would like to discuss?

Note:

1. It would be well to plan the interview for a time when the employee is not involved in work which cannot readily be put aside. Further, a more satisfactory result will be obtained if strict privacy, free from any interruptions, is observed.
2. It is important that no commitments as to salaries, duties or other matters be made except to assure the employee that further thought and consideration will be given to any points raised by him.
3. An expression of appreciation should be made to the employee for his cooperation during the interview.

Periodic Review of Individual
Performance Standards

When an individual is employed, it may be highly desirable to have a "trial period" of one month to three months. At the end of this time the work of the individual will be reviewed and if all is satisfactory, it will be indicated that the arrangements henceforth are of a permanent nature. The advantages of such an arrangement are several. In the event the employee is not efficient, the termination can be made with a minimum of feeling. It has the further advantage of stimulating the employee to do well. The initial period can be one of high concentration and more rapid adaptability to the job. If this item is understood at the beginning of employment, it should be spelled out in writing in the detailed letter of invitation.

In addition to an annual review by the personnel committee, it may be useful for the chief administrator to review the employee's work periodically with him, noting any changes in the job description and seeking to discover if the employee is happy and offering any suggestions as to how the work might be improved.

3. Supervision of the Staff

Staff Meetings, Worship,
Social Affairs

The good administrator will constantly seek to create good morale among his staff members. Adequate communication is a significant item in achieving that end. People need to be informed. A weekly staff meeting may be in order. The meeting can be held at noon time with a simple lunch, or it may be during working hours at a convenient time when one of the group will cover the switchboard. One purpose of the meeting is to review the immediate past programs in the church and to ask how such may be improved for future occasions. Notes should be taken of the meeting. One member of the staff should prepare the minutes and see that they are distributed to the other members of the staff.

A further purpose of the meeting will be to review the immediate future programs of the church. Assignments of responsibility will be made.

The staff meeting further can provide an opportunity for the stimulation of creative suggestions and ideas. It should be a clearing house for any questions involving the various departments and activities of the church. The minister customarily serves as chairman of the staff meeting and he will regularly report on the decisions of the Official Board. Then, too, he should have his own thinking and vision for the welfare of the church.

The staff meeting provides occasion when errors may be rectified and when improvements in the policy and program can be discussed.

Many churches are enriched through occasions when the staff gathers for worship. This may be done at the opening of the office day, five times a week. The worship may be in the sanctuary itself, or a small chapel, or in the church office or a board room. A brief reading of scripture and a prayer may suffice.

One church holds a regular ten-minute service at 8:50 A.M. each weekday in the chapel. The congregation is notified and all are invited to share in this brief period of morning prayer. The staff members are particularly invited, but it is not required that they be present. Asking the Lord's blessing and guidance on the work of the church and on the individual tasks of the staff members can inspire a sense of commitment and elevate the tone of the church office and all departments of the congregational life.

Occasional social affairs for the staff members and their husbands or wives may be a source of deepening friendship and camaraderie among the individual members. It can mean a great deal to the staff to have an evening occasion in the pastor's home and to come to know him and his family. A picnic, an outing at some distance from the church property, and where the spirit and intent of the occasion is just fun and conviviality, may prove worthwhile.

Paper on Staff Relationships

A paper on staff relationships which shows concern for desirable morale can be set up as follows at desirable times:

March 19___

STAFF RELATIONSHIPS IN CHRIST CHURCH

Our role as leaders in the life of this congregation can be summed up in the words of St. Paul: ". . . Each has his own special gift from God, one of one kind and one of another." Our concern is for people within and without the walls of what we call the organized church. In our committed service to all people whom God must love, we find ourselves and the mission of the church.

The church is a means of God's salvation to the world and we are His instruments each with our own talents. It is the cause and purpose for which we are organized that is "the first and last item."

1. As members of the staff of Christ Church we function to-

gether in a team ministry. We are one working fellowship serving in and for a cause greater than ourselves, either individually or corporately. Our chief loyalty is to Jesus Christ, the great head of the church, for whom we labor in this particular place. At the same time, we seek to fulfill our calling through a humble and loving ministry to those with whom we work and the congregation we serve.

2. Our loyalty to one another is a reflection of our loyalty to Christ. Our emphasis in this mutual responsibility is on unity, harmony and cooperation. We mutually stimulate each other, develop program together, worship and work and play together, so we will have a part in causing the church to move forward, fulfilling its destiny in the world. Accomplishments are achieved by the total staff. However, each individual will have certain areas for personal achievement, but most always well complemented by the total staff.

3. Every team must have a captain. This is the role of the senior minister. He is called by the congregation to administer the entire program of the church for which he is ultimately held responsible. Obviously, this is not something one person can do alone. Thus, we have a team of individuals, trained and qualified, to serve in particular areas of specialization, with responsibility for that area. At the same time, every aspect of the church is a concern of the entire staff. As we share together in this intense relationship of a group ministry we develop a sensitivity toward each other and our work which expresses itself in a unique rapport with one another and with the entire congregation.

4. We carry a heavy load, individually and together. Each person's time is extremely valuable in the economy of service. Respect for the work and study time of each person is important. Plan carefully and in advance. Seek to avoid changes in schedules once established and the ensuing last-minute pressures. Anticipate problems and conflicts and have practical suggestions in advance where possible. Attention to all details is of utmost importance. Double-check rather than take a chance.

5. Let us operate together as economically as possible. We are all servants of the church. We should never be miserly; neither should we be careless. Thoughtful ordering is important. Careful use of equipment and supplies is essential. Simple practices of economy can show a marked saving

in the budget at the end of the year. Plan generously, but with as little waste as possible.

6. If acute problems develop, it may be best to consult with the senior minister. Where problems come up in a given area of responsibility, use good judgment in working them out. Call on the minister for his aid or counsel only when the problem is complex or may be a matter involving other areas of the church life.

7. Regular staff meetings will be held to discuss program, projects and detail of administration. Questions, reviews, and announcements should be cleared through this mutually shared time. It is essential that we keep each other informed. Free communication, both formal and informal, gives us insight into the various activities and the spirit behind them.

8. Help to see that the church is neat and in good order at all times. An immaculate church indicates Christian concern for the appearance of God's house. Encourage others of the congregation to leave areas of activity neat, attractive and uncluttered. Please see that your desk gives the appearance of order.

9. The personal touch is important in maintaining good public relations. The way we deal with people personally, by telephone or by letter represents our entire church and its good name. In the service of the Master, we deal in service. Every contact we make, the way we make it and how we handle it, speaks for all of us.

10. Let us deal with our common faults, mistakes and needs in Christian love and charity. Above all, let us seek to be creative and always helpful. At some points, dialogue in depth may help ease tension and renew spiritual bonds.

11. In order to have a uniform understanding of administrative procedure, these points of policy are noted.

   a. Any special time-off periods should first be discussed with the minister. Regular days off have been established and as nearly as possible normal personal needs should be cared for on these days. Vacation plans will be worked out individually with all members of the staff by the senior minister.

   b. Salaries are determined by the Personnel Committee, taking into consideration total church budget and all factors relating to a particular position. Salaries are personal and if for any reason there may be need for discussion, this should be done with the senior minister.

c. Staff hours will vary because of the particular demands of the various areas of service. Each person will want to establish and maintain his own discipline in regard to a pattern of working hours and then give his best. Each person who has a specific time commitment will want to do his part by being on time. Any departures from what has become our regular schedule should be noted with the office so that one may be contacted in case of an emergency or callers may be informed where one can be reached or the expected time of arrival. Keep the church office informed during regular working hours when you leave your point of contact for any length of time.

d. Messages taken for another member of the staff should be placed on that person's desk immediately. Report every telephone call to the person for whom it was intended, even if no message was left. Return all telephone calls promptly.

12. Programs

a. Recommendations from the staff regarding any aspect of the church should be cleared through appropriate board committees. Where such reference is not feasible, the senior minister will present the recommendations.

b. All activities and programs for which staff members have responsibility should start promptly. Be present in advance of every appointment to see that all is in readiness. At times when a staff member cannot be present for a meeting where he has responsibility, another should be notified and briefed completely.

c. All committee meetings and activities or any use of the building should be noted in the parish date book.

d. Personal use of church equipment should be approved by the business administrator. The borrowing of equipment can be done only in keeping with the principles outlined by the Maintenance and Operations Committee.

e. All supplies are ordered through the administrator, so that a proper inventory and budget check can be accurately maintained.

Staff Meeting Agendas

It is helpful to have an agenda for the staff meeting. Each staff member, with a copy of the agenda in his hands, can make notes at the side of any item, particularly so when a decision is made concerning his department or responsibility. Minutes of each meeting are distributed to all members. The following agenda proved useful in the church where it was developed, and can be revised to fit the needs of any particular church:

STAFF MEETING AGENDA

CHRIST CHURCH

January 16, 19___

  I. Dates and schedule

  II. Building and grounds

    Special setups

    General maintenance

    Lockup arrangements

  III. Office supplies and procedures

  IV. Calling

    Hospital

    Regular

    Prospective member

  V. Church weekly

    Assignments

    Special deadlines

  VI. Sunday schedule

    Worship assignments

    Adult education program

    Special events

  VII. Program and committee review

    Boards and their committees

    Budget

    Educational program

    Men's program

    Membership seminars and receptions

    Music

    Seasonal events

    Senior citizens

    Women's program

    Youth

  VIII. Old business

    (Review items from last meeting)

  IX. New business

  X. Adjournment with prayer

Organization of the Annual
Staff Conference

The entire work of the church for the coming year can be synchronized, the yearly church calendar established, and many matters of policy can be effectively organized at an annual staff conference.

The minister is the key leader in such a conference. Throughout the year he will be available to individual staff members and will make a point of being accessible for personal and group conferences to his staff. He will remember Stevenson's comment: "Extreme busyness is a symptom of deficient vitality."

But at the staff conference he can create a unique atmosphere of relaxation and at the same time, one that stimulates the thinking and action of the entire group.

Certain individuals will be assigned responsibility for bringing proper materials to the staff conference—notebooks, pencils, typewriter, etc. Careful notes will be taken and the results of the conference will be put in a memorandum for each member, and, where appropriate, for the Official Board and other major committees.

Careful preparation will have been made for some months prior to this staff conference. Regular weekly staff meetings will have an item on the agenda concerning the staff conference. One staff member will have been assigned the part of compiling all items mentioned during the year which are appropriate for discussion at the conference. These will be incorporated into an agenda.

The staff conference should open and close with worship. Often it is meaningful to have a final service of dedication with the celebration of the Lord's Supper.

There should be opportunity for interdepartmental discussions and occasion for the clearing of relationships in program between the various departments of the church, as for example between the Music Department and Christian Education. Occasion should be provided for quiet and for group fun.

Many items beyond the yearly calendar, and agreed-on major emphasis for the coming year, may be evaluated in detail at the staff conference. One church developed at its annual staff conference an office work schedule for the financial and church secretaries. It was put in condensed form, with additional elaborations and explanations further spelled out, as will be noted in the following work schedule and notes:

Typical Office Work Schedule

OFFICE WORK SCHEDULE
CHRIST CHURCH

	Church Secretary	Financial Secretary
Monday	*TELEPHONE RESPONSIBILITY* *a.m.* Posting changes in membership file, addressograph file, zone file, church register. *p.m.* Letters of transfer, visitor letters, dictation.	*a.m.* Counting money. *p.m.* Posting pledges. ONLY EMERGENCY PHONE CALLS MONDAY.
Tuesday	*a.m.* Hospital listing; activity schedule. *p.m.* Church register until done; ONLY EMERGENCY PHONE CALLS.	*TELEPHONE RESPONSIBILITY* *a.m.* and *p.m.* General weekly work on Board of Trustees and Board of Deacons reports, minutes, notice of meetings, etc.
Wednesday	*a.m. TELEPHONE RESPONSIBILITY* *p.m. Church Weekly* addressed, folded.	*a.m.* Bookkeeping and notices regarding the Church School, Young People's Society, etc. *p.m. TELEPHONE RESPONSIBILITY*.
Thursday	*a.m.* Hospital listing; work on *Church Weekly*. *p.m.* Church Register until done; ONLY EMERGENCY PHONE CALLS.	*TELEPHONE RESPONSIBILITY* *a.m.* Work of director of Christion Education. EMERGENCY PHONE CALLS ONLY. *p.m.* Payment of bills.

Friday

TELEPHONE RESPONSIBILITY

a.m. Work on board minutes, mimeo minutes; board committee needs.

p.m. Monthly mailing Friday after W.A. board meeting.

a.m. Counting money and posting receipts. ONLY EMERGENCY PHONE CALLS.

p.m. Completion of all correspondence of the assistant minister and the director of Christian Education.

Saturday

8:30 a.m. to 12 Noon

Hospital listing; mimeographing for Sunday for Chr. Educ.; Men's Club mailing last Saturday of month; dictation.

Notes on Schedule

The foregoing schedule merely indicates periods during the week when secretaries give priority to certain responsibilities. It is also to indicate who has responsibility for the telephone, and times when secretaries are to be free from interruption.

Professional staff members, unless they agree or in case of bona fide emergency, are not available for telephone calls on Monday, at the office or at their homes.

WHEN TAKING TELEPHONE MESSAGES, TAKE DOWN FULL NAME OF PERSON CALLING AND THE TELEPHONE NUMBER WHERE THE CALL CAN BE RETURNED.

Church secretary's hours are 9 a.m. to 5 p.m. and the financial secretary's, 8:30 a.m. to 4:30 p.m. They alternate Saturdays from 8:30 a.m. to 12 noon in the church office. Neither secretary is expected to work overtime except in case of emergency. Overtime work shall be reimbursed at the rate of $1.75 per hour.

THE USE OF OTHER PAID OR VOLUNTEER ASSISTANCE IN THE CHURCH OFFICE ON ANY BASIS SHALL BE CLEARED WITH THE PASTOR IN ADVANCE OF ANY FINAL ARRANGEMENTS.

The director of Christian Education and the assistant pastor (visitation) give their work to the financial secretary, as does the music staff. The pastor and assistant pastor give their work to the church secretary. Any professional staff member can use the IBM dictating equipment; two identical combination recording-transcription machines are available—one in the pastor's office and the other either at the church secretary's desk or the assistant pastor's office. Both secretaries can transcribe material from these machines.

The church office will make every effort to care for needs of committees and organizations within the church, and such groups as the Ministerial Association or Association of Churches. Work will be done in sequence received by the secretaries; questions concerning priority of work orders shall be decided by the pastor, or, in his absence, the assistant pastor.

IN ANY EVENT, WORK FROM COMMITTEES, CHURCH OFFICERS, ORGANIZATIONS IN THE CHURCH SHOULD BE GIVEN FORTY-EIGHT HOURS BEFORE NEEDED, LONGER IF IT IN-VOLVES A CONSIDERABLE WORK LOAD. CHURCH ORGANIZATIONS ARE REQUESTED TO CARE FOR ENVELOPING OF THEIR MAILINGS.

Questions in specified areas are always to be referred to the staff members indicated below:

CHURCH SECRETARY

Official Board records	Flower orders
Membership records	Hospital calling
Official Board committees	Building schedule
Addressograph plates	Regular church files
Church register	Baptism and Communion
Changes in membership	The Sunday Bulletin

FINANCIAL SECRETARY

All financial records	Postage meter
All trustee records	Mailing permits
All deacon concerns	Inventory on paper, etc.
Maintenance contracts	Emergency calls on building
Office equipment	maintenance

DIRECTOR OF CHRISTIAN EDUCATION

Church School	Nursery care
Weekday kindergarten	Senior citizens
Audio-visual equipment	Youth Council, jr. high group

PASTOR

Worship and preaching	Adult education, Library
Membership seminars	Church board organization

ASSISTANT PASTOR

Prospective members   Athletic program
Mariners Club   Youth communicant class
Senior high program   Shut-in members

Relationship of the Staff
Members to the Congregation

Good morale will be assisted in a healthy relationship of the staff members to the congregation. A warm and dignified introduction of the staff to the church membership as a whole is in order. When new staff members are employed, a biographical sketch in the Sunday Bulletin or magazine will be of interest to all concerned. At annual meetings of the congregation, the minister may make a point of introducing each staff member to the congregation and indicate the areas of his or her responsibility. He may use such occasions to express appreciation.

The minister should protect the staff members against unwarranted intrusion by individuals. It should be clear what responsibility the staff member has to individual committee chairmen and board members. It should be a clear policy that any special request for the time and services of a staff member, if it has not been previously ascertained, should have the approval of the business manager or pastor.

The pastor will remind the staff of the basic rules of courtesy and will teach such simple rules as rising from one's seat when a member of the congregation comes to one's desk. The pastor will encourage staff members to make note of pertinent information regarding the individual church member, which may be useful in the family record file or to the pastor when he calls. Such information should be given to the pastor in brief written memos.

The recognition of long and loyal service by a staff employee may fittingly be done before the congregation at the annual meeting or some other significant time in the church year.

Office Hours and General
Deportment of Staff Members

Every member of the staff should be promptly at his office at the agreed opening time of the office and will be expected to fulfill the work schedule of the day by the time the church office closes. If an employee is habitually late or otherwise delinquent, the pastor should speak to that individual directly and privately, requesting a more adequate fulfillment of the responsibility.

The staff member should be expected to be neat in appearance, wearing clothing that is not too gaudy.

Courtesy toward other staff members and all who enter the church will be expected. Loud talking will be discouraged, as well as long personal conversations between staff members during office hours.

Statement of Employment
Regulations and Policies

Aspects of the employee's relationship to the church will probably have to be changed from time to time. Employment policies, sick leave, holidays, etc., of course will be spelled out and put in writing for each staff member. An example of detailed further points that were helpful to employees of one church, is the following:

DETAILS OF STAFF EMPLOYMENT

CHRIST CHURCH

January 1, 19____

I. HOLIDAYS

Employees shall be entitled to the following holidays with pay as they fall on a regular work day:

New Year's Day (January 1)
Good Friday (the afternoon free)
Memorial Day (May 30)
Independence Day (July 4)
Labor Day (first Monday in September)
Thanksgiving Day (fourth Thursday in November)
Christmas Eve, one-half day (December 24)
Christmas Day (December 25)

If holidays fall on the weekend, the Personnel Committee will determine if a prior or subsequent day will be designated as a holiday.

II. VACATIONS

1. Not more than one member of the office staff shall be on vacation at the same period.

2. Vacations should be planned in advance with the approval of the minister and office administrator.
3. Inasmuch as peak work periods exist at certain seasons of each year, vacations should be planned so staff members will not take vacations during the times of heavy work loads.
4. Vacation days accumulated by an employee for future use shall not exceed ten working days.
5. Compensation for accumulated unused vacation will be paid only at the time when employment is terminated.
6. Modifications of the foregoing shall be presented to the Personnel Committee for consideration and decision.
7. Records of vacation and sick leave credits and debits for each employee will be kept by the financial secretary.

III. OFFICE HOURS

1. The work day for *office* employees shall be as follows:
   9 a.m. to 12 noon; 1 p.m. to 5 p.m. Monday through Friday.
   The church office also will be open on Saturday from 9 a.m. to 12 noon.
2. Be prompt at all times and in all relationships and responsibilities.
3. If you are to be away from your desk during office hours, let the switchboard operator know where you may be reached.
4. Keep your desk neat.
5. Observe every rule of courtesy and helpfulness to church members.
6. Keep your promise on every commitment.
7. Learn all aspects of the church life so you can be an interpreter to any visitor or member of the congregation.
8. While your assignment and job description has been described specifically, be flexible and cooperative in assisting other staff members at times of demanding responsibility.
9. Constantly seek to let the spirit of Christ be reflected in your attitude toward your work and the men and women and children of the congregation whom you are called to serve.

Weekly Schedule of Events

There is merit in preparing a weekly schedule of all events for every staff member. The schedule should indicate the hour of each meeting or activity and designate the staff member responsible and all details regarding required assignments. The details will include answers to these questions:

1. What chairs and tables are to be set up, and in what arrangement?
2. A lectern?
3. Loud-speaking system?
4. Any special materials on the chairs or tables or by the entrance?
5. What special equipment, such as screen, slide projector, sound movie equipment, blackboard, etc.?
6. Who may be contacted for further instructions?
7. What is the adjournment time?
8. Any kitchen equipment to be used? If so, who is in charge of refreshments? When is it to be served and where? Who is responsible for the clean-up?

4. EXAMPLES OF JOB DESCRIPTIONS OF
PRINCIPAL STAFF POSITIONS

The Minister and Assistant Ministers

It is good for the minister to have a specific outline of his responsibilities, as it is for the assistant and/or associate. The "call" of the minister will state his responsibilities, but as in the case of developing bylaws for a congregation, there may be merit in detailing the expectations for the pastor and assistants in a specific print. The outlines or specific job descriptions may take some such form as the following examples:

JOB DESCRIPTION OF THE SENIOR MINISTER

CHRIST CHURCH

July, 19__

The senior minister is elected by the congregation to lead the spiritual life of Christ Church in accordance with the constitution of our national denominations and the sectional judicatory.

DUTIES

1. Provide spiritual leadership in conducting worship services, preaching of the Gospel, administering the sacraments and conducting the Holy Rites of the church.
2. Perform pastoral responsibilities by visitation of the sick, shut-ins, and the bereaved; counsel on marriage and varied personal needs of individuals.

3. Oversee the Christian Education program and conduct young people's communicant classes.
4. Be responsible for the general coordination of all church activities. Act as moderator of the congregation and Official Board, advisor to the Board of Trustees, and administrator of the church staff, and coordinate the worship aims with the music program.
5. Advise and work with the various organized groups of Christ Church, such as the Women's Association and the Men's Council. See that all church affiliated organizations act in accord with the purposes of the church and are placed under the oversight of the Official Board.
6. Conduct training of church officers and oversee the stewardship program.
7. Edit the monthly magazine and Sunday bulletins. Direct church publicity and oversee the selection of books and periodicals for the literature desks and library.
8. Promote the efficiency and morale of the church staff and encourage the development of individual staff members in their respective areas of responsibility.
9. Represent Christ Church in the judicatories of the denomination. Participate in the wider relationships of Christian mission work in the community, nation, and the world.
10. Submit written quarterly reports on activities, plans and accomplishments to the Official Board.
11. Assign portions of the duties of the senior minister to staff or lay personnel when necessary and with approval of the Official Board.

JOB DESCRIPTION FOR ASSISTANT/ASSOCIATE MINISTER

CHRIST CHURCH

January, 19__

The assistant-associate minister of Christ Church shall support the senior minister in the pastoral responsibility of the church in harmony with the philosophy and practices of our denomination and in conformity with the authority of the Official Board of Christ Church.

DUTIES

1. Perform these pastoral duties which create, develop, and enhance the evangelism program, by visitation calls, by training lay groups in fellowship evangelism. Train lay leaders for a parish program involving all members. Be the staff

coordinator of the work of the evangelism committee of the board. Conduct classes for the assimilation of new adult members.

2. Assist the senior minister in the conduct of adult communicant classes. Serve as staff coordinator of the "Outreach Committee" of Christ Church.

3. Serve as moderator of the deacons and deaconesses, and as staff adviser to designated organized adult groups of the church, and assist groups in furthering the fellowship activities of Christ Church.

4. Assist the senior minister in the preaching mission by filling the pulpit in the absence of the senior minister and preaching a minimum of one Sunday each six months. Provide a ministry to young people in overseeing the Youth Chapel. Assist the senior minister in the conduct of worship, administration of sacraments and rites as called upon.

5. Assist in the Christian development of Christ Church through sponsored family programs, education, study groups, prayer meetings, and other programs to enhance the growth of the spiritual life of Christ Church.

6. Represent Christ Church and the Official Board in various denominational activities when commissioned thereto, and coordinate, disseminate, and train in the general mission and program of the church.

7. Share in the assigned administrative tasks of the church and assist in the development of and training for the Every Member Canvass program.

8. Submit a written quarterly report on his activities, plans and accomplishments to the senior minister and Official Board.

A Simplified Outline

Another more simplified outline was prepared by an Official Board in a growing church when a third minister was added to the staff and the areas of responsibility for each clergyman should appropriately be clarified.

AREAS OF RESPONSIBILITY OF OUR MINISTER

CHRIST CHURCH

March 1, 19___

In order to develop the smooth functioning of the three ministers of the church, it seems desirable to set forth the particular duties of each. This job analysis should facilitate handling of various duties by the ministry, avoid unnecessary duplication, and insure the maximum of cooperation and coordination, both with ministers, church personnel, and laymen. It is believed that such a job analysis, approved by the Official Board, will be helpful to this and succeeding boards when changes or additions to ministerial duties come up for consideration.

1. *The Senior Minister*

   Has overall charge of and responsibility for:
   a. Church services, including preaching, special services, music.
   b. Church administration.
   c. Church School administration.
   d. Pastoral calling.
   e. Church organizations.
   Reports to the Official Board.

2. *The Associate Minister*

   a. Assists the minister when called on and should be prepared to handle any services or duties of the minister.
   b. Is responsible for pastoral calling, both present and prospective members, calls on sick, bereaved and special cases.
   c. Preaches and conducts services when called on by the minister or the Official Board.
   d. Works with organizations as requested by the minister or the Official Board.
   Reports to the minister and the Official Board.

3. *The Assistant Minister, Minister of Education*

   a. Takes charge of the Education Department.
   b. Secures and trains teachers.
   c. Organizes and supervises the Sunday School.
   d. Organizes and supervises adult education classes, etc.
   e. Assists with other church functions when called on by the minister or the Official Board.
   Reports to the minister and the Official Board.

It is the hope of the Official Board that each minister will have a working knowledge of the duties of the other ministers to the end that each may assist, and, if need be, take over the duties of another minister should the occasion arise.

It is our further hope that in our growing parish there may be a "team ministry" with the highest degree of cooperation between our ministers to the end that our leadership may give the maximum spiritual guidance to our congregation and the cause of Christ.

Organist, Choirmaster

The Director of Music, if he combines in himself the position of organist and choirmaster, will certainly have the following items incorporated into his "job description":

Responsibility to the Official Board for the music of the church through the Music Committee.

Oversight of the organ and the playing of it for all worship regular and special services of the church.

The training of the choir or choirs.

The care of the music library and the ordering of music within the budget provided for the purchase of new music.

General administrator or executive secretary of the Choir Guild and choir organization.

Oversight and direction of the office for the choirmaster and any secretarial help that may be employed to assist in the musical program.

Responsible for sending out notices to the choir members and the development of all written materials regarding the choirs.

In charge of planning and executing any special musical events, such as organ recitals, choir festivals and others.

Organist for weddings, funerals, baptisms, and other private occasions. Other musicians requested by parishioners shall use the organ only on approval by the organist.

The organist and choirmaster may use the organ for the giving of private lessons, but shall permit the use of the organ for practice by his pupils on a limited basis.

Director of Christian Education

A key staff member in the growing church that seeks to develop a strong educational program for its children and adults is that of director or "minister" of Christian Education. One fairly inclusive job description of this staff position is as follows:

DUTIES OF THE DIRECTOR OF CHRISTIAN EDUCATION

CHRIST CHURCH

November 7, 19___

The director of Christian Education shall have overall responsibility for providing and promoting a program serving the educational needs of the entire congregation, consistent with the philosophies and practices of this denomination as directed by the senior minister and the Christian Education Committee, and in conformity with the authority of the Official Board.

DUTIES

1) Provide supervision and planning for the Sunday Church School, Vacation Church School, Sunday Evening Youth Program, weekday Christian Education activities for youth and adult organizations, and other special projects or programs which are considered essential to the educational life of the congregation.

2) Assess the personnel needs of the educational program. Revise and execute means for recruitment and assume responsibility for teacher and staff on-going training.

3) Assess the literature, audio-visual aids, church library and other educational equipment and materials needed for instruction, and insure that adequate stocks and supplies are requisitioned and on hand. Promote the use of materials and equipment which are considered useful to the success of the educational program.

4) Call and promote calls on families and individuals to strengthen relationships between families and the Christian Education program.

5) Represent Christ Church in, and provide leadership for, various denominational and ecumenical youth activities and training programs.

6) Act as staff representative on the Christian Education Committee.

7) Promote and arrange leadership schools, conferences, and programs related to Christian Education.

8) Attend staff meetings called by the senior minister and keep him briefed on plans, problems, and other matters regarding the conduct of the Christian Education program. Coordinate all activities with the senior pastor to insure there are no conflicts of effort and dates.

9) Be responsible for initiating suggestions for the annual budget items for Christian Education.

10) Submit written quarterly reports on activities, plans and accomplishments to the senior pastor and the Official Board.

11) Coordinate the use of church facilities with other organizations, such as the weekday kindergarten and the Women's Association.

12) Consult with the Christian Education Committee on prob-

lems concerning school programs, teacher recruitment, new educational materials, training programs, promotional plans, and budget requirements.

This office should be given every possible recognition in the church. Ideally, the director or minister of Christian Education should be installed before the congregation and all possible should be done to gain support from the entire membership for the educational mission of the church.

Administrative Assistant

As needs in the individual church change, it may be wise to assign a staff member to certain business and administrative duties in the church operation that will relieve the senior pastor from undue details.

If the title is that of administrative assistant, it is likely that this individual will work directly under the minister and his or her assignment will be the duties classified as "business," and may previously have been performed by the minister and other staff members working with a Building and Grounds Committee or a Maintenance and Operations Committee.

Items to be considered by the pastor and the committee for selection of an individual for this office are the following:

The administrative assistant should have a commitment to the cause of Christ and the Church. While the work of the administrative assistant will have little to do with the preaching and prophetic aspects of the church and it may appear that there is a minimal responsibility for the spiritual emphasis of the church, yet here, as with all staff positions, the cause of Christ will be strengthened through individuals who are dedicated to serve Him.

It is important that the areas of authority of the administrative assistant be carefully defined:

1) In what specific ways will he have oversight of the sextons and housekeeper?
2) What will be his relationship to the Maintenance and Operations Committee?
3) Will he have any oversight of the church office or the work of such employees?
4) What about the business and financial aspect of the church program? If the administrative assistant is given

the assignment of bookkeeping, financial records, and liaison representative to the Official Board and to the Finance Committee for the Every Member Canvass, all these points should be clearly spelled out.

5) Will he be responsible for the rental or borrowing of church property, the assignment of rooms and the responsibility of setting them up for regular and special occasions?

In this instance, as with all other staff positions, the more detailed the job description, the more helpful will be the relationship of the employee to his work.

Business and Office Manager

As the staff is enlarged and the work in the church may become more specialized, there may be need for an individual bearing the title of office or business manager, with specific relationship to the Official Board and the Finance Committee. He would be responsible for the supervision or overseeing of the property and might also be charged to give assistance in making arrangements for weddings, funerals and other services and programs that would relieve the pastor.

Other duties may include the following:

1) Keeping the records of all employees. This would involve an account of time off, sickness, and vacation time.
2) Interviewing new employees.
3) Overseeing the work-loads of employees and modifying responsibilities as required by circumstances.
4) Planning the work of the office staff for the day, week, month, and year.
5) Maintaining and ordering all supplies for the church office.
6) Supervising the storeroom.

There are some churches with sizable membership and programs where there is an overall church administrator, but where the specific overseeing of the employees in the church office may be assigned to an individual with the title of office manager. Most churches will have but one such individual.

Secretaries

In 1963, Prentice-Hall Inc. (Englewood Cliffs, N.J.) published a book written by me entitled, *Handbook for the Church Secretary.*

That volume has innumerable suggestions for church secretary, and I would recommend some such volume for each individual who comes into the professional life of the church and is given responsibility in its office and program.

The specific duties of each secretary should be carefully detailed in job specification. Usually the secretary is directly responsible to one individual. As far as skills are concerned, she will be called upon to demonstrate the same kind of technical competence any employee in any business or industry should provide. These skills include typing, shorthand, knowledge of filing and effective office procedures. Beyond mechanical skills, the good church secretary will manifest a higher degree of dedication, enthusiasm, flexibility, imagination and cooperativeness. He or she should have a love for and respect for individuals.

The good secretary will have a sense of stewardship and a constant desire to seek ways of improving the organizational program of the church. Her promptness and self-imposed high standards in her work will provide many happy dividends to herself and to the church as a whole.

Sextons

Usually the sexton and his assistants will be under the direction of the minister and, if there is such, the business manager, and the Maintenance and Operations Committee. The lines in his supervision should be carefully spelled out and the sexton himself should know definitely to whom he is responsible.

Those who oversee the sexton's work should be careful in protecting him from unusual or unwarranted demands from the congregation or organizations using the church. On this particular matter, it should be clear which individual will receive requests concerning the use of the rooms and has authority to approve such for the church calendar. All details regarding a specific meeting should be cleared through this staff member, who in turn will notify the sexton. The sexton should not be responsible for such decisions.

Ideally, there should be a schedule made out for each day and each week. Seasonal work should be detailed under the supervision of the Maintenance Committee and reviewed quarterly with the head sexton.

Problems of interpersonal relationship may be placed properly in the hands of the Maintenance and Operations Committee.

A high standard of cleanliness in the sanctuary and all rooms of the church should be maintained. The sexton should be instructed that the supplies he uses are provided by the benevolent gifts of many people and are to be used with a sense of stewardship. He should also be fully informed of all rules regarding the church property. He probably will be charged with the responsibility to see that the buildings are properly locked at night and suitably opened at appointed hours during the day.

Though the sexton's work may involve some hard physical work, every effort should be made by him to maintain a neat appearance, particularly when there are meetings in the church and many people are present. He should strive to keep his appearance as pleasant as his working conditions will permit.

While the sexton may not be included in regular staff meetings, his immediate superior or administrative supervisor will confer with him regularly with regard to his work and give him the sense of relatedness to the whole church program.

Housekeeper and Kitchen Personnel

If the church has substantial property with a number of rooms to be cared for, it may be found desirable to have a housekeeper on the staff. As a rule she will be responsible for the supervision of cleanliness throughout the rooms of the church. She will supervise the kitchen and kitchen personnel, and be responsible for the maintenance of kitchen equipment and supplies. If the kitchen is generally used by women's groups of the church, it may be desirable to have the housekeeper oversee the use of the kitchen and check to be sure the equipment is used properly. She may also be charged with the care of equipment for sewing groups or other such supplies.

5. VOLUNTEER STAFF MEMBERS

Many important services may be rendered to the church, even the large and highly organized church, by various volunteers. Many retired men have energy, skill, and time that can happily be given to the service of the church. This is also true of women whose children are grown and have left home.

A survey among church members asking for contribution of time and listing various skills or interests may be useful. A sizable "pool" may be obtained of people who could do much to relieve the professional staff members.

If individuals are used on a volunteer basis they should have recognition for their work. What is expected of them should be made clear. There should be one person to whom they are responsible and who oversees the work. If a number of people are involved, it may be desirable to appoint a chairman for the volunteers and to have that person work closely with one of the staff members in laying out the work program for the day, week, month, and year.

4

The Church Property

This chapter will be concerned with the administration as to the care, maintenance and conservation of the real estate and personal property belonging to the church.

1. House and Grounds Committee

This committee may be also called the Operations and Maintenance Committee. It is charged with the responsibility for the property maintenance of the church, the church hall, and any related buildings. Also the committee may be made responsible for the grounds. Many churches find it helpful to appoint a committee of women who are interested in gardening to oversee the care of the grounds of the church. Individuals interested in gardening often find it a source of joy and satisfaction to be made responsible for the planting and care of bushes, shrubs, vines, and flowers growing on the church or rectory properties. Of course, the sexton or some particular individual should be responsible for the cutting of the lawn and the week-to-week labor required to keep the grounds neat.

The committee will oversee the sextons, and will, through the chairman or other appointed representative, authorize the payment of bills for maintenance and repairs.

The committee may also be charged with the responsibility for the care of the manse, parsonage or rectory.

2. Periodic Inventory and Appraisal

Once a year the Official Board should receive an estimate of the value of the church and the church property. This is extremely helpful in determining whether the insurance coverage is adequate. It is a wise investment to have an approved appraiser list all of the furnishings in the church with an accurate statement as to their replacement cost. Such an appraisal should be done once every few years. Any new furnishings or equipment, together with their cost, should be added to the list as these are added to the church.

3. Annual Maintenance Inspection

Once a year the Maintenance Committee should thoroughly inspect the church property on the interior and exterior. A list of needs should be made and a plan devised to meet them.

The inspection will include the heating and plumbing systems, storerooms, workrooms, supply closets, the condition of the roof, the guttering, any walks or roads, the organ, etc. Appropriate reports and recommendations will be made to the Official Board.

4. Principles of Effective Property Management

In addition to thorough and periodic inspections and appraisals, the Maintenance Committee will continually supervise the care and repair of the church property. Any contract for specific work should be overseen by one appointed member of the committee, and his approval should be received before any bills for specific work are paid. The cooperation of the congregation in the care of the property should be enlisted.

Established Rules for Care of Church Property

Rules for the care of the property will be established by the Maintenance Committee, with the approval of the Christian Education Committee and the Official Board. The Women's Society and other groups and committees that use the church facilities with regularity should present suggestions through one of these committees.

One church prepared the following form for the guidance of individuals and groups using the church property:

FOR YOUR GUIDANCE
ON USING THE CHURCH PROPERTY

This is *your* church. Its effective use by your group and many others depends on your thoughtful cooperation. If you have occasion to use any of the church facilities, or are responsible for one of the many groups that meet here, please observe the following directives:

1. Turn off all unnecessary lights, especially when leaving the building. Check restroom lights and electrical appliances such as record players, fans, coffee urns, etc. Parking lot lights and spotlights are on automatic timing clocks.

2. Close and lock all windows before leaving. Check doors to special sections or rooms that you may have used and see that they are locked. If you unlock any outside door, it is your responsibility to see that it is locked again when the last member of your group departs.

3. If rooms are rearranged or furniture and other items are moved from one room to another, make sure that such items are replaced and the rooms left in the same condition as you found them.

4. If your group engages in crafts or handwork, please see that the floor and tables are properly cleaned before you leave and all materials used are put away in assigned storerooms or cabinets.

5. If you have occasion to use the kitchen, please observe the rules for proper use. Clean up thoroughly. Leave the kitchen in as good or better shape than when you found it. When the large coffee urns are used they should be left clean. Empty the grounds in the large garbage disposal and thoroughly wash and dry the urns.

6. If you turn a thermostat up to warm a room, please set it at its original position when you leave.

7. Youth groups are expected to stay in the location where their activities are scheduled. Other parts of the church are "off bounds."

The sexton or janitor should thoroughly check the buildings at the beginning and end of the day. Is the thermostat set at the proper temperature? Are the windows properly opened and later suitably closed? Doors locked? Lights off? Have the washrooms been checked?

Are the rooms set up for the work and program of the next day?

The Maintenance Committee may properly prepare a checklist for the janitor or sexton. A high standard should be set for the church office. All desks should be cleared at the day's end, typewriters put away, machines covered, and supplies in order for the next day.

5. TYPES OF INSURANCE PROTECTION

The Official Board should appoint an Insurance Committee. Three members are usually sufficient. Ideally, a man specializing in the insurance of property should be on the committee or an adviser to it. The committee should report at least annually regarding the insurance program to the Official Board. The maximum coverage against loss by fire or other calamity should be maintained. Special policies for the stained-glass windows, the organ and other specific or valuable possessions of the church may be in order. The committee will consult with the annual Appraisal Committee, builders, and any others whose experience and judgment will assist in determining an adequate insurance program.

The church should be protected against possible suit for injury sustained by anyone on the church premises. The employees and any workmen should be covered against accident. Some churches have found it desirable to offer a group life insurance program to staff members.

The insurance policies should be kept in the safe deposit box.

6. CARE OF FURNISHINGS AND EQUIPMENT

Under the Maintenance and Grounds Committee, special oversight and care will be given to the church equipment, supplies and furnishings so that they will provide maximum usage to the church. The importance of an inventory has been mentioned. A copy of this statement will be in the hands of the Maintenance Committee, and annually, if not more frequently, the committee will check to be sure that no equipment has been lost or stolen. Proper replacements or repairs will be made as needed.

Snow Plows and Lawn Mowers

All equipment for the care of the grounds of the church should be stored in a suitable place. In building a new church, the pastor and

Building Committee should make provisions for adequate storage of all equipment needed to maintain the grounds. Lawn mowers, snow plows and all mechanical equipment should be cleaned and properly stored at the end of the season. Instructions in the care of equipment should be followed, such as drainage of gasoline tanks of motors used seasonally, proper greasing and oiling of the mechanism, both when in use and during the time of storage. Manufacturer's instructions should be kept in an accessible place together with any further information regarding the use of the equipment. Seasonal tools such as rakes, hoes, pruning shears, etc., should be oiled and put away with care during the off-season. Each piece of equipment and all tools should have a special place, and when not in use should always be in that place.

The Organ

The church is well advised to make an annual maintenance contract with a reputable organ specialist for regular checking, tuning and repair of the organ. It must be recognized that organs from time to time require major repairs and their life span is limited. The Music Committee will report regularly to the Official Board regarding the organ maintenance and condition.

Some congregations have established an estimated life span of the organ, and annually place into a special fund a portion of that total amount so that at the time of major rebuilding or replacement of the organ, the matter may be handled with a minimum of financial burden.

The organ should be under the care of the organist. He alone, should have authority to grant permission to others to use the organ. When not in use, the console should be closed and locked. The Music Committee customarily grants the organist permission to use the organ for teaching purposes. The committee should determine any rental or contribution schedule for students who may use the organ for practice.

Heating System

The furnace, flues, chimneys, boilers, ducts and vents should be cleaned at least once a year. One individual is designated, usually the sexton, to be in charge of the heating system. No one else should seek to operate the furnace or boilers without his oversight and approval.

Church Kitchen

In view of the fact that the women of the church frequent the kitchen, the Maintenance and Operations Committee may put the kitchen under charge of the Women's Society. While the Maintenance Committee and the Official Board may be responsible for the major equipment in the kitchen such as stoves, freezers, refrigerators, and dishwashers, the women may take responsibility for supplying the kitchen with china, glassware, cutlery, cooking utensils and linens.

No equipment should be loaned or taken from the premises. Rules should be clearly established. One woman should be appointed to oversee the kitchen when it is used by outside groups. Replacements should be made for any breakage. An established rate should be made for the use of linens and any special equipment such as silver tea service, candelabra, punch bowls, and an established contribution should be expected from groups using the kitchen which are not directly affiliated with the church.

Woodwork

Many of our churches have fine woodwork, particularly in the chancel. There may also be memorial cabinets and other special woodwork such as pews and architectural details in the narthex and chapel. The builder and woodworking specialists should outline for the Maintenance Committee and sexton a program for the proper maintenance of all woodwork. Certain woods, depending on the geographical location of the church, climatic conditions, and the heating situation in the church, must receive special treatment.

An annual survey should be made of all specially carved woodwork in the church, and the proper use of oils and suitable preservatives should be applied. Attention should be given to proper dusting and cleansing week by week as well as the periodic "feeding" of the wood.

Stained-Glass Windows

In addition to providing proper protection for the stained-glass windows from outside breakage and also sufficient specific insurance coverage, a periodic maintenance program for the windows should be established. The architect and the fabricator of the windows should be consulted as to the proper method of maintenance and preservation. The Maintenance and Operations Committee should prepare such recommendations and, as with the care of the woodwork, should see that a copy of such procedures is filed in the church office in its own "operational procedure" file, and of course, regularly see that the requirements are fulfilled.

Rugs, Carpets, Hangings

Many churches may have special rugs of particular value, placed in the chancel, sanctuary or other areas of the church where the use may be limited. The Maintenance Committee will see that such rugs receive the required treatment and, if needed, repairs. Valuable rugs may properly have a plastic cover when there may be excessive wear. Rooms that have carpeting should be vacuumed weekly and cleaned at least once annually. The housekeeper should have particular instructions to remove spots, and should consult a rug maintenance organization if there are major problems.

Hangings such as draperies, tapestries, flags, banners or other related items must have special attention and care. Instructions for each item should be established with the best possible counsel from specialists, and such instructions be incorporated in the annual oversight by the Maintenance Committee.

Choir Robes

Choir robes should always be fresh in appearance, cleaned and pressed. Usually the Choir Guild or a specially designated individual or committee will be in charge of this project.

Each robe should be assigned to an individual chorister, and the name placed in that particular robe.

Suitable storage facilities for robes are necessary, and the Maintenance and Operations Committee should provide such closets or cabinets for the proper hanging of choir robes. When, as during the summer, the choir may be disbanded, robes should be housed in darkness with protection against moths and sunlight.

If cottas and collars are used, the person in charge of the robing should see that such are properly laundered and on hand for the worship services.

Vestments

Our churches vary as to the number of vestments and the ownership of same. Often the individual minister procures his own robe, cassock, and other ecclesiastical vestments. These may be housed in his study or in a small vestry closet. The Chancel Committee may be helpful to the clergyman in seeing that his robe is in proper condition, suitably cleaned and pressed.

In our churches of a more liturgical background, more elaborate vestments may be common. In this instance it should be determined by the Official Board whether the vestments are provided by the congregation and will then be the property of the church, but for the use of the local clergy. Usually an Altar Guild may be delegated the responsibility of seeing that all such vestments are on hand and in proper order. Stoles, surplices, and special garb worn for high and holy occasions will receive all possible attention for their preservation.

Communion Service

All accoutrements having to do with the Sacrament of the Lord's Supper will be treated with great love and respect. A proper room or cabinet for the housing of all communion ware should be established and maintained with meticulous order. Drawers for the housing of altar linens should be provided. The Altar Committee will see that chalices, patens, and individual communion glasses are immaculate for the celebration of Holy Communion.

Some churches have in their possession silver communion services of historical significance. It may be meaningful to exhibit these in a permanent display case, or perhaps on special occasions, in a place where they may be viewed by the maximum number of parishioners and visitors. All linens used in the Sacrament should be laundered promptly and carefully housed for the next occasion of their use.

The Official Board usually delegates to the Altar Guild the authority to purchase any replacements or supplies required for the proper celebration of the Lord's Supper.

7. THE MINISTER'S STUDY AND OFFICE

Location

The location of the minister's study should be made in terms of the following principles:

a. Accessibility to parishioners and the staff.
b. Seclusion where study and sermon preparation may be done in quiet. It may be impossible to meet both requirements in one location. Some clergymen find that their sermon preparation and study must be done in the rectory, manse, or some withdrawn room in the church, whereas their office for counseling and administrative program will be more accessible to parishioners and staff.
c. A third aspect involves the minister's own temperament and work schedule, and the particular demands of the individual parish.

Equipment and Furnishings
of the Study

The "study" should be a place of refuge. Any parishioner entering for counsel should find it a place of dignity and repose. All equipment and furnishings should be of good quality. A comfortable chair for the seating of a visitor to the pastor should be placed for open and relaxed conversation. The telephone, dictating equipment (if used), and all other instruments for efficient work should be placed for maximum efficiency and with a minimum of intrusiveness when the study is used for conference.

Items of religious symbolism may most properly be in the minister's study for his own inspiration and for those who come to consult him there.

The Official Board will be well advised to provide for the pastor any equipment that will facilitate his spiritual labors, such as dictating equipment, an interoffice communicating system, a recorder, or such other instruments that may further his efficient ministering to the parish. It may be highly desirable to place in the pastor's study any work of art or esthetic treasure of the parish.

Files for the Minister

For his efficient leadership, the minister will have a number of files in his study. These may include the following:

1) A card file of the church members.
2) Prospective members.
3) Shut-ins.

4) A record of weddings, baptisms, and deaths.
5) A special file having to do with the Official Board and all major committees.
6) A "Confidential File" containing notes of counseling problems with individuals.
7) Ideas for sermons.
8) A file of clippings from magazines and periodicals arranged under alphabetic subjects.
9) A catalogue file of the minister's personal library.
10) A file of sermons preached by topic and by text.

These are indicative of a number of files and records that the individual pastor may suitably prepare and keep up to date for the conducting of his administrative, preaching, and pastoral offices.

8. THE CHURCH OFFICE

Lighting and Ventilation

For the most efficient work of the church staff, the office should be pleasant in every respect. The maximum exterior lighting is desirable. If this is not possible, suitable interior lighting that will minimize eyestrain is an absolute necessity.

The office should have an even temperature. If the church is located in a hot, humid climate, air-conditioning is an essential. The Official Board and Maintenance and Operations Committee can do much for the morale of the staff by providing warmth from the cold and coolness from the heat.

Proper Desks and Equipment

For efficient work, any staff member needs the best kind of equipment. The Maintenance and Operations Committee will be well advised to confer with the head of an office equipment company as to proper chairs and desks for office workers. Many improvements have recently been made in posture chairs and typewriter desks that add to the comfort of the worker and so to increased efficiency.

Types of Machines

Beyond suitable dictating equipment and typewriters, the local parish office, as its requirements increase, may well use the following types of machines:

a. Mimeograph or some other type of reproducing machine.
b. Addressograph.
c. Graphotype.
d. Postage meter.
e. Copying machines.
f. Letter opener.
g. Sealers.

Other machines and specialized equipment will be considered as a particular demand is put on the church staff and as needs in the parish develop where mechanized equipment can facilitate the church program.

Handling of the Mail

One individual should be designated to sort and distribute all mail coming to the church.

It is an inviolate rule that all mail marked "personal" or "confidential" shall not be opened by anyone other than the person to whom addressed.

If the church has a staff of more than two or three members, it is well to have a designated place where the mail or messages for each will be placed.

Many churches will receive mail for individual members of the Official Board, the Women's Society, or other church organizations. The person in charge of the mail should telephone such individuals, notifying them that they have mail at the church office.

Correspondence

There are several rules about correspondence that must be observed:

1) Every letter should be answered promptly.
2) A carbon of the response attached to the original letter should be placed on file for easy reference.
3) There should be warmth and the most attentive concern manifested to the writer of the original letter.
4) Annually the correspondence file should be checked to eliminate all correspondence that is not relevant to the present or possible future life of the congregation.
5) Correspondence concerning specific topics, committees, or individuals should be filed under specific headings. It may be neces-

sary to make notations in certain files referring to such specific correspondence for cross-reference.

6) Where correspondence may concern individuals or departments of the church other than the person who receives and responds, carbons of responses and, if needed, copies of the original letter should be sent to such.

Files for the Church Office

The effectiveness of the church office will depend on proper files, through which pertinent information is maintained regarding the members and the church activities. Suggested files are the following:

1) *An accurate card file of the members of the parish.* The membership card file will contain a maximum amount of pertinent information and at the same time will require the minimum of effort to keep up to date.

Typical cards for the membership record are shown in Examples 1 and 2 on pages 119-121.

2) Some churches have found it valuable to have a file showing the *contributions of church members.* Such a file may be of significance at the time of the yearly membership canvass.

One such pledge history card is illustrated in Example 3.

3) *An up-to-date file should be maintained on prospective members of the church.* The minister and "Calling Committee" will see that this file is kept accurate and pertinent information concerning the individual and family is entered on a prospective member card. When the prospect joins the church, the card should be removed from the prospective file and a card made for the church membership file. Such other records as are required will receive proper notation in this change of status.

4) Correspondence files should be maintained alphabetically, containing the original letter and a copy of the response.

5) If the church engages in mailings to specific groups such as the Church School or the Women's Society, the addressograph files for such groups should be kept up to date through continual coordination with the church office and the designated member of the particular group.

Many other specialized files may be maintained in terms of the church program. These may include files for the music department, young married group, shut-ins, senior men's program and many others.

Example 1. Form of Individual Church Membership Record.

1 2 3 4 5 6 7 8 9 10 11 12 13 14 15 16 17 18 19 20 21 22 23 24 25 26 27 28 29 30 31

NAME BIRTHDATE CARD DATE

ADDRESS

APARTMENT NUMBER HOME PHONE PARISH ZONE

OCCUPATION

FIRM ADDRESS BUSINESS PHONE

SINGLE MARRIED (DATE) WIDOWED SEPARATED DIVORCED

RECEIVED BY

DATE NO.

LETTER FROM

REMOVED DATE REASON

NAMES & RELATION OF OTHERS IN HOME. BIRTHDATES OF MINOR CHILDREN. RELIGIOUS AFFILIATIONS OF OTHER ADULTS.

ACTIVE IN

REMARKS

OFFICIAL CALLS PLEDGE ATTENDANCE

1960
1961
1962
1963
1964
1965
1966
1967
1968
1969
1970
1971
1972
1973
1974
1975
1976
1977

1 2 3 4 5 6 7 8 9 10 11 12 13 14 15 16 17 18 19 20 21 22 23 24 25 26 27 28 29 30 31

Example 2.   Alternate Form of Membership Record (Side 1).

CHRIST CHURCH

FAMILY NAME

Address

Tel. No.

	Birth	Baptism	Member	Death
Mr.				
Mrs.				
Miss				
Children				
Others in household				

Example 2. Alternate Form of Membership Record (Side 2).

CHURCH INTERESTS — A—Present, B—Past, C—Future

	Mr.	Mrs.		Mr.	Mrs.
1. Elder	□	□	10. Church School Teacher	□	□
2. Deacon	□	□	11. Choir	□	□
3. Trustee	□	□	12. Choir Mother	□	□
4. Women's Guild	□	□	13. Evangelistic Calling	□	□
5. Couple's Club	□	□	14. Boy Scout Leadership	□	□
6. Men's Group	□	□	15. Girl Scout Leadership	□	□
7. Adult Study Group	□	□	16. Ushering	□	□
8. Sewing Group	□	□	17. Youth Advisor	□	□
9. Cancer Dressings	□	□	18. Loyalty Sunday	□	□

	Mr.	Mrs.
19. Secretarial Work	□	□
20. Offering Tellers	□	□
21. Public Relations	□	□
22. Maintenance Jobs	□	□
23.	□	□
24.	□	□
25.	□	□
26.	□	□
27.	□	□

MR.

Occupation and/or Training

Chief Interests, Skills, and Hobbies

Available for Service

Morning □ Afternoon □ Evening □

MRS. or MISS

Occupation and/or Training

Chief Interests, Skills, and Hobbies

Available for Service

Morning □ Afternoon □ Evening □

Example 3.   Pledge History Record (Side 1).

Example 3.   Pledge History Record (Side 2).

Rules for special files. Certain principles should govern the establishing and maintaining of special files:

a. The files should be as simple as possible, containing only the information needed for maximum efficiency.

b. One person should be in charge of and responsible for the accuracy of the files.

c. A method for providing the necessary information should be established, and all members of the staff should cooperate in providing such information to the one responsible for the files.

To assist in reporting accurate information for changes in membership, prospects, affiliates or special groupings, it can be of value to circulate a sheet on which are listed all changes that may affect the files to the church staff and members of the Official Board. The sheet may list the name and address of the individual, with a series of items to be checked, such as change of address, date of reception as a new member, marriage, death, a prospect, and any other category that may be of value to the church office.

Various Forms and Supplies

The church office should be supplied with proper stationery and other supplies necessary to efficient office operation. One individual should be in charge of the supply closet, its inventory, and should have authority to order supplies as needed.

The stationery of the church should be dignified. It is desirable to have several types of stationery for business and social use. Business stationery should have the name of the church, the full address with zip code, and the telephone number with the area code number. It is usual to list the ministerial staff in the letterhead.

Where the writer of a letter is not identified in the letterhead, it is desirable to type the name and position under the signature.

Many mimeographed forms can facilitate the office procedure. These should be kept in adequate supply on the desk of those who are to use them. Some of these forms are as follows:

1) A form for telephone messages. This should include date, hour, name of person calling, when he can be reached, at what number, further details, etc.

2) A form noting the weekly or monthly payroll.

3) A form on which the minister may note items for the coming

Sunday's service, such as Scripture reading; hymns; psalter and other items.

4) Forms for recording information on marriages, deaths, and baptisms.

Telephones

Several principles should govern the location and use of telephones.

1) An active church with many parishioners should provide a pay telephone for people coming and going. The church staff should have a ruling from the Official Board that church office telephones are for official church business only.
2) Every member of the church staff should read material prepared by the telephone company regarding the use of the switchboard or intercom system.
3) Telephone courtesy is most important, and every employee should be instructed regarding the manner of answering the telephone and the rules for good telephone manners.
4) Telephones should be located for maximum use and efficiency. An adequate number of extensions should be installed for the church office and for the clergy. There should also be extensions at strategic points for the use of the sextons and those serving in the kitchen and other areas of the church and related rooms.

Problems Between Staff Members

The pastor will provide leadership that will minimize friction between individuals serving on the church staff. Many potential areas of disagreement can be anticipated and resolved in regular staff meetings and in continuing communication between the pastor and individual staff members. Each employee should have the sense that his ideas are welcome regarding any aspect of improvement in the church operation, and that any detail can be "talked over" with the minister.

The minister, sensitive to any disagreement or unhappiness on the part of a staff member, or any area of potential friction, will wisely meet the situation by conferring with the individual or individuals involved. Often this can be done indirectly. The philosophy should be that there is no problem that cannot be solved, and potential problems will be met before they become acute.

Supply Closet

The following general points should be observed with reference to working supplies for the church:

a. A supply closet should be established, and kept under lock and key.

b. The closet should be kept neat. Items that have not been used for two years should be discarded.

c. One individual should be in charge and responsible for ordering supplies and issuing them to individual staff members.

d. The use of supplies should be anticipated and orders made ahead of time to insure adequate supplies at periods of heavy use.

e. Requisitions for supplies should go to the individual in charge and orders for replacement or for new supplies should be approved by the proper committee chairman.

Machine Room

In churches that develop a membership of over 1,500 it is often desirable to have a separate room to house the various mechanical equipment such as duplicating machines, mimeograph equipment, addressograph plates and machines, etc. Ideally, one person should be assigned to operate and care for such equipment. The room should be well lighted and ventilated, and it should be maintained with maximum attention to its efficiency and neatness.

Service contracts for the maintenance of machines and equipment are desirable. The sexton or janitor should have special instructions for the cleaning of the machine room. The room should be locked when not in use.

5

The Sanctuary
and Chancel

The church is "God's House." It should be a place of sanctuary
and repose where men lift their souls in worship. It is a place for
private prayer, rest, and meditation. It therefore will be treated with
deep love and respect. All who are responsible for it will do their
duties with quietness, dignity and dedication.

The church should be open throughout the week. Announcements
in the Sunday Calendar or the bulletin board will indicate that the
church is open for private prayer and devotion.

Preparation for Public Use

For all occasions of public worship, the sanctuary must be immaculate. The pews should be dusted and, if kneeling cushions are
used, they should be arranged symmetrically. Hymn and prayer books
should be arranged in careful order. If there are cards placed in the
pew racks, the sexton or some appointed individual should see that
there are sufficient cards and sharpened pencils. The Chancel Committee will see that flowers are suitably arranged, if it is customary
to have them. The Bible will be opened to the proper place for the
Scripture reading.

A meaningful service to the church can be rendered by a dedicated
Chancel Committee, in charge of all details of the chancel. Each

church, no matter what denomination, will profit by such a women's group. They should be properly instructed in their duties and the occasions when they are to be in charge of the chancel.

The church should be well ventilated. If the season is winter, it will be comfortably heated. In summer, if there is no air-conditioning, the windows will have been opened and adjusted for maximum comfort. If it adds to the comfort of the worshipers, hand fans will be placed in the pews.

The Order for Public Worship will be given to each worshiper by the usher, or placed in the pew or narthex prior to the hour of worship. If there are cloakrooms, an appointed individual will check them for orderliness and neatness before the congregation arrives.

Elsewhere in this volume, the maintenance of the church property is discussed. Every item of furnishings, from pew to communion table, will have been treated with such thoughtful maintenance that the entire fabric will tell each worshiper that it has been cared for with great concern.

Uses for Holy Rites

Our churches vary in their definition of Sacraments and Holy Rites. While the majority of Protestant churches name Baptism and the Lord's Supper as "Sacraments," still there are other holy rites and ceremonies that will be conducted with infinite regard.

Information Sheet for Weddings

So that the church wedding will be beautiful and fulfill its high spiritual purpose, a number of practical items must be covered. Many churches find it helpful to ask the bride and bridegroom to fill out an information sheet. Examples to guide a local pastor in preparing an appropriate form that will provide necessary information for a wedding are the following:

CHRIST CHURCH

Application for Marriage

GROOM

Name .... Age ....
       First   Middle   Last

Residence .... Zone ...... Phone ....

Residence after marriage ....

Business or Profession .... Business phone ....

Member of .... Church, Address ....

Have you been married before? .... If yes, divorced or widower? ......

If divorced, date of divorce .... Any children ...... Ages ......

BRIDE

Name .... Age ....
       First   Middle   Last

Residence .... Zone ...... Phone ....

Residence after marriage ....

Business address .... Business phone.......

Member of .... Church, Address ....

Have you been married before? .... If yes, divorced or widowed? ......

If divorced, date of divorce .... Any children ...... Ages ......

CHURCH DATA

Date and hour of wedding .... Single ring ... Double ring ...

Place: Sanctuary ...... Chapel ...... Other ....

Minister .... Estimated attendance ....

Conference date with minister ....

Number of Ushers .... Bridesmaids ....

Date ....

CHRIST CHURCH

WEDDING CHECK LIST FOR OFFICE AND STAFF

Wedding of .... and ....
Bridegroom's full name   Bride's full name

Bride's address .... Phone ....

Groom's address .... Phone ....

Date of wedding .... Day of week .... Time ....

Date of rehearsal .... Day of week .... Time ....

Place: Sanctuary .... Chapel .... Require use of kitchen .... Hall ....

If use of kitchen and hall are desired, inform bride of charges involved and how payment is to be made:

Kitchen .... Hall ....

Custodian .... Supervisor ....

If a Saturday wedding, are the flowers to be left for church use on Sunday? ....

Is the service of the church organist required? .... If yes, give her the name and phone number of the organist and inform her it will be her responsibility to inform the organist of rehearsal time, wedding time and payment for services.

Is the bride informed that there is to be no picture-taking during the ceremony? ....

Date for bride and groom to see the minister ....

Minister performing the ceremony ....

Single-ring ceremony .... Double-ring ceremony ....

Attendants .... Ushers .... Ring bearer ....

Flower girl .... Name of person to give bride away ....

Best man .... Maid or Matron of honor ....

Names needed as witnesses ....

Address after marriage ....

Notify the following:

Flower Chairman .... Whether flowers will be used in the church on Sunday.

Custodian .... To arrange for his services at rehearsal and for proper arrangements at the wedding.

Worship Commission .... To change pulpit hangings if needed.

Reception Chairman .... If there is to be a reception in the church hall following the marriage.

Kitchen Chairman .... If kitchen is to be used for reception.

IMPORTANT: All dates should be cleared with the church calendar to be sure the church is available at the times needed.

CHRIST CHURCH

WEDDING INFORMATION SHEET

BRIDE

Name .... Age ....

Address .... Phone ....

Parents ....

Address ....

Church affiliations ....

Previous marriage ....

GROOM

Name .... Age ....

Address .... Phone ....

Parents ....

Address ....

Church affiliations ....

Previous marriage ....

Counseling date .... Rehearsal date ....

Wedding date .... Officiating minister ....

Address after wedding ....

Services requested: Church .... Tower bells ....

Chancel .... Rehearsal ....

Organist .... Sexton ....

Soloist .... Candles (14) ....

Best man .... Maid of honor ....

Number of ushers .... Number of bridesmaids ....

Disposition of flowers ....

....
Minister's approval   Date of approval

The bride and bridegroom should be informed as to regulations and procedures for a wedding in the church.

A mimeographed sheet, such as the following, may help all parties concerned with the wedding in expediting a harmonious handling of the details of the occasion:

WEDDINGS IN CHRIST CHURCH

PROCEDURAL GUIDANCE AND INFORMATION

The minister and staff at Christ Church will guide and assist you to make your marriage a truly high and holy occasion in your lives.

Marriage, according to the beautiful ritual, is "instituted of God, regulated by His commandments, blessed by our Lord Jesus Christ, to be held in honor among all men." Your wedding will mean more to you, your families and friends when there is careful concern for all the reverential aspects of the holy occasion.

Certain policies have been established by the Official Board to accomplish that purpose and to assist the bride and groom and their families in answering questions regarding the wedding ceremony.

SCHEDULING

Plan in advance for the use of the church. The pastor will help you with your personal wishes concerning the wedding. A time for counseling should be arranged, and the date for the wedding set before any other plans are made.

No weddings are scheduled in Christ Church on Sunday, during Holy Week, on Christmas Eve or Christmas Day.

OFFICIATING

The pastor or assistant pastor of the church will officiate at all weddings. If a family desires another clergyman to conduct the ceremony, the request should be made to the pastor. It is his prerogative to extend an invitation to the other clergyman to assist at the wedding.

The pastor will meet with the wedding party for rehearsals and explain all procedures. Please be prompt at all rehearsals.

The marriage license must be in the minister's possession before the ceremony, and preferably should be given to him at the rehearsal time.

MUSIC

Music is an important part of a wedding ceremony and should be in keeping with the reverence observed in the House of the Lord. All music shall be approved by the pastor and organist. Only the appointed church organist may play the organ in the sanctuary.

The organist should be consulted by the bride well in advance of the wedding date. If a soloist is desired, the organist will be able to furnish names of able singers. Should the family desire a particular singer, arrangements should be made with the organist for adequate rehearsal time.

DECORATIONS

It customarily is the responsibility of the bride's family to make arrangements with a florist for the wedding decorations. The church suggests simplicity, with a minimum of decoration. Ribbon or simple floral arrangements may be used to mark pews. No nails or thumb tacks are to be used on the church woodwork. Masking tape is suggested and may be used.

Non-drip candles only are to be used in the candelabra. If desired, a white runner may be rented from the florist for the aisle.

WEDDING CONSULTANTS

Wedding consultants who assist the bride should understand that the wedding ceremony is in charge of the minister. They are not to assume direction of any portion of the wedding rehearsal or service. It is the responsibility of the bride to make this known to her consultant.

PHOTOGRAPHERS

The bride is asked to instruct her photographer that flash pictures are not permissible in the sanctuary during the ceremony. A time-exposure of the ceremony may be taken from the rear of the sanctuary.

WEDDING RECEPTION

If the church hall facilities are desired for the reception, arrangements should be made through the church office. The church staff can give the names of several reputable caterers if such service is desired.

It is suggested that arrangements for such service be made at least eight weeks prior to the date of the wedding.

If refreshments are served by a caterer, the bride's family shall be responsible for the use of the kitchen and equipment, and for damage or breakage.

Alcoholic beverages cannot be served on the church premises of Christ Church.

WEDDING CONTRIBUTIONS

When the bride or groom, or one of their parents are active members of the church, the following contributions are suggested. With the exception of the pastor's honorarium, which is given by the bridegroom through his best man, the following contributions are customarily taken care of by the family of the bride:

Use of sanctuary	—no charge	
Fellowship hall	—no charge	
Organist (wedding and one rehearsal)		—$35
Soloist (if provided by the church)		— 25
Custodian		— 15

When neither the bride or groom or their parents are members of Christ Church, the following contributions are suggested:

Use of sanctuary	—$15
Use of fellowship hall	— 10

If the services of an outside caterer are used, there will be a $15 charge for the use of the kitchen.

There is no fee charged by the pastor. The gift to the pastor is a token of appreciation for his time spent, including the counseling session, rehearsal and wedding, and is the responsibility of the bridegroom.

The bride and bridegroom are required to sign the enclosed application form agreeing that they understand and will comply with the foregoing rules.

Reservations for the church and hall will be considered firm when the signed confirmation form is returned to the church office.

Any variations to the regulations can be made only at the pastor's discretion.

The minister or some representative designated by him is in charge of the rehearsal. Some churches find it helpful to prepare a list of reminders for ushers and others who will have some responsibility for the wedding ceremony.

An example of such guidance is the following:

FOR THOSE IN CHARGE OF WEDDING CEREMONY
IN CHRIST CHURCH

(A checklist for important details)

1. Make sure ushers have boutonnieres.
2. Check that ushers light all candles (including ones on altar) before people begin to arrive (about twenty to twenty-five minutes before the hour).
3. Give first signal light to the organist when the bride's mother is escorted to her seat. (Bridegroom's mother is seated first.)

4. Make sure ushers unfold white runner after bride's mother is seated.
5. Line up bride, her father, and bridesmaids in narthex.
6. Start bridesmaids down the aisle as soon as the minister, bridegroom and groomsmen are in place; allowing about eight pews between each bridesmaid. (If there is a flower girl or a maid of honor, she precedes the bridesmaids.)
7. Remind photographers not to take pictures during the service in the sanctuary. Pictures can be taken in the narthex after the benediction.
8. Give the organist the second signal light just as the bridal party (other than the bride) start down the aisle.
9. As the bride, on the arm of her father, starts down the aisle, the wedding march is increased in volume.
10. Latecomers are to be seated quietly in side aisles if there are pews available.
11. After the benediction, when the bride and bridegroom, the bridesmaids and groomsmen have recessed to the narthex, the ushers will immediately go down to escort the bride's mother (first) and the bridegroom's mother from the nave.
12. Remind ushers to go down the aisle two abreast to conduct people out of the sanctuary pew by pew, beginning from the front.
13. See that the reception line forms properly if such is to be held.

In general the bridal couple should be given a copy of the wedding service and a carefully prepared certificate attesting to the marriage.

The thoughtful clergyman will write to the young couple, keep in touch with them, and perhaps send a letter of felicitation on their first anniversary. If the individuals married are members of the church, proper changes on the membership roll will be made and needed records promptly made for ecclesiastical and civil authorities.

Baptisms—General Procedure

The time of Baptism is an occasion of deep significance. Adequate announcement should be made of the occasion for public and private baptisms and all needed information should be given to parents. One pastor sends out a letter prior to public Baptism which reads as follows:

CHRIST CHURCH

April 23, 1968

Dear Parents:

This letter is in regard to infant Baptism which will be conducted in your church on Sunday, May 5, 1968, at the 11 A.M. Worship Service.

The elders have directed me to conduct an information class before Baptism, in order that parents might have a better understanding of the vows which they are taking. This class will last for just one hour. I will try to explain the Biblical basis and long historical background of this Sacrament, what is expected of the parents of baptized children, and answer any questions that may be in your mind. *All fathers and mothers* who plan to take the baptismal vows are expected to attend one class session.

Our class, preparatory to the administration of the Sacrament on May 5, will be held on Sunday, April 28, at 3 P.M. in the chapel.

Enclosed is a card which we ask you to return immediately, so that we may know if you are planning to attend the class on April 28.

Sincerely yours,

The Minister

The baptized child is properly registered on the roll of the church and will receive pastoral and congregational attention and care. A form that proved to be helpful in obtaining information for the baptismal service and subsequent records is the following:

BAPTISM PROCEDURE NOTES (For All Staff Members)

CHRIST CHURCH

1. Refer call to the pastor's secretary if he is not available.
2. When taking a call be sure to obtain all information indicated.
3. See that information is promptly relayed to the pastor.
4. Usual steps   Check

      Request is received from the family.   _____

      Baptismal date is given.   _____

      Pamphlet and pastoral letter on baptism sent.   _____

Appointment is made for pastor to visit family. ———
Church officer sponsor is included in the visit. ———
Complete permanent record for pastor and
Christ Church files is prepared.   ———

Date Information Received . . . .

FULL NAME . . . . (double-check spelling)

BIRTH DATE . . . . BIRTHPLACE . . . .

CHECK ONE: *Infant Baptism* . . . .

Adult Baptism . . . .

PARENTS' FULL NAME: *Father* . . . .

Business Address . . . . Telephone . . . . . .

Church Affiliation . . . .

Mother . . . .
(maiden name)

Home Address . . . . Telephone . . . . . .

Church Affiliation . . . .

DATE WHEN PASTORAL LETTER & PAMPHLET SENT . . . .

SCHEDULED PASTORAL VISIT TO HOME . . . . PASTOR . . . .
Date   Time

OTHER INFORMATION ABOUT FAMILY:

Names and ages of brothers and sisters

. . . .

. . . .

. . . .

CHURCH OFFICER SPONSOR . . . .

DATE AND TIME OF SERVICE PLANNED FOR BAPTISM . . . .

date

. . . .

hour

. . . .

Date Baptism   Pastor Officiating   Date of Official Recording

Another simple card which seeks necessary information and indicates procedures is the following:

INFANT BAPTISM

Date of Baptism . . . .

CHILD'S NAME . . . .

FATHER'S NAME . . . .

MOTHER'S NAME . . . .

PLACE OF BIRTH . . . .

DATE OF BIRTH . . . .

PLACE OF BAPTISM . . . .

PARENTS' ADDRESS . . . . TELEPHONE . . . .

ENTERED IN COMMUNICANTS' BOOK . . . .

CRADLE ROLL NOTIFIED . . . .

REPORT TO OFFICIAL BOARD . . . .

CERTIFICATE DELIVERED . . . .

. . . .

A dignified certificate of Baptism should be given to the parents of the baptized child and they should be told that the document is of importance and should be put with the child's birth certificate and other vital documents. The parents should be informed that a permanent record of the Baptism is made in the church archives.

Funerals

The matter of a "Christian funeral" in the church is worthy of careful planning by the minister and the Official Board. Various church boards have prepared a summary of items for the guidance of the church leadership responsible for the conduct of funerals, and the congregation as a whole in participating in this holy rite. Following is an effective setting out of necessary facts and suggestions for the church membership.

SUGGESTIONS FOR A CHRISTIAN REGARDING DEATH AND THE FUNERAL

CHRIST CHURCH

Approved by the Official Board May, 19__

The Official Board feels a responsibility in making certain reminders and suggestions to all members of Christ Church regarding death and the most wholesome and Christian way in which this inevitable event can be met.

1. *Think through the Christian view of death and the life eternal.*

   Our official denominational documents affirm that ". . . in the presence of death (Christians) witness to their faith that God, in Jesus Christ, has conquered death and raises his children from death to life eternal . . . In this belief, Christians should make of the occasion of death a time in which the hope of the gospel is reaffirmed by them with solemn joy."

2. *Formulate your plans in advance.*

   This need not be morbid or depressing. Making a will and arranging financial provision for one's family is evidence of a sense of responsibility and sound intelligence. Discuss with members of your family your desires regarding a Christian burial and disposition of your property.

3. *Notify your pastor immediately when a death occurs.*

   ". . . that he may help the bereaved in relating the reality of death to the sustaining reality of the Christian community and the hope to which it witnesses. The pastor and other members of the congregation have a special responsibility not only to pray with and for the bereaved, but to be of practical assistance to them."

4. *Choose your funeral director in advance.*

Your pastor, lawyer, physician, or memorial society may be able to guide you.

5. *Are there special requests?*

Special requests, such as eye bank, kidney transferral, postmortem, and other such wishes should be discussed and decided before the time of death.

6. Write such desires in clear detail and give copies to your family physician, a medical school of your choice (its Department of Pathology will provide necessary papers for you to indicate your instructions), or funeral director, your lawyer and your minister.

7. For the Christian *"the service should normally be held in a church."*

If the casket is present, it should remain closed. This is ". . . all in order that the worship of those assembled may more naturally be directed to the Author and Finisher of their salvation."

The service may be a *memorial service.* In such a service, held either in the church chapel or in the church sanctuary, the casket or ashes need not be present. In counseling and comforting the bereaved prior to the service, the minister will try to help the bereaved accept the reality of bodily death and let grief "work itself out" until any sense of unreality or shock is replaced by the assurance of God's love unending, and of the Christian hope of resurrection into life eternal.

A committal service is usually conducted by the minister at the cemetery or crematorium for interment of a casket or of an urn. This service may follow or precede the memorial service. In certain circumstances the committal service may be a part of the church or chapel service.

8. *Avoid ostentation and unnecessary expense for the casket and flowers.*

Although the human body is the temple of the Holy Spirit during earthly life, "flesh and blood cannot inherit the kingdom of God" (1 Corinthians 15:50). The person having left the "earthly house" means that while the "house," the body, should be treated with respect, it should not be the occasion of extravagant expense.

9. *Encourage friends to express their sympathy and affection by a contribution to a worthy cause.*

Your church has a Memorial Fund to which gifts may be sent. Such gifts are recorded in the name of the person in whose memory they are given. When a fund is used for a specific purpose, the family is consulted. We honor the dead best by caring for the needs of the living.

10. *For the funeral or memorial service.*

The minister will be glad to receive suggestions as to favorite passages of scripture, hymns, etc. The service provided by the church in *The Book of Common Worship* contains Bible selections and prayers which are part of our great heritage. The minister may give a brief message expressing the Christian faith and hope when we confront death at the funeral service. Eulogies are usually not given, although in the prayer of thanksgiving for the one who died, it is right to include those qualities and graces which characterized the one now in the Church Triumphant. If it is possible to have the congregation sing a hymn of faith and comfort, it provides more participation in the service of worship, and often proves "a means of grace." If friends and relatives come from great distances, the bereaved may meet friends in the church parlor immediately following the service. An announcement of this informal reception may be given by the officiating minister if it is deemed appropriate. Remember the promise: "Neither death nor life . . . will be able to separate us from the love of God in Christ Jesus our Lord" (Romans 8:38).

*Pastoral Guideline Leaflets
for General Distribution*

Death so often comes as a shock. Those immediately related to the deceased have many items for decision at this time of duress. Other family members and close friends may come to the home and rather than contributing to the ordered direction of the house, may add confusion. No decisive blueprint can be given as to how to prepare church members for such an hour, but the pastoral leadership can be a great blessing and strong ridgepole for the family at this time.

It may be completely inappropriate to present any typed or printed material to a family at this time. The warm, strong, personal guidance cannot be replaced by stilted literature. Yet the preparation of a brochure or leaflet, constantly available to parishioners on the literature table of the church, can be helpful to those who may read it. A suggested form offering guidelines regarding funerals to a local congregation is contained in the following brief but informative communication:

CHRIST CHURCH

GUIDELINES CONCERNING FUNERALS

Our denomination and our local Christ Church are dedicated to ministering to the needs of our people in the name of Jesus Christ. Among the occasions when its ministry is needed is when death comes to a family, and a funeral service must be planned and conducted. Few times in a person's life are more charged with emotion, fuller of feeling, and in greater need of tender sympathy and helpful guidance.

Our funeral directors have high ethical and moral standards. We accept their dedication to serve the needs of the bereaved with sympathy and dignity. We apreciate their services. Many people, especially those with no church home, hold the funeral service in the accommodations provided by the funeral director, in which case the minister adapts himself to the conditions of place and surroundings.

Church members, however, are turning increasingly to the church sanctuary for funeral services. The Official Board of Christ Church respectfully calls attention to the standards and regulations of the church for funeral services to be held in the sanctuary or the chapel of Christ Church.

> Funeral services are in the charge of the pastor of Christ Church. He will remember that the purposes are the recognition of divine providence in the affairs of men, the goodness and mercy of God under all varying conditions, the consolation of the living that they may be comforted in their sorrow, and that their affliction may be blest to their spiritual good. Whenever appropriate, the joy and triumph of the believing dead should be emphasized.

>> No funeral should take place on the Lord's Day except in cases of absolute necessity.

>> Everything which savors of vain display or fulsome eulogy should be avoided.

> When the funeral is for a member of the church, the pastor ordinarily will have been ministering to the deceased and

his family at the time of the approaching death. Members should call him at any hour when his ministry is desired, and as soon as possible after death.

The minister will assist in making the necessary arrangements for the use of the church. There is no charge for its use or for the funeral, although the family may wish to remember the services of the organist and the custodian. The chapel may be used for small funerals involving not more than 100 worshipers. The sanctuary should be requested for any service where the anticipated attendance is more than 100 people.

Although the funeral services are left largely to the discretion of the minister, he will welcome suggestions concerning Scriptural and other passages of literature to be used in the service. Opportunity should be arranged by the family for privately consulting with the minister concerning details of the service.

Personal loss is great, and sorrow is real, but if the deceased is a Christian we can rejoice to remember "how precious in the sight of the Lord is the death of His saints," and we can lift our hearts in thankfulness for those blessings of God which have enriched the life of the one now gone and which made the world richer for his presence. In the service, "we do not mourn as those who have no hope," but rejoice in the goodness of God, and find our strength in that which comes from the Holy Comforter.

A Christian funeral is never a performance staged for morbidly curious or indifferent spectators.

The service may involve the singing and praying in unison of those present, for they are essential parts of "the recognition of the divine providence in the affairs of men, and the goodness and mercy of God under all the varying conditions of life." In order that the music may express our faith, the same standards are to be used in the selection of hymns to be sung and music to be played as are used in the worship held on the Lord's Day. All decisions concerning music to be used are to be made in consultation with the pastor and the minister of music.

Flowers are widely used as the language of sympathy and memory. However, some families request that no flowers be sent to the funeral, and if some expression of sympathy is desired, that it be in the form of a donation to a memorial. For this purpose Christ Church has a Memorial Fund which is used for various purposes such as planting trees and other landscaping, for furnishings for the building, and for similar projects. Many worthy charities also have Memorial Funds. When a contribution is made to one of these, a permanent record is made, and the family is officially notified of the gift. If a request for memorial contributions instead of flowers is to be made, it should be included in the newspaper notice of the death and the funeral service.

The use of flowers in Christ Church sanctuary or chapel is limited to a covering for the casket if desired, and a simple arrangement at each side of the casket. Cut flowers may be placed in matching arrangements in the vases on the Holy Table. All other flowers are to be arranged in the narthex, in the tower entrance, and the halls, if necessary.

The old custom where the casket is placed at the head of the center aisle at right angles, before the Holy Table, may be followed.

All members of the family and friends should take leave of the body, if desired, before the beginning of the funeral service. For this purpose, the body should lie in state for an announced period of time. The casket should not be opened following the service except in the case of an extreme emergency and then not at the front of the sanctuary or chapel. To "view the remains" after the service is over is to take the spirit away from the contemplation of heavenly things and return to the viewing of the physical. Often this destroys the comfort brought to the bereaved through the funeral service. Christians will want to keep their minds fixed on God and in Him find their strength and help in time of trouble.

Those present at the funeral service will want to stand out of reverent respect when the members of the family enter the sanctuary or chapel at the beginning of the service, and again at the end when they leave, following which the people are to leave quietly and reverently.

A Helpful Form for Accumulating
Funeral Information

It is highly important that when the church office is notified of a death, the proper information be obtained and the pastor be notified immediately. One church developed a mimeographed form that proved to be helpful in obtaining information at the time of the initial call, and also for the recording of subsequent items regarding the funeral and place of interment. Following is the manner of setting up such a form for basic funeral procedure:

FUNERAL PROCEDURE NOTES   CHRIST CHURCH

1. Refer call immediately to the pastor; if he is not available then to his secretary.
2. When taking a call be sure to obtain *all* required information.
3. See that information is promptly relayed.
4. Check membership directory while phoning if possible.
5. For your convenience list three major local funeral directors:

   Jenkins Funeral Home, 5 Linden Lane   NO 8-1377
   Muller Funeral Home, 765 Second Street   NO 8-5984
   Thompson Funeral Home, 274 Mountain Ave.   NO 8-2602

   Christ Church makes no recommendations on funeral directors. These names are listed "for information only."

---

1. DATE AND TIME OF CALL   FROM WHOM
2. IS ANY PARTICULAR MINISTER REQUESTED FOR THE SERVICE?

The following information should be obtained by the pastor:

1. FULL NAME OF DECEASED
2. DATE AND CIRCUMSTANCE OF DEATH
3. CHURCH MEMBERSHIP—WHERE?
4. NEAREST RELATIVES—HOW TO REACH THEM
5. PREFERRED DATE AND HOUR OF SERVICE
6. PLACE OF INTERMENT—IF OUT OF TOWN, IS PASTOR EXPECTED TO GO?
7. FUNERAL DIRECTOR AND/OR STAFF MEMBER IN CHARGE OF ARRANGEMENTS

---

8. INFORMATION RELAYED TO WHOM?
9. FLOWERS ORDERED   WHAT FLORIST?
10. CONFIRMED PLACE AND TIME OF SERVICE
11. PLACE OF INTERMENT

   OTHER NOTES OF IMPORTANCE

The Lord's Supper

The Sacrament of the Lord's Supper is the universal Sacrament of deepest spiritual significance to the devout Christian. Where the Sacrament is administered as the congregation remains in the pews, a careful rehearsal of procedures is in order for the church officers who will assist in serving the elements.

A diagram should be prepared showing the position of each officer and the section of the congregation which he is to serve. Typical of the care to be exercised in preparing the documentation and procedure for the Communion can be seen in the following mimeographed bulletin to participants in the ceremony:

COMMUNION PROCEDURE

CHRIST CHURCH

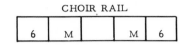

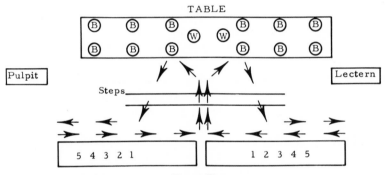

1) Elders assemble for prayer before Communion in the minister's study.
2) Enter sanctuary as a body—half of the group on each side. 6-5-4-3-2-1.
3) Elders Number 6 will sit in chair alongside ministers' seats in chancel.
4) At singing of hymn before Communion, they will remove the tablecloth covering the bread and the tops from the wine trays (B and W) on the Communion Table.
5) After Words of Institution, as minister nods his head slightly, elders will rise in a body.
6) Elders Number 1 will march together up the steps and the other elders will move to center and march up in subsequent order. Wait until party ahead of you has reached first step before you move forward. Move with dignity and take your time.

7) After receiving tray, move in semicircle toward the pulpit or lectern and go down steps to your position.

8) When coming back after elements are served, move in opposite fashion to the way you started: Start your semicircle wide, near the pulpit or lectern, give tray to minister—wait for your partner and then move down the steps shoulder to shoulder. Reach the first pew and separate to sitting positions. All elders will sit together when Number 6 men are in place.

9) Move in this fashion after receiving elements:
Number 1's will go directly to the back and thence to balcony, if needed. Number 1's serve balcony and then come downstairs and give help at back where needed.

10) Number 2's will receive trays and move up center aisle to designated pew approximately halfway up center aisle.

11) Number 3's will receive trays and move to front row, center aisle.

12) Number 4's will receive trays and move up the outside aisles to a pew directly opposite Number 2's.

13) Number 5's will receive trays and move to the front row, outside aisle.

14) *When in position, turn and face Communion Table.*

15) Number 6's will receive elements and the one on pulpit side will serve bread to minister. *That is the cue for all others to begin serving.*

16) Number 6's will serve choir and then go out side entrances of chancel and move down far side aisles to back of church sanctuary. They will serve those sitting against wall on very last pews, then go to the back and help where needed.

17) Make absolutely certain everyone is served.

18) When all are served, regroup outside sanctuary to return to the Communion Table—5-4-3-2-1-6.

19) Allow about 10 to 12 feet between those in front of you. Walk slowly and with dignity.

20) Repeat with serving of wine—except Number 6 on lectern side will serve the wine to minister.

21) The following are only suggestions:
    a. The men should wear dark suits, shoes and ties—dark blue preferably—and white shirts.
    b. Women should wear dark dresses or suits—dark blue preferably.

22) Approach this solemn task with personal prayer and examination. As you perform this holy duty with humility and dignity, the entire congregation will be more deeply moved by the occasion.

23) Following the service, particularly the early service, help the deacons to collect the empty glasses as soon as possible.

Functions and Procedures of
Chancel Committee

The Chancel Committee responsible for the preparation of the elements for Holy Communion should prepare detailed instructions for the guidance of its members. There are wide differences in the conduct of the Sacrament. Where communicants come to the rail and one chalice is used, the Altar Committee should have written instructions approved by the clergy. A congregation where 800 may receive the Sacrament and where the elements are taken by church officers from the clergy to communicants in their pews, may profit from instructions along the following lines in the necessary detail:

CHANCEL COMMITTEE

COMMUNION SERVICE DETAILS

I. INVENTORY

Serving equipment:

20 deep silver trays containing 40 glasses	800	glasses
3 deep aluminum trays containing 40 glasses	120	glasses
2 deep aluminum trays containing 44 glasses	88	glasses
3 shallow aluminum trays containing 40 glasses	120	glasses
Loose glasses plus 2 new boxes, approx.	30	glasses
Total	1158	glasses
(3 boxes, 28 glasses per box—odd sizes)	84	glasses

10 new silver bread plates — 6″ center
2 silver bread plates — 7″ center
6 plates, unmatched — 7″ center
1 aluminum tray cover
4 Communion altar cloths

Preparation equipment:

6 transfusion bottles or pitchers for filling glasses

Maintain inventory of:

1 package 6″ paper doilies for bread plates

1 package 7″ paper doilies for bread plates
1 roll scotch tape

II. PREPARATION—*Saturday Afternoon*

    A. Material required:

        1) Two large sandwich loaves of white bread (1 loaf per 600 people.)

        2) Four bottles Welch's (or similar) grape juice (1 bottle per 5 trays.)

    B. Preparation of bread:

    The bread should be cut into ⅜ inch to ½ inch cubes. By special arrangement this will sometimes be done at a bakery. Cubes received from a bakery should be checked for uniformity of shape and size and trimmed if necessary. Otherwise, freeze the sandwich loaf, trim off the crust, and slice into cubes. Crumbs should be removed by screening through a collander or other device, and the bread cubes stored in polyethelene bags in the refrigerator.

    C. Preparation of glasses:

    Be sure each glass cup is sparkling clean. Pour bottle of grape juice into transfusion bottle, add water to fill mark, shake bottle, attach transfusion kit and invert bottle over sink in auxiliary kitchen. With glasses in tray, fill each with juice to level half way between tray and top of glass. Fill 20 trays (40 glasses in each tray). Cover the trays and store in a cool place. DO NOT REFRIGERATE!

    D. Inventory:

    Glasses, trays and plates are kept in parlor in cupboards to left of fireplace. Check condition of Communion cloths in lower left drawer in auxiliary kitchen. Check supply of 6″ and 7″ doilies for bread plates, replenish if necessary. Purchases can be charged to the church or a bill submitted to the office after paying cash.

III. PREPARATION—8:30 *Sunday Morning*

    A. Preparation:

    Obtain bread plates from parlor storage cabinet. Get doilies for the bread plates, using the 6″ doilies on the silver plates with the 6″ center, filling each with approximately 70 bread cubes.

Prepare two of the 7" plates with the larger doilies
to be used for the balcony, if necessary.

Use the 20 silver glass trays for the table.

B. Table arrangement:
1) The cloth should be balanced in good symmetry
on the Communion Table.
2) Location of trays and plates on the table:

B	B	B	6		6	B	B	B
			trays		trays			
B	B	B	(cups)		(cups)	B	B	B

C. Between services the silver trays and plates will be
returned to the kitchenette, replenished and the table
reset.

IV. After the Sacrament

A. Between services the ushers will remove the used
glasses from the pews and assist the Chancel Committee wherever possible.

B. The glasses will be washed, rinsed, dried, and placed
in the aluminum serving trays for storage.

C. The trays will be stacked in the vestry cupboard and
covered.

D. After the second service, the silver trays with the
cleaned glasses will be stored in polyethelene bags,
stacked and replaced in the parlor cupboards to the
left of the fireplace.

E. The Communion Table cloth will be left in the storage
drawer, unlocked, for washing.

F. The Chancel Committee will notify Mrs. James that
the cloth needs washing.

*Procedure for Communicants
at Chancel Rail*

In churches where the communicant comes to the chancel rail for
the Sacrament, the minister will be largely responsible for the pouring
of the wine and the selection of sufficient bread or wafers to serve
the worshipers. In this case he will rely on the properly trained acolyte
and the Chancel Committee to prepare the elements suitable for the
Holy Sacrament.

V. Points to be observed in setting up a uniform procedure for the sanctuary are the following:

1. *Regulations and Rules*

The chancel and nave are hallowed and set apart from secular and nonreligious purposes.

The Official Board should prepare a statement of policy regarding the use of the chancel and sanctuary. It is advisable to make the minister and the chairman of the Worship Committee responsible for any modification of the rules in a particular situation.

2. *The Chancel Committee*

The Chancel Committee or Altar Guild will be charged with the maintenance of the chancel furnishings. Usually this committee prepares the elements for the Sacrament of the Lord's Supper, oversees the placing of memorial flowers in the chancel, and the sharing of those flowers with the ill and shut-ins following the service of worship.

It can be a meaningful experience to dedicate in a simple ceremony those who will serve on such a committee. This committee will organize itself so that one or more individuals are responsible for every occasion of public worship.

The expenses entailed by this committee will be paid by the Official Board and will be included in the annual budget. It is a proper form of recognition to publish the names of the members of the Chancel Committee who are responsible and on duty each Sunday.

3. *Hymn Books, Prayer Books, Pew Cards*

Every worshiper should have a hymn book, a prayer book and any other items that will assist in participation in the worship of God.

The hymn and prayer books should be in good repair and placed in an orderly fashion in the pew racks. If they become frayed or soiled, they should be replaced. Any pew cards, such as ones to be signed by visitors, should be fresh. There should be notice in the Sunday Bulletin and perhaps also through verbal announcements as to the procedure regarding the signing of the pew cards.

4. *Painting and Cleaning*

The care of the church fabric is usually placed under the Maintenance and Operations Committee of the Official Board. The annual budget will include a sum to provide for adequate janitorial and housekeeping service. The pews should be dusted once a week, the floor cleaned and, where needed, waxed. The pews and kneeling cushions should be vacuumed as required. A regular cleaning schedule will be given in writing to the individuals responsible. The ministers or chairman of the Maintenance Committee or some other designated individual will check weekly to see that the church is clean.

The annual budget should make provision for periodic painting and other major maintenance items in the church and chancel. Ideally, the Official Board should set aside certain "anticipatory" maintenance funds for this purpose.

5. Cloak Rooms

If the church has no provision for the placing of winter garb, the floor should be immaculate, so that if necessary, hats and coats may be placed under the pews.

If there is a cloak room, the sexton will check it weekly for cleanliness and tidiness. There should be adequate hangers. These should be of good quality and in good repair. One of the ushers or someone assigned for the specific purpose will watch the cloak room during the worship service.

There will always be items left in the cloak room or in the sanctuary. A program for lost and found materials should be established. Usually any item left in the cloak room or in the pews should be taken to the church office. Periodic announcements should be made regarding lost articles. If an item has not been called for within a year's time, after announcement in the Sunday Bulletin, such items may properly be given by the church to some worthy agency.

6. Heating and Ventilation

The Maintenance Committee will oversee the heating and ventilating systems of the church. The sexton or some other designated individual will prepare the heating and ventilating system sufficiently ahead of time so that worshipers arriving will find the sanctuary comfortable.

The ushers should take assignment to check the ventilation during the worship hour. At certain seasons of the year, opening the windows during the singing of a hymn may add to the comfort of those who worship. In cold weather the ushers will be attentive to the opening and closing of doors so that drafts may be minimized.

The Maintenance and Operations Committee must consider in its budget a plan to provide for major heating and ventilating repairs and improvements not alone annually, but over a five- and ten-year period.

7. Ushers

A key group of individuals who contribute much to the significance of worship are the ushers. One church adequately instructed the ushers on their important place in worship through the following communication:

CHRIST CHURCH

A COMMENT FOR USHERS

We must clearly understand the relation of church ushering to the worship service. It is a service rendered to God and deepens our personal commitment to Him. When we gather to worship God, we do so to receive from Him His Grace and Presence through Word and Sacrament, and to offer Him our sacrifices of prayer, praise and thanksgiving.

A church usher is part of the worshiping congregation. He has his particular acts to perform in the divine service, as does the minister, the organist, and the choir members. What he does is done not "as unto man, but unto God" (Col. 3:23). When he sees to it that an atmosphere of reverence and order is maintained before, during, and after the service, he does it for God. When he gathers the offering he serves God. Everyone, and especially the usher, must realize that his task is a service and contribution to the worship of God.

The ushers can have a significant part in seeing that the people assemble in an orderly way, and that a spirit of quietness and reverence prevails in and around the church building. It is written: "The Lord is in His Holy Temple; let all the earth keep silence before Him" (Habakkuk 2:20). Orderliness and reverence are instruments to prepare worshipers for a meaningful experience of worship.

The Head Usher

To achieve these ends one individual, usually the head usher or chairman of the ushers, will have the duties clearly outlined. These may be assigned in detail to individual members of the ushers group, but the chairman or head usher has responsibility to see that all assignments are completed.

A suggested outline may be structured as follows:

HEAD USHER'S CHECKLIST

1) Check the lights—sanctuary, narthex, balcony, stairways, cloak rooms, basement stairs, writing tables, entries.
2) Check public address system. Are control and volume dials properly set? If distortion occurs, turn amplifying system down, or off if distortion persists.
3) Check ringing of the tower bell fifteen minutes before service (ring for one minute.)
4) Procure bulletins and report card from table in narthex—check order of service.
5) Check ushers, including those responsible for balcony; equip them with boutonnieres, assign their positions.
6) Check the ringing of the tower bell five minutes before service, ring ten to twelve times.
7) Check the lighting of the candles.
8) Signal organist by red light that choir is ready to process; also see that the signal is given when the ushers are ready to return offering plates for dedication.
9) Close center doors after the processional.
10) NO ONE IS TO BE SEATED AFTER WORSHIP BEGINS EXCEPT DURING HYMNS OR AT SEATING INTERVALS INDICATED IN BULLETIN (definitely not during anthems, prayers, or scripture reading).
11) Seat latecomers on side aisles.
12) Maintain two ushers on main floor and one in balcony for any emergency. A stretcher should be kept in the men's washroom or in the cloak room.
13) See that offering plates from the table in the narthex and on the Communion table are in order—cleaned and in proper number.
14) Instruct ushers to count attendance while taking the offering.
15) See that side aisle lights and lower sanctuary lights are turned down before the sermon. Be sure lights are turned up again for the closing hymn.
16) Open doors at the end of each service. See that ushers assist in tidying the sanctuary—hymnals should be neatly replaced in racks, bulletins picked up. This duty may be assigned to the sexton, but the head usher should make sure it is done.

17) Lights and sound system should be turned off after the second service.
18) Candles should be snuffed out.
19) The attendance card should be filled out and placed on the work table in the office.
20) Be prepared to usher people into assembly hall on overflow Sundays. Have extra offering plates ready for such occasions.

Good Ushering Means a Richer Spiritual Experience for Worshipers.

Ushers' Meetings

The ushers should meet at regular intervals, and the head usher or chairman of the Ushering Committee should chair the meeting. The minister should be present in an ex-officio capacity. The meeting should be conducted with dignity, opening with prayer. An inspirational talk may be given regarding the presence of the ushers in the worship service. Any problems noted by the group should be discussed and appropriate action taken. If such a meeting is held annually only, this is an appropriate time to make assignments for the year. A mimeographed sheet listing the assignment of each usher should be placed in the hands of each member. It should be clearly indicated what to do, and whom to call if the individual usher cannot keep the assignment of a particular Sunday.

Usually at this meeting any past outline of ushering responsibilities and details should be reviewed.

One form to indicate and develop ushering responsibility is the following:

CHRIST CHURCH

USHERING

1. Ushering is not a duty to perform. It is one of the most important services you can offer, and the manner in which you carry out this service can be largely responsible for the impression people have of our church. You are the one officer that our members and visitors most often contact at public worship. Be as friendly as possible and yet maintain a reverent and worshipful atmosphere in the church at all times. Many people come to the sanctuary early for prayer and meditation, and it is the duty of the ushers to go about their

ushering chores in such a way that it will not create distraction.

2. The attached floor plan of the church shows the identifying numbers of each usher. There are eleven ushers required for each service. Usher schedules are made every two months and several alternates are listed for each service. Please get your own replacement if you cannot usher as scheduled. If that is not possible, call the head usher so he can prepare in advance for your absence. Your cooperation in this matter would greatly relieve your fellow ushers of the difficult task of trying to fill in for those who fail to appear as scheduled.

3. It is requested that all ushers wear dark suits and ties. Carnations are provided and may be obtained at the main literature table. The ushers at the 9:30 A.M. service must return the carnations for the next service. Ushers at the 11 A.M. service may keep the carnations. Ushers are to report twenty-five minutes before the service.

4. Before the service starts, the front ushers (2 and 3) seat people. The rear ushers (5, 6, 7 and 8) toward the rear will seat people in the rear or send people up to the front ushers. At this time all doors to the sanctuary are open.

5. As soon as the processional leaves the narthex, all doors to the sanctuary are to be closed. Ushers 1 and 4 remain forward to seat people coming in late through the south doors. Ushers 5 and 8 come out into the narthex to hold people there until the proper time in the service to usher them in. Ushers 2 and 3 remain in the rear of the center aisle and 6 and 7 come out into the narthex to hold people until the proper seating time. Those ushers in the narthex should give people who are waiting a bulletin, and explain to them that they will be seated as soon as possible.

6. After the service has started, no one should be ushered to seats except at points marked in the bulletin with asterisks and during the singing of the hymns. At no time are people to be ushered to seats during:

   a. the singing of an anthem by the choir;
   b. the reading of the Old or New Testament lessons;
   c. prayers;
   d. the singing of the Gloria Patri, or the Apostles' Creed.

7. Do not group together and talk in the narthex, as every word carries easily into the sanctuary even with the doors closed. Use sign language when possible.

8. When the offering is announced, ushers 6 and 7, followed by ushers 2 and 3, go forward in pairs and stand four abreast

on the lower platform of the chancel. At the same time, the side ushers go forward to take their positions. After the offering prayer, the minister will hand two plates to each of the four center aisle ushers. Ushers 6 and 7 turn about-face toward each other, and leave for their positions halfway back in the aisle. Ushers 2 and 3 also turn toward each other and go to the first pews and start the collection.

9. The collection plates for the balcony are kept in the balcony at the rear of the side aisles. The side aisle ushers in the balcony pick up these plates at the time the first floor ushers go forward for the offertory prayer. Begin the collection in the front pew, working two rows at a time. The center usher has to handle four plates and keeps advancing them back to the side ushers.

10. The two side aisle ushers in the balcony, 9 and 11, return with the plates to the narthex and go down the aisle behind the first floor ushers to the chancel for the Doxology. At this point six ushers are standing six abreast on the lower step of the chancel. After the Amen, they go single file through the sacristy door to the main office, where the treasurer or some other designated officer will receive the collection.

11. After the collection the ushers return to the service and remain near the rear of the sanctuary, so they can open the doors as soon as the service ends.

12. At the close of the service, each usher cleans up his section. Pick up all bulletins and replace all hymnals and prayer books face up in the racks.

13. The usher captains are responsible for the service to which they are assigned:

   a. See that all ushers are in their proper place.
   b. See that all ushers have carnations.
   c. See that bulletins and special flyers are available for all ushers.
   d. Check and see if the collection plates are in place before the service begins.
   e. See the minister before each service for any special instructions.
   f. Check heating and ventilation for comfort.
   g. Check any adjustments to the loud speakers that might be necessary.
   h. See that all doors are unlocked, especially the second-floor cloister hall door and the door to the sacristy.
   i. See that all corridor traffic is orderly and that no unnecessary noise is being made.

    j. See that the attendance count is taken and recorded in the attendance book.

    k. See that all exit doors are opened at the end of the service.

    l. See that the sanctuary is put in order after the service.

Ushering Assignment Follow-Up

The most careful and orderly assignments made to individual ushers, in thoughtful planning for the church year, should be reviewed by the chairman from time to time. Prior to each Sunday's assignment a simple reminder card should be sent. The notice should be sent early Monday morning preceding the service, as is indicated by this form note:

Dear Fellow Usher:

According to our yearly outline of assignments for ushering, you are to serve next Sunday morning (date) at the 11 A.M. worship service. If you cannot be present please notify Mr. A. J. Moore before Wednesday. Phone 638-3827.

Please be present before 10:40 A.M.

Looking forward to seeing you and sharing with you in the conduct of our worship service at Christ Church.

Faithfully,

Chairman, Ushers

The Atmosphere for Worship

Beyond the details discussed previously and elsewhere in this volume, the following items can be significant in creating a dignified and expectant attitude for the worship service:

Item 1—If there is a church bell, it may be rung fifteen minutes before the worship hour, calling the community to prayer.

Item 2—If there are hymn boards, the hymns for the Sunday service should be placed on the board on Saturday.

Item 3—The Altar Guild will have arranged the flowers in the chancel before any worshipers have assembled.

Item 4—The offering plates will be polished and in place.

Item 5—The ushers and any other appointed church officer will greet the worshipers with warm solemnity as they enter the church.

Item 6—The Prelude will be selected with care and be played reverently.

Item 7—The pastor will instruct the congregation in the ways of meditation that will prepare them for the corporate worship experience. The period before the call to worship should be one of prayerful preparation.

Item 8—The bulletin can carry in it helpful guiding thoughts for the worship.

Item 9—For newcomers and strangers, descriptive materials regarding the sanctuary can assist in creating a fine worship atmosphere. One church, with an unusual sanctuary, prepared the following statement for the new worshiper, which was handed to each by an usher as he entered the church:

FOR NEWCOMERS TO OUR SERVICES
THE SYMBOLISM OF THIS SANCTUARY
OF CHRIST CHURCH

We welcome you to the worship of Almighty God. Your relationship to Him and His direction of your life is a matter of prime meaning that brings us together.

Our particular church is unique in its architecture and symbolism. The following explanation may be helpful to you:

The floor plan of the sanctuary is in the shape of a fish, which was an early Christian symbol. Ichthus is the Greek word for fish. The first letter of the words "Jesus Christ, God's Son, Savior" come from this word in the Greek language.

The large marble communion table in front of the dramatic thirty-two-foot cross forms the center of worship. Wood for the cross came from the Canterbury Cathedral Library. In front of the table rests a millstone, gift of Dr. James Miller. The lectern and pulpit on either side of the chancel are important centers of focus. A stone from the Iona Community, off the Scottish coast, is embedded behind the lectern, and a stone from Wartburg is in the floor of the pulpit. The sounding board above the pulpit is in the shape of an open Bible, signifying the fact that the minister speaks under the authority and judgment of "The Word."

The one-inch thick colored glass on the north side of the nave has been designed to represent the crucifixion of Christ.

Three huge crosses (1) of white glass may be seen. On the beam of the center cross are the letters I N R I (2) signifying Pilate's words "Jesus of Nazareth, the King of the Jews."

To the far right is shown in red the curtain of the Temple (3) which at the crucifixion was rent from top to bottom. Just below this is a falling Roman column (4) in light-colored glass. On the far left at the top are the rooftops of the city of Jerusalem (5). Below this at eye level is portrayed the hand (6) of a Roman soldier throwing dice (7) for the robe of Christ.

The south side of the nave depicts scenes from the resurrection. Near the center slightly above eye level may be seen the empty tomb (8) in blue glass. Emanating from this is shown the angel as lightning (9) which stabs the sky in three directions. Figures of the women (10) and the frightened centurions (11) may be seen to the right and left of the tomb. A Roman's horse (12) in blue glass is shown at the far right. Again at the top left of the scene is the suggestion of the Holy City (13). The large hands of red on the left sides symbolize sunset at the crucifixion (14) and sunrise at the resurrection (15). The glass in the narthex suggests the sacraments and teachings of our Lord. At the peak is the word PAX. Two chalices, several loaves of bread and symbols of fish may be discerned, all representing the life and living presence of our Lord.

Item 10—Instructions should be given to the worshiper regarding any unusual form of the worship service, so that he will be at ease as to when to sit or stand or kneel.

Item 11—The church will be properly lighted, and if it is suitable to the sanctuary and for the worshipers, rheostats may be used to increase or decrease the lighting at various points in the worship service.

Item 12—The choir and clergy will conduct themselves with a spirit of great reverence.

SPECIAL ROOMS AND EQUIPMENT

A. *The Church Kitchen*

Principles regarding the church kitchen should be clearly outlined with the approval of the Official Board. Some items for clarification will be the following:

1. An individual or small committee of the Women's Society should be in charge of the kitchen.
2. Rules regarding use of the kitchen by church groups and outside groups should be established and placed in the hands of the church office and all others who may be in a position to answer questions or receive requests for the use of the kitchen.
3. Usually the Maintenance and Operations Committee of the Official Board will be responsible for major replacement and maintenance, with clearly established lines as to the responsibilities of the Women's Society.
4. Organizations using the kitchen should be responsible for the replacement of any breakage.
5. If the church is engaged in a new building program, properly appointed women from the Women's Society should be invited to consult with the architect and a kitchen planning specialist in the layout of the church kitchen.

B. *Stage and Stage Equipment*

1. Only competent and designated individuals should use the electric and other equipment of the stage.
2. Beyond the sexton, one individual or a small committee from a drama organization should oversee the sets, costumes, and other materials used in presentations on the stage.
3. It is desirable to have a long-term plan for obtaining additional stage equipment and for the replacement of present equipment.
4. Usually a group of people interested in drama, properly organized, may be assigned to the overall care and development of the stage and its equipment. Such a group should be properly related to the Official Board, the Maintenance Committee and to the minister.

C. *Recreational Areas and Facilities*

Some churches have acquired summer camps or may have land that is used for recreation. Other congregations may develop Nursery Schools where areas adjoining the church may be used for play and exercise. In administering such, the following points are worthy of consideration:

1. If the area is near or adjacent to the church, the equipment used should be camouflaged by hedge or fencing.

2. A responsible appointed individual should see that recreational equipment is stored and locked when not in use.
3. Rules should be established regarding the use of the area and facilities by neighboring children.
4. Summer camps should have the attention of one professional member of the church staff, and a special committee should be appointed to oversee all the details involved in an effective camping program.

D. *Projectors, Recorders*

The church should be "generous" in the use of its equipment for worthy causes and programs in the community. However, experience indicates that there may be more problems in being "casually generous" than in being restrictive in the lending of special equipment. Costly motion-picture projectors and recording equipment may properly be restricted to church use. The Official Board should prepare policies regarding the loan of church equipment. Sound motion-picture projectors should be operated only by competent and properly appointed individuals. The same rule is true of sound-recording equipment. Usually such equipment will be assigned to a particular department such as the Christian Education or Music Department. The staff member in charge of this department will be responsible for the equipment.

E. *Board Room*

It is desirable to have a room designated for the Official Board and for important conferences.

1. If at all possible the room should have a religious symbol dominating the area.
2. The room should be well lighted and always freshly ventilated.
3. Chairs should be comfortable.
4. The seating should be arranged for maximum attention to the business that calls the group together.
5. Notepaper and pencils, together with agendas and other items pertinent to the business of the meeting, should be neatly arranged at each place.
6. Any item in the way of pictures or paintings that would contribute to the dignity of the room should be properly placed.
7. A suitable place for the hanging of hats and coats should be furnished.

F. *Music and Choir Rooms*

Determined by the number of musicians in the church, there may be a choir rehearsal room, an office for the director of music, a choir library room, and a suitable robing room. The rehearsal room should contain the most desirable type of piano, good acoustics, suitable lighting, good ventilation, proper chairs for the musicians, and if needed, a series of step elevations for the seating of choristers. The office for the director of music should be developed in terms of his needs and desires. The music library should be carefully catalogued with a central cross-reference guide system, so that any desired music may be quickly found. One individual should be appointed as music librarian. The music should be housed and stored for maximum protection and clearly identified by a numbering system that offers the maximum simplicity and efficiency.

G. *The Church Parlor*

Usually used primarily by the women, but also as a reception room and for various committee and small group meetings, the church parlor should meet the following checklist:

1. All requests for the use of the church parlor should be cleared through the church office or a properly designated person who is in charge of the complete church calendar.
2. Definite rules for its use by outside groups should be established by the Official Board.
3. If outside organizations are permitted to use the parlor, a suggested contribution toward the cost of maintenance should be established.
4. If the use of the kitchen and the housekeeper (as, for example in serving tea) are required, a definite procedure for compensation and for clean-up should be outlined by the Maintenance and Operations Committee.
5. Ideally, a closet or cabinet in or near the parlor should be kept to house materials helpful to those using the church parlor. These items may include hymn books, worship materials, books of prayer, paper and pencils, and whatever additional items are needed to further the use of the room. It is helpful to have a small lectern readily accessible for use by a speaker or chairman at small meetings.

6. The room, including furniture, rugs, pictures, drapes, windows, should be immaculate. If it is needful in the administration of the church property to have assistance in keeping parts of the building clean, this policy should be made clear to those using the parlor. The Maintenance Committee should check the room from time to time to see that the highest standards of orderliness and cleanliness are met.

7. The parlor should be an "inviting" room, meeting the standard of good taste and offering in its atmosphere warmth, dignity and informality. As the room is a part of the church, it should have some religious emphasis to remind the eye and heart of all who enter that "this, too, is part of God's House."

8. If the parlor is large enough to require voice amplification for a chairman or speaker, mention of a microphone should be made in instructions for the preparation of the room before the scheduled meeting. The sexton or housekeeper or some designated person should "double-check" before the appointed hour to see that this and all other requirements are met.

9. If the parlor serves as a reception room or a place where individuals may rest or wait, an unobtrusive table containing literature and reading material may be appropriate.

10. All individual gifts for the furnishing of the parlor or any part of the church should be acknowledged by the pastor and the Official Board and recorded in the permanent records of the church.

H. *Literature Racks and Tables*

To develop the literacy of the church members, a church library and the development and upkeep of literature racks and tables are indispensable. Principles to create an effective program of literature distribution are the following:

1. A keen-minded committee, related to the Official Board for "Literature Promotion," should be appointed.

2. The committee should be reviewed annually and replacements made as required.

3. The committee should meet regularly and constantly seek for and review leaflets, pamphlets, folders, cards, magazines that will further the aims of the church.

4. The literature racks should be placed throughout the church premises where the maximum number of people may pass them.

5. If contributions toward the cost of the literature are desired, an offering container, with lock, should be a part of the rack or attached to the table.

6. The suggested cost or contribution for each piece of literature should be indicated by a neatly printed card or noted in pencil on each pamphlet.

7. The tables should be kept in neat order and well supplied. A member of the committee should be responsible for tidying the racks after every service or major church event.

8. The literature material should be current. Leaflets, unless they are classic and permanent, should not remain on the racks gathering dust after they are out of date.

9. The appearance of the literature racks and tables is important. Not alone neatness, but the creation of "interest" should be considered. A quotation, suitably printed, concerning reading or religious development could be placed by the literature and might be helpful to this end.

10. The Sunday bulletin should be utilized to call people's attention to the literature materials. New leaflets and pamphlets particularly should be called to the attention of the parishioners.

11. The cost of the literature program should be underwritten through the budget of the Official Board. However, contributions toward the program can assist in meeting this budgetary item.

I. *Restroom Facilities*

1. Ushers, the church staff, and all responsible for activities in the church should know the location of restroom facilities for both men and women.

2. All restrooms should be checked on a regular schedule, and items such as soap, towels and tissue should be replenished.

3. A program for cleaning the facilities should be prepared under the Maintenance Committee and the sexton should be required to check periodically as to whether the schedule is maintained and adequate in terms of the use of the restrooms.

4. Proper disinfectant should be used in scrubbing the floors,

lavatories and toilets, and the use of deodorants should not be neglected.

5. Supply and work closets should be kept in order.

6. Proper inventory of soap, towels and toilet tissue should be maintained.

7. The Maintenance Committee should prepare a policy for purchasing. Often members of the church may be in a position to effect considerable savings in the purchase of supplies. Such information should be in the hands of the Maintenance Committee.

J. *First-Aid Equipment*

Accidents do occur in spite of all precautions. To avoid these as much as possible, the entrances to the church and related facilities should have every available safety factor. These will include railings at steps, white lines indicating risers, rubber or cocoanut matting as required, fire extinguishers at strategic points. In spite of all precautions, people will become injured or ill on the church premises. Items that should be included in a checklist are the following:

1. The head usher at every worship service or major church gathering should note where a doctor in the congregation is located, so that he may be quietly called for any emergency treatment.

2. Every area of the church and church house where numbers of adults and children may be present should have basic first-aid items, and the location should be familiar to the person in charge. Special departments are:
   a. The church narthex.
   b. The church office.
   c. The kitchen.
   d. Office of the director of Christian Education.
   e. Work room for the sexton maintenance staff.
   f. The vestry and sacristy.

3. The narthex should have a closet where a stretcher, wheelchair and two blankets are available. Also here and in the other areas, a first-aid kit containing disinfectant, smelling salts, bandages, tape, cotton and scissors should be kept. The kit should be checked for needed replenishment of any item at regular intervals. All items should be in usable condition.

K. Rooms for Youth Activities

This type of facility will vary with the terms of the church program and the numbers of young people involved. Special rooms may be designated for the Boy Scouts, teen and high school groups. Most churches cannot fulfill the desire of some specialized youth groups to have a room "just of our own." But anything that can be done to prepare facilities for youth activities with appropriate furnishings is desirable. Across years of experience, certain guiding thoughts and observations have been helpful on this item:

1. Young people like to "do things their way." They want an opportunity to express their likes and dislikes. Give them a chance, under guidance, to express their preferences, and let them share, in-so-far as possible, in the responsibility of furnishing the room they will use.
2. Use furniture that is sturdy, easily cleaned, and can take abuse not likely to be suffered in the board room or the ladies' parlor.
3. Through the individuals in charge of the youth programs, develop within the young people's groups a sense of responsibility for maintenance. A "house committee" or a "clean-up brigade" should be established to go into action at every meeting of the group. Any special equipment used should be put in its proper place, including items for games, hymn books, and record players or projectors.

L. Chapels and Classrooms

Certain principles for the facilities used for worship and education in the church are basic:

1. The room or chapel should be designed for the activity for which it is to be used, and then prepared for it. If it is a classroom, the blackboard should be clean. Chalk and erasers should be available. Any leaflets or study books to be used during the class session should be at the end of the table where the students will sit—or a copy placed at every seat. If visual aids of any kind, such as maps, slide or strip projectors, or charts are to be used, the individual in charge will have seen that these items are available and on hand and in working order before the class meeting.

2. The chapels should be set aside primarily for worship. If they are used for lectures or necessary church meetings, such occasions should open and close with prayer, and the sacredness of the place of worship should always be honored.

3. As with the use of all church facilities, the scheduling of classrooms or chapels should be done through one individual who oversees the complete church calendar.

4. Proper lighting and ventilation are very important. Windows should be clean. Lights should be at the proper setting and drapes suitably adjusted. The chapel will have adequate lighting so worshipers may follow the hymn book and participate in the acts of worship without eyestrain. It is desirable to have the chapel lighting adjustable through a rheostat so that various lighting effects may be obtained for different conditions of day or evening.

M. *The Church Library*

Many congregations are benefited by a library, designed to provide books and literature to assist in meeting the educational and spiritual aims of the church. From experience and consultation with a number of churches, the following checklist should be covered to provide a usable library in the church:

1. A responsible committee should be in charge, under appointment by the Official Board. The committee will oversee purchasing, cataloguing, and lending of books. It will be in charge of keeping current periodicals, leaflets and similar materials available. The appearance and order of the library will be its responsibility.

2. Location is important. The library should be easily accessible to the majority of users. It should be well lighted and ventilated.

3. A system for check-out and return of books should be established and strictly adhered to.

4. To further the adult and youth group, and individual educational aims, the several departmental leaders of the church should be consulted about their required or recommended books and study materials.

5. Special sections of the library may be set apart for particular groups or for special seasonal emphases such as Advent, Christmas, Lent and Easter.

6. The committee in charge shall set the aims of the library, and donations of books shall be accepted only if they are suitable to such aims. Usually the church library should be a specialized library. A few basic reference works may be appropriate, but the centering of the library should be on religion. Sections will include prayer and devotional materials, church history, religious education, denominational reference works, Bible study, hymnology, church symbolism and liturgy, philosophy and theology, books on the relation of religious principles to contemporary life, and other categories that may be suggested by the needs and program of the particular congregation.

7. The various avenues of public relations in the church should be used to inform the congregation of new books and materials available for inspiration and study.

8. The financing of the library may be accomplished in various ways, determined by the particular congregation. In most churches there are individuals who have interest in libraries and books, and their support can be enlisted. One church began its library with an initial "memorial gift" of a church member, which was accepted and acknowledged by the Official Board. This official body should underwrite the operational cost of the library in its annual budget. This may be done under the particular budget of one department, perhaps that of the Christian Education Department. However, the value of having the library program related to the entire church cannot be overestimated.

N. *Fire and Safety Equipment*

Usually the Maintenance and Operations Committee will oversee all safety aspects of the church and related buildings on behalf of the Official Board.

It is wise to place on this committee church members who are experienced in property oversight and maintenance. Such individuals should be co-opted from any segment of the congregation to see that proper protection is established and maintained.

Consultation with the local fire department officials is advised for proper protection against fire hazards. All exits should be identified according to local fire laws. Electrical wiring outlets and electrical equipment should be checked periodically. Ushers should be instructed as to procedures in the event of fire or any other public hazard.

Helpful counsel on safety measures can be received from insurance specialists, and such advice should be sought in regular surveys of the property. Fire extinguishers should be placed at strategic positions on the church premises and a regular check should be made as to their usefulness.

Hand railings, step markings, the use of rubber or cocoanut matting, and the display of clear instructions at points of possible danger are recommended for consideration by the Maintenance Committee.

CARE OF MEMORIALS AND SPECIAL GIFTS

In the course of the years the congregation will acquire special gifts of furnishings and equipment, or special contributions for particular causes or parts of the church building.

a. All such gifts should be approved and acknowledged by the pastor and the Official Board.

b. Every memorial gift, with all details regarding it, should be recorded in a special permanent file. If the church has a "Book of Memorials" all gifts of a special nature will be recorded therein. The book should be kept up to date. It may be helpful to exhibit it from time to time to the congregation.

c. The congregation, through the church magazine or Sunday bulletin, should be informed of memorial gifts.

d. Where it is appropriate, a special ceremony of dedication can be meaningful to donors, the cause for which they have given, and the deepening spirit of stewardship among all the people.

e. Major gifts, as for an organ or a special room, may properly be memorialized through a permanent brass or bronze plaque or tablet. Dignity and simplicity should be guiding principles in the selection of such a marker and the wording it contains.

RULES REGARDING THE USE OF CHURCH PROPERTY

Many problems can arise for the pastor, staff and church officers if there is no clear-cut outline of principles and detailed rules regarding the use of the church and related buildings.

Points to be cleared and covered in the policy statement are the following:

a. Will church-sponsored or related groups have priority in the use of church facilities?

b. What about groups which are identified with a political party or some secular issue that is controversial among church members?

c. Will the church facilities be available to individuals or groups which charge fees for their services, such as a non-church-sponsored nursery school or dancing class?

d. What of "contributions toward the cost of maintenance" to be made by groups other than church members, using certain rooms or facilities?

e. Will the Official Board permit the lending of church furnishings and equipment such as chairs, motion-picture equipment or ecclesiastical objects?

f. What rules will govern the use of the kitchen and its equipment, together with special items such as tablecloths, silver, dishes and glassware?

g. How will the scheduling of the church facilities be handled?

h. Will the pastor and the chairman of the Maintenance Committee have authority to modify expected contributions in unusual circumstances?

i. Will any inquirer receive full rules regarding the use of the church property, including baptisms, weddings, funerals in the church?

6

New Building Projects

Enlarging or modifying the sanctuary, or creating new facilities of whatever nature requiring capital funds, poses a number of problems and details to challenge the competent church administrator. Following is a suggested checklist for basic consideration of personnel concerned:

I. INITIAL STUDIES

No building program should be contemplated without careful surveys and evaluations. Questions that must be asked and answered include:

a. What are the demonstrable needs of the congregation that cannot be met by the existing facilities?

b. From random checking among the members, what will be congregational response? What questions do the church people raise that warrant full and convincing answers?

c. If the capital program involves improvement or replacement of present aspects of the church, such as a new organ, heating system, or remodeling of the chancel or nave, has there been adequate consultation with non-interested specialists? For example, on the matter of the organ—what have been the costs for maintenance and repair over the immediate past years? Is there a written report on its condition from the builder of the organ or the maintenance specialist? What is the opinion of the organist? Have other competent organists expressed their opinion on the condition of the organ?

If the matter concerns the fabric of the building, the question should be raised, "Has a survey of the condition of the building been made by two reliable builders or specialists in the maintenance of property?" "What is the recommendation of the Maintenance Committee?" "What is the judgment of the Official Board to these reports and recommendations?" If the program is to consider the erection of additional new facilities such as a church hall, added Sunday School rooms, or improved office facilities, an outline of all facts should be made. If the Official Board feels it advisable, a special "Study Committee" may be appointed on the recommendation of the pastor and the Maintenance Committee. This committee will survey the needs and discuss the situation with leaders of all related departments of the church and staff members. The committee will observe first hand the program for children, young people and adults, and in light of these observations put itself in a position to speak with the authority and facts that can come alone from a thorough study.

The initial study will not be primarily concerned with costs, but any estimates and information in this area can be helpful. Also, suggested ways and means of raising funds may appropriately be proposed in the initial study. These latter items are to be purely informative and the further decision on fund-raising shall remain for the Official Board and usually congregational approval.

II. THE BUILDING COMMITTEE

When it is agreed by the Official Board that a building program is required, a report should be made to the congregation and approval received to proceed.

Where ecclesiastical law requires it, a report should be made to the proper judicatory and the necessary procedures should be fulfilled.

In most of our churches the appointment of the Building Committee is made with the approval of the congregation. The committee should represent all departments and programs of the church, including Music, Christian Education, men, women, and youth activities.

These departments should explore fully the building program as it impinges on their particular interest. For instance, if a new kitchen is a part of the program, the head of the Women's Society probably should be named to the Building Committee. She in turn will consult with a subcommittee or other officers of the Women's Society on kitchen needs. She will then report the women's recommendations to the Building Committee. As specific plans are suggested by the architect, the kitchen details should be approved by the women.

If the committee is larger than twelve, it will be helpful to name a smaller executive committee.

The committee should have regular stated meetings. In some phases of the building schedule it may be necessary to meet as often as once a week. Once a month is the minimum needed to cover all aspects of a new building and capital program.

III. THE ARCHITECT

Points to consider in engaging an architect are these:

a. Consult the denominational department on church architecture, if there is such, for recommendations.
b. The National Council of Churches can provide materials and suggestions.
c. Raise the question, "Is there a local architect, trusted by the community, and who has a proved record of good planning?" There can be an advantage in having an architect in close proximity.
d. The committee should invite at least two, and preferably more, architects for individual conferences. Attention should be given to each architect's background, experience, personality, and particularly his knowledge of church life and church architecture. The fee should be discussed. The committee should present the church's needs and have the individual architect offer suggestions and proposals as to how those needs can best be met. On the basis of these conferences one architect should be selected and a contract signed for his services.
e. The committee should have the contract approved by a lawyer on behalf of the church.

IV. THE BUILDER

As with the architect, several builders should be consulted. Each should, in the presence of the committee, give his background, experience, and response to the specific building needs of the church.

The committee, with legal counsel, should select the builder whose proposal and contract would be most advantageous to the church.

The Building Committee will include the builder and the architect in all its meetings.

V. THE FUND RAISING

The raising of capital funds must be considered in relationship to the annual budget of the local church. An opportunity is presented in a Capital Fund Program to raise the level of giving.

Depending on the goal of the capital needs, the capacity of the local congregation and the aggressive and trained local leadership available, the engagement of a professional fund-raiser should be considered. With a major capital fund need, the engagement of a responsible professional fund-raising firm has been found to be desirable by an increasing number of churches.

Whether with lay or professional leadership, the fund-raising effort may involve these aspects:

a. The cause and need must be presented to the widest number of people who will be the sources of response.

b. A major gifts committee must be established.

c. A congregational dinner where the pastor will announce his gift and several major gifts will be reported, can be helpful.

d. The potential of every giver should be established by a small, confidential committee, and the assignment of names, "who approaches whom?" must be developed by this committee.

e. The fullest possible report to the congregation via newsletters, Sunday bulletins and special reports should be kept up during the program. Every likely giver should be contacted. No letters! The personal call is the best, with the aim and need in the heart of the caller, and with full information to answer any question.

f. The church engaged in a Capital Fund Program may well prepare material that will answer the questions "What, Why, Where, When?"—"Why?" is the key question.

VI. CEREMONIES AND DEDICATIONS

The congregation can be inspired as the various steps in the building program are marked with appropriate ceremonies. These include:

a. The ground-breaking.
b. Dedication of the cornerstone.
c. Special ceremonies as certain stages of construction are completed, such as the raising of the last piece of steel for the tower, the closing in of the roof, the completion of the work of a particular trade, such as stonemasons; the replacing of memorials from a previous building into the new structure.
d. Most thrilling can be the dedication of the completed structure. A Dedicatory Committee should be appointed, far in advance, to meet with the pastor and prepare plans for this high occasion. Many special services and ceremonies may be developed that will serve the whole cause of the church and its people. Seminars, conferences, musical events, lectures, dramatic presentations, and scores of other programs, in terms of the structure that has been built, should be developed.

The following examples of dedicatory services may serve as useful guidelines to be adapted to individual church use.

1. GROUND-BREAKING CEREMONY.
   Prelude
   Call to Worship
   Hymn—"Old Hundredth"
   Presentation of Spade—Building Committee Chairman
   The Breaking of the Ground
   Remarks
   Response by Architect
   Response by Builder
   The Apostles' Creed—(in unison)
   Minister: The Lord be with you.
   Congregation: And with thy Spirit.

Minister: Let us pray,
Prayers of Thanksgiving and Dedication
The Lord's Prayer
Hymn—"The Church's One Foundation"
Benediction, Choral Amen, and Silent Prayer
Postlude
Note: All are invited to the fellowship period on the lawn
following the service.

2. ORDER FOR THE LAYING OF THE CORNERSTONE
Christ Church
12 noon, Saturday, October 14, 1967
The people, being assembled at the place where the church
is being built, shall stand, and the Reverend Thomas Jones
shall say:

> "Our help is in the name of the Lord, who made heaven
> and earth. Except the Lord build the house, they labor
> in vain that build it."

Following shall be a responsive reading.
The Reverend Charles Larson shall say: "Let us pray:

> O LORD JESUS CHRIST, who art the one foundation
> and the chief cornerstone of Thy Church, bless what
> we now do in Thy name, and let this stone, planted in
> this foundation, be to us and to our children the symbol
> and pledge of Thy presence. Direct us, O Lord, in all
> our doing, with Thy most gracious favor, and further
> us with Thy continual help; that in all our works, begun,
> continued, and ended in Thee, we may glorify Thy holy
> name, and finally, by Thy mercy, obtain everlasting life;
> through Jesus Christ our Lord. Amen."

Reading of the Epistle
Reading of the Gospel
Hymn—"The Church's One Foundation," congregation
standing.
The congregation, still standing, shall repeat the Creed.
The Reverend John Forsyth, placing his hand on the stone,
shall say:

> "In the name of the Father, and of the Son, and of the
> Holy Ghost, we lay this stone of the building here being
> erected under the name of Christ Church, and devoted
> to the worship of Almighty God. Other foundations can
> no man lay than that is laid which is Jesus Christ.
> Let us pray:

Almighty and everlasting God, who has built the living temple of Thy Church upon the foundation of the Apostles and Prophets, Jesus Christ Himself being the chief cornerstone: We beseech Thee to confirm and bless that which we have now done in Thy name. Establish this stone which we have laid and prosper the work to which we have set our hands, for the upbuilding of Thy Church and the glory of Thy Kingdom."

Prayers of thanksgiving and dedication.
The Lord's Prayer in unison.
Hymn
Benediction

7

Church Finances

I. THE ANNUAL BUDGET

Behind the preparation and presentation of the annual budget should be a strong Finance Committee.

Churches vary in the formation of the Finance Committee, and in the specific duties assigned to it. The following format as to rules and regulations worked effectively in one church, and may suggest procedure to any congregation seeking to lay out the purpose for the Finance Committee.

CHRIST CHURCH

FINANCE COMMITTEE

RULES AND REGULATIONS

As Amended by Congregational Meeting, June 4, 19__

INTRODUCTION

At the January meeting of the Congregational and Corporation Meeting in 19__, a church Finance Committee was established to facilitate (1) the handling of all church income, and (2) the preparation, presentation, raising, and administration of a Unified Annual Church Budget.

The establishment of a church Finance Committee does not abrogate the already well-established duties and responsibilities of the various boards and organizations of the church. However, a central Finance Committee has been needed to plan and over-see the total financial program of the church. The following rules and regulations governing the relationship of the Finance Committee to the various boards and organizations will help to strengthen the entire stewardship program.

A copy of these rules and regulations will be retained in the permanent files of the church, as well as the files of each board and organization in the church. Each subdivision will be discussed in turn, according to the following Index:

CHRIST CHURCH
FINANCE COMMITTEE

INDEX

I. Purpose
II. Membership and Voting Rights.
III. Responsibilities and Authority of Finance Committee
IV. Responsibility of Participating Boards and Organizations.
V. Handling of Funds
VI. Budget Format and Financial Statements
VII. Duties of the Director of the Every Member Canvass

CHRIST CHURCH
FINANCE COMMITTEE

PURPOSE

The purpose of the Finance Committee is to facilitate:

a. The handling of all church income and expenses on a consolidated basis, and

b. The preparation, presentation, raising, and administration of a Unified Annual Church Budget.

MEMBERSHIP AND VOTING RIGHTS

1. The Finance Committee shall be composed of ten members as follows:

   a. Two members from the Board of Trustees
   b. Two members from the Board of Deacons
   c. Two members from the Administrative Board
   d. Two members from the Christian Education Board
   e. The church treasurer
   f. The chairman of the Finance Committee

2. Each board or organization represented shall elect its own representatives from its membership for a term of two years, one representative being replaced each year.

3. The chairman of the Finance Committee shall be elected by the congregation and shall be a member of the Official Board.

   The church treasurer shall be elected by the congregation and shall be a member of the Board of Trustees.

   In the event of a mid-term vacancy of either of these offices, the Official Board shall elect a replacement to finish the term.

4. Each member of the Finance Committee shall be entitled to a vote.

RESPONSIBILITIES AND AUTHORITY OF FINANCE COMMITTEE

1. The Church Finance Committee shall be responsible for:
   a. The coordination of the preparation of both the tentative budget and the final budget.
   b. The presentation to the congregation for its approval of both the tentative and the final budget.
   c. The raising of funds to meet the annual church budget.
   d. The administration of the final budget as approved by the congregation.
   e. The exchange of financial information between the various boards and organizations of the church.
   f. The preparation of quarterly financial reports to all members of the church.
   g. The handling of gifts and bequests for specially and non-specifically designated purposes, if such gifts are approved by the proper governing bodies of the church.
   h. The review of special requests for funds other than budgetized items for presentation to the Official Board.
   i. The appointment of a director of the Every Member Canvass.

2. To facilitate the accomplishment of these responsibilities, the Finance Committee shall have authority to:
   a. Reallocate the use of funds where nceessary, subject to board approval.
   b. Review the detailed budgets submitted to it and revise them where necessary.
   c. Appoint a permanent Audit Committee of three (3) members to certify accuracy of financial records an-

nually—or as required by the Finance Committee.
(These "authorities" are subject to the review and approval of the Official Board.)

RESPONSIBILITIES AND PARTICIPATING BOARDS AND ORGANIZATIONS

It shall be the responsibility of each participating board or organization to:

a. Prepare its own budget, which shall be submitted to the Finance Committee not later than July 31 annually, for the preparation of the tentative budget.
b. Advise and assist the Finance Committee in making any revisions in the budget which may be necessary.
c. Administer its own individual budget within the limits of funds allocated to it.
d. Submit a monthly financial report to the Finance Committee.
e. Assist in the Every Member Canvass.

HANDLING OF FUNDS

The collection of monies shall be made by the financial secretaries of participating organizations and boards or approved fund-raising project.

a. All monies collected shall be deposited to the account of the Finance Committee of Christ Church.
b. The receipts shall be allocated as follows:
   1) Bequests, special gifts, special offerings or other receipts for specifically designated purposes shall be allocated by the church treasurer to specific purposes for which they were given. All allocations are subject to regular review by the Official Board.
   2) Bequests or special gifts which are not specifically designated shall be held by the church treasurer for eventual specific allocation as directed by the Official Board.
   3) All receipts such as annual pledges, youth pledges, loose-change offerings and miscellaneous items shall be considered to be "general income." The church treasurer shall allocate the "general income" to the current expense, benevolence, and capital accounts as provided in the annual budget.
      Any changes in the budget shall be made only on the

recommendation of the Finance Committee, subject to the approval of the Official Board.

c. The church treasurer shall disburse funds only on receipt of signed vouchers from the current expense financial secretary, the benevolence financial secretary or the capital funds financial secretary.

d. The chairman of the Finance Committee shall be considered the official alternate for the church treasurer and shall be authorized to sign checks in the absence of the church treasurer.

BUDGET FORMAT AND FINANCIAL STATEMENTS

The following format shall be used both in presenting the budgets to the congregation for approval and in making the quarterly financial reports to the membership of the church:

Current Expenses
    a. Salaries
    b. Operating Expenses
        1) Supplies
        2) Communications
        3) Fixed Charges
    c. Plant Maintenance
        1) Supplies
        2) Repairs

Benevolences
    a. General Assembly
    b. Synod
    c. Presbytery
    d. Local
    e. Special

Capital
    a. Debt Retirement
    b. Expansion Fund
    c. Capital Improvement

Note: It will be seen from the foregoing outline for the Finance Committee that it has an important and complex task involving all aspects of the church development and church life. Its relationship to the Official Board and to the congregation should be constantly cultivated.

II. The Every Member Canvass

Items that will be significant in the planning and execution of a successful Every Member Canvass are the following:

1. The chairman or director of the Every Member Canvass should gather around him a strong and competent committee for advice and planning for the canvass. Suggested duties of the director may well be these:

   a. Make plans for Loyalty Sunday.
   b. Arrange an educational program prior to Loyalty Sunday for the congregation and for the follow-up canvassers.
   c. Arrange for a follow-up by trained canvassers on those who did not pledge on Loyalty Sunday.
   d. Appoint a permanent canvass committee to contact new members to obtain their pledges. The director shall serve on this committee.
   e. Submit a report to the Finance Committee by the end of January including:

      1) Number of pledges as compared to total membership. Both youth budget and adult pledges shall be included in this report. (A joint pledge by husband and wife shall count as two pledges.)
      2) A written report of the effectiveness of the canvass methods used.

2. A timetable of dates should be prepared. The timetable will include a first general letter that may be mailed to the entire congregation. The date of Loyalty Sunday should be clearly indicated. The dates for the meeting of team captains and the dates for final reports and all other items having to do with the initiation to the completion of a good house-to-house Every Member Canvass should be outlined in detail.

3. All communications to the congregation should be simple. Eliminate long sentences, adjectives. Give the facts. State the needs. Try to show how each individual member is needed and involved in a generous response!

4. Most effective Every Member Canvass programs involve the enlisting of team captains, who in turn will enlist other callers for the Every Member Canvass.

One church that has conducted for years a successful Every Member Canvass, has devised the following instructions, which are given to all canvassers:

CHRIST CHURCH

INSTRUCTIONS FOR "EMC" CANVASSERS—19__

What to do on Every Member Canvass Sunday—November 15:

1. Attend 11 a.m. worship service.
2. Attend meeting of all EMC workers in the assembly room immediately following the service (approximately 12:15 p.m.).
3. Attend district meetings with your captains. Signs will be posted and sheets distributed indicating meeting places. Captains will distribute materials for your calls and answer any questions.
4. Please note the following:

    a. It is important that you make your calls *this afternoon,* since members of the parish have been asked to remain at home to receive you. In the past, we have been criticized by people whose canvasser failed to appear. If you cannot complete your calls this afternoon, be sure to telephone those you cannot see and arrange another date with them.

    b. Keep in mind that a 5 per cent increase in *all* pledges is needed.

    c. Be sure to note on the canvass card any facts that may be helpful.

       —If persons listed at address have moved, get their new address where possible.

       —If members of a family have married (or otherwise changed their name), obtain new name and address.

       —If members say they have transferred membership to another church, or say they are not members of Christ Church, note name and location of the church where they do belong.

       —If there is illness or other difficulty that may need ministerial attention, note this on the card, and if someone is in the hospital, note name and location of hospital.

       —If telephone numbers are available, note them on cards.

    d. Please report the results of your calls *today*. Reporting desks in the assembly room will be manned until 7 p.m. After that, report to the church office, which will be open until 8 p.m. You are requested to retain canvass cards of your incompleted calls until they are finalized either with a pledge or a statement that no pledge will be made.

What to Do After EMC Sunday

  1. Complete any remaining calls as rapidly as possible.
    a. Mail or deliver cards to the church office as they are completed.
    b. Remember that incompleted calls remain your responsibility and your district's responsibility until completed. Try to help your district be the first 100 percent report.

Please return all unused materials to the church office.

For your information, the church office telephone number is 238-6877.

Specific Instructions for District EMC Captains

To make such a program come off successfully, the district captains must have specific and careful instructions. The following instruction sheet prepared by one church proved to be highly successful and may be useful to many others:

CHRIST CHURCH

INSTRUCTIONS FOR EMC DISTRICT CAPTAINS—19__

  I. *Each district kit will contain the following:*
    1. List of district workers.
    2. District list of member families, adherents and non-member Church School parents.
      a. List is alphabetical by member family name. Names listed underneath the address indicate other persons (children, relatives, etc.) who are living at that address. In some instances only the children or others living at that address are members.
      b. Included in the member listing may be some non-

members who might normally be expected to pledge, marked as follows:

> Adherents—those who contribute to the church but do not have membership here.
>
> Church School parents—persons who are neither members nor adherents but have children enrolled in our Church School. (Some Church School parents are also adherents and would be so listed.)

c. Disregard names which are blocked out; these are persons who have moved, transferred membership, deceased, already pledged, or otherwise should not receive a call. Some names will be marked "Church office mailed pledge card. Follow up later." The district captain is asked to follow up on these if the church office does not receive the pledge within a reasonable time. They remain the district responsibility until there is a conclusive pledge or a statement that no pledge will be given.

3. Canvass cards. There should be one canvass card for each family unit corresponding with your district list.
4. Pledge cards.
5. Copies of the budget message which were mailed out earlier to the congregation.
6. "Will call again" cards.
7. Return envelopes.
8. Printed manila canvasser envelopes.
9. Copies of "Instructions and Timetable for Canvassers —19___."
10. Church directory.
11. District map.

II. *Preparation of Canvassers' Envelopes.*

1. Make up manila envelope for each canvasser, indicating on the front the district number, name of canvasser, and names of families to receive calls.
2. Assign calls by street or convenient area if possible.
3. Indicate on the district list the name of the canvasser assigned to each family. This list should be maintained by the district captain, as it will be the only record of calls assigned to each canvasser and will be vital for follow-up work later.
4. Insert the following in the canvasser's envelope:
   a. Canvasser's own card if not already pledged.
   b. Canvass cards—one for each family unit.

     c. Pledge cards—at least one for each family unit.

     d. Budget message.

     e. At least three "Will call again" cards.

     f. Three return envelopes.

     g. "Instructions and Timetable for Canvassers—19___."

5. It is recommended that canvasser envelopes *not* be distributed until the district meeting on Sunday, November 15, so that last-minute deletions may be made.

6. Telephone all canvassers to remind them to be present on EMC Sunday.

III. *What to Do on EMC Sunday, November 15:*

1. Attend 11 a.m. worship service.

2. Attend EMC dedication service and final briefing in assembly room immediately following worship service (approximately 12:15 p.m.).

3. Attend district meetings with canvassers after dedication service. Signs will be posted and sheets distributed indicating district meeting places. It is well to post a list of canvassers and district areas for those who may have forgotten in which district they will be canvassing.

4. Before going to district meeting, check with the EMC director for a "pull list" and eliminate names from all canvasser envelopes that do not need to receive calls.

5. Distribute canvassers' envelopes, and

     a. Emphasize with your canvassers the importance of making their calls this afternoon, since members of the congregation have been asked to stay at home to receive them. Telephone if you cannot see everyone.

     b. Stress the need for a 5 per cent increase in *all* pledges.

     c. Point out the importance of noting on the canvass card any facts that may be helpful to the church staff:

       —if persons listed at address have moved, get new address if possible.

       —if members of family have married, get new name and address.

       —if members say they have transferred membership to another church, or say they are not members of Christ Church, find out the name of the church they belong to and its location.

       —if there is illness or other difficulty that may need ministerial attention, note this information on card. If someone is in a hospital note this information and name of hospital.

—if telephone numbers are available note on cards for future use.

6. Request your canvassers to report the results of their calls *today*. Reporting desks in the assembly room will be manned until 7 p.m. After that, they should report to the church office, which will be open until 8 p.m. Explain to all canvassers that incompleted canvass cards are to be retained until contact is made with each and either a pledge is received or a statement that no pledge will be made.

7. For canvassers who do not appear, it will be necessary either to deliver their envelopes to their homes or to distribute their calls among remaining members of your group. In case of redistribution, be sure to add names to the envelope of canvasser who is to call on each.

8. If you have a shortage of canvassers for your district, contact the EMC director. Likewise, if there should be an oversupply of canvassers for your district, be sure to contact the EMC director so that some may be assigned to another district.

IV. *What to Do After EMC Sunday:*

Responsibility for follow-up calls rests with the district captains.

1. Check your open items at the church office on November 22 (the following Sunday) either after the 9 o'clock or the 11 o'clock service.

2. Contact canvassers who have open items and urge them to complete them as soon as possible.

3. Repeat 1 and 2 on the following three Sundays.

4. At this point all cards not completed should be returned to the district captains and become their responsibility.

5. It is advisable to keep a constant check with the church office and/or the EMC director on open items at this period, to avoid calls where pledges have been sent in.

6. PLEASE RETURN ALL UNUSED MATERIALS TO THE CHURCH OFFICE.

As the canvass progresses it is highly important that reports be given to the district captains. The following report sheet may be suggestive:

CHRIST CHURCH

EMC Director's Report on Every Member Canvass for 1969
as of (date)

To: District Captains
From: Director Ray Wilson

Number of pledges received	1,156
Amount of pledges received	$247,106
Amount of same pledges last year	231,135
Amount of increase	15,971
Percentage of $270,761 goal attained	91%
Overall percentage of increase	6.9%

Last year on the same day, we had 1,197 pledges amounting to $254,890, which was 92 per cent of the $275,360 pledge goal. Here is how the districts line up as to "open items":

DISTRICT	CAPTAINS	NUMBER OF OPEN ITEMS	1968 PLEDGES
6	Southerland	2	none
11	Jones	3	none
13	Edwards	3	$125
1	Kendall/Lee	5	none
2	Smith	7	$412
4	Thompson	7	$505
3	Johnson/King	7	$102
8	Kane	8	$310
14	Wiley/Kemp	8	$267
5	Miller	9	$320
7	Peterson	10	$285
9	Williams	10	$1,182
10	Freeman	12	$257
12	Wooster	15	$861
15	Henry	15	$241
District Totals		121	$4,867
Other		1	1,200
		122	$6,067

Enclosed is a list of your "open pledges." Please follow up on them over this weekend. Tom Nelson or Henry Allen will be in touch with you during this next week.

If a Pledge Sunday or Loyalty Sunday is used where the individual members of the church make their pledge and have the pledge dedicated at the regular worship service, a proper pledge card should be prepared. It is strongly suggested that the card be one that has a fold on the top so that the amount of the pledge remains private. One church preparing such a pledge card printed the theme on the front:

YOU . . .

YOUR SUPPORT . . .

To fill our timeless needs

The inside of the card is shown at the top of page 193.

III. EXPRESSING APPRECIATION FOR PLEDGES

An individual cannot be thanked too much for his contribution. This certainly applies with regard to support of the church. The director of the Every Member Canvass should express appreciation to the congregation in some kind of public way, either orally at a church service, or through printed media that will go to all the members of the congregation. Also, each individual pledge should be acknowledged with warmth and gratitude. Ideally, this should be a personal letter, and if the director knows the individual to whom the acknowledgment is sent, some additional handwritten postscript may be very desirable.

For office use only
No. _____

Last Name   First Name   Initial | District
No. _____

In order that the ministries of worship, music, Christian Education, service and benevolences may be carried forward, my pledge to Christ Church for 1969 will be $_____ payable weekly:

_$20	_$8	_$5	_$2
_$10	_$7	_$4	_$1
_$9	_$6	_$3	_other

Signature _____
Address _____
Telephone _____ Date _____

Keeping the pledger informed of the status of his pledge throughout the year also involves another opportunity for contact, and for a constructive or a negative response. One such reminder that is simple and reports the facts, is the following:

CHRIST CHURCH

QUARTERLY REPORT—1968 OPERATING BUDGET

For your information, our records show that, of the $___ pledged by you for the 1968 church year, $___ has been paid up to date hereof, leaving $___ payable during the remainder of the year.   John T. Maguire, treasurer

Please understand that this is NOT a bill, and that it is sent solely in the interest of helping you and the church office to keep the records in agreement.

The entire Every Member Canvass program and its follow-up should be guided by the principle of "constantly informing" those who are the participants in the support of the church.

At the time of the quarterly statement it may be appropriate to enclose a bit of information about some aspect of the church that is exciting and constructive. One church enclosed a slip of paper the exact size of the quarterly report. From quarter to quarter it would simply report one aspect of the church life. One quarter, the statement might read, "Do you know that your contribution to our church budget made possible 10,000 cataract operations in Southern India?" The next quarter, a simple statement might center on education of children and young people.

IV. EDUCATION IN STEWARDSHIP

Literature that tells the story can be very helpful in educating the members of the congregation. Of hundreds of pieces of literature and brochures related to the church financial program, and seeking to gain the response of members, the best have been those that have been the simplest and have been strong in the use of pictorial presentation. As I am writing this I have before me a simple leaflet with four pictures. It shows, in one of the four pictures, a group of teenage youngsters around a piano, singing. The second picture shows a teacher with second-graders. The third picture portrays the Sunday worship service, with the pastors and choirs and people together. The fourth picture represents a specialized group of adults who are together in the church hall, and listening to a speaker from another country.

These pictures tell the story—"Our church is involved with our boys and girls, and our men and women, and is seeking to serve them in the name of Christ." Above, and surrounding the pictures, is the annual budget. One gets the sense, in looking at the leaflet, that it is not alone dollars and cents, it is people and program that one is supporting. This is good.

Among the many pastors and able church administrators with whom I counseled in the preparation of this book, one friend in California sent a letter that reads in part:

> Because we have no formal or written procedure, I herein simply indicate that a "stewardship counseling" committee comprised of approximately fifteen to twenty men, some ordained church officers, others not, meeting approximately every two

months and working closely with the treasurer of the church, are able to determine those who lag behind in stewardship and proceed to make a counseling call immediately on the family. In no case have we found this to be objected to, and from almost every visit we have been able to determine attitudes, trends, etc., from our people. We have been delighted with this response and have found surprisingly few churches using this kind of procedure. Obviously, if we discover cases of permanent or temporary hardship, these families are counseled to either modify or discontinue their pledge, but in most cases the reminder of concern works wonders.

Educating the Congregation on Stewardship

Education in stewardship is done in many different ways. I have always felt that to let the congregation know what is the expectation in terms of percentage giving is extremely helpful to them, and of course to the overall stewardship program. The following simple statement and graph prepared by one church is a very powerful means of education and stewardship:

GIVING AN ADEQUATE SHARE OF YOUR
SUBSTANCE TO THE WORK OF THE LORD
IS A MEANS OF EXPRESSING FAITH IN
YOURSELF AND IN THE FUTURE OF YOUR CHURCH

If your total income is	THEN: your weekly pledge might be		
	AT 1%	AT 2½%	AT 5%
$ 5,000	$ .96	$ 2.40	$ 4.81
10,000	1.92	4.81	9.62
15,000	2.88	7.21	14.42
20,000	3.85	9.62	19.23
30,000	5.77	14.42	28.85
40,000	7.68	19.23	38.48

Education with Pastor's Leadership

Education in stewardship can be furthered by the effective use of the pastor's leadership. Dr. Paul S. Wright, of Portland, Oregon, in a publication that went out to his people regarding the annual budget appeal, wrote the following editorial preceding the annual budgetary appeal.

PAUL'S LETTER TO FIRST CHURCH

At last it is coming through to us that (1) the laity are the church, (2) the laity carry out the church's mission, (3) this mission is accomplished not within the walls of the church but beyond it, in opportunities offered by our daily work, and that (4) going to church is not the sum and substance of a Christian's duty.

With this we are in full agreement. Membership in the church means a commitment to serve Jesus Christ. The continuance of the ministry of our Lord in our times is entrusted to the whole people of God. Each disciple enjoys the distinction and bears the responsibility of being an instrument of his Master.

The pastors have their calling within this scheme of things. It is to help the people to be ministers! To "minister" means to "serve." The pastors are the servants of the servants. We all are in it together. As the pastors must be diligent and faithful in performing the work Christ has assigned them to do, so the laity must fulfill their vocation with equal zeal.

If Christian mission is the laity witnessing by word and work in the world, how is this related to "going to church"? In this way. The church is the body of people whom Christ has bound to Himself and to one another. Another way of putting this is to say that the church is the community of faith which knows what God has done in Christ to make them His people. To worship the God of their salvation is their highest privilege. To worship willingly and joyously their deepest desire. From such worship spring the incentives and goals of action. Worship and service cannot be separated if either is to be real.

As ever,
Paul S. Wright

An idea and a point of view such as represented by Dr. Wright can have strong and lasting influences in the lives of many people. It is like the "arrow shot into the air."

Forms Re Stewardship for
New Members

It is very desirable that at the time individuals join the church they have some instruction, or at least some indication of what is expected of them in terms of their stewardship response.

One church, at the time new members were received, not alone had the chairman of the Finance Committee speak to them briefly about the budget of the church, its program and its needs, but put in each new member's hands the following statement:

CHRIST CHURCH

Our Philosophy of Financial Support

When you promise financial support to Christ Church . . .

1. You are fulfilling a part of your membership vows . . . "Do you promise . . . to give of your substance as the Lord may prosper you?"

2. The pledge card you will receive after you join the church is a record of your intended investment. It is a voluntary statement of your intention upon which your church bases its expenditures, makes its plans and carries forward its total program.

3. Your "investment" may be raised or lowered as your personal financial circumstances change significantly. One needs only to call the financial secretary and adjustments will be made in a courteous and gracious manner.

4. You will be participating in a truly Christian plan of financial giving. This is what we call proportionate giving. All gifts are given in proportion to one's worldly means . . . "in proportion as the Lord may prosper you."

5. The Church of Jesus Christ is "big business" in every sense of the word. What the church does, its members make possible through their prayers, service and tangible support of the program. The vast and far-flung areas of spiritual concern at home and abroad are maintained by the sacrificial sharing of those who are deeply concerned in the Christian sense of the word.

6. You will be given offering envelopes, for they make all gifts equal in the sight of men.

7. The church budget is arranged in three categories: Local Mission, for the work of the local church; General Mission, for the work of the church world-wide; and Capital Funds, for an on-going physical improvement program in our own large building. One may divide the pledge so that amounts are given to each of the categories, or one may choose to give a total amount to be used as needed. All pledges are held in the strictest confidence.

8. You are assured of a policy of limited special offerings. As members of Christ Church we will always participate in the "One Great Hour of Sharing" during Lent for world relief.

Any other special offerings must be approved by the Official
Board.

9. In considering a total pledge to the church one should also
keep in mind that children and youth are invited to contribute to the Youth Budget as a method of developing good
stewardship habits while in Church School. Also, the Wom-
en's Association supports its budget largely by pledges from
its members. These things should be taken into consideration when planning for your pledge to the church.

10. You will receive a financial receipt every three months indicating the church's record of your giving. This is not a "bill."
Rather, it is a record for your income tax needs or for any
file you may wish to keep. It is an accurate report on the
church records and perhaps, at times, a friendly reminder.

THE CHURCH OF JESUS CHRIST CAN BECOME WHAT
IT WAS INTENDED TO BE, NOT THROUGH "TOKEN
CONTRIBUTIONS," BUT BY DEDICATED, REALISTIC
AND LOVING STEWARDSHIP.

*Education in Self-Giving for
the Congregation*

One church that was very successful in the united love and response of the congregation to the overall program of the church had
a pastor who repeatedly sought to educate the parish on the basic
principles of self-giving. One of his strong editorials preparatory to
the Every Member Canvass is the following:

SPIRITUAL ABUNDANCE

Here is a simple, direct way to enrich your life—a strange,
paradoxical, wonderful way, guaranteed by the Word of God and
proved by all those who venture it. "You will be enriched in
every way for great generosity . . ." (I Cor. 9:11).

Great generosity for Christ's sake issues in great enrichment.
Note carefully II Corinthians 9:6-15. The Scripture makes clear
the experience of the one who sacrificially shares what he has
with others. He is enriched:

By the love of God (vs. 1).
By the supply of God's resources (vs. 8).
By the satisfaction of assisting those in need (vs. 11, 12).

By praise lifted to God from grateful hearts (vs. 12).
By bearing true witness to Christ (vs. 13).
By the love and prayer of others (vs. 14).
By a glad and grateful heart (vs. 16).

God's way of enrichment is not through pulling in all we can get or holding on to all we possess. Rather it is in the opposite direction—"For God so loved the world that He GAVE His only begotten Son" (Jn. 3:16). Then let's open wide our lives to God's enrichment. "The point is this: he who sows sparingly will also reap sparingly and he who sows bountifully will also reap bountifully. Each one must do as he has made up his mind, not reluctantly or under compulsion, for God loves a cheerful giver. And God is able to provide you with every blessing in abundance, so that you may always have enough of everything and may provide in abundance for every good work" (II Cor. 9:6-8).

In a crisis hour of human need with the saving Word to be shared with the world, supported by God's promise, provision and presence, let us pray through our Christian stewardship with a new sense of its high privilege.

At the closing of the morning worship services opportunity will be given for us to indicate our stewardship intention for 1969 by means of the pledge cards in an act of united dedication of ourselves to Christ and His cause.

Note: Men and women grow by their gifts and by their commitments. Wise and able leadership in the church will challenge and call out deep dedication of stewardship.

V. DEDICATION OF GIFTS AND PLEDGES

If the local church determines to have a Loyalty or Stewardship Sunday, pledges are dedicated on this day. After the sermon, and a statement from the chairman of the Stewardship or Every Member Canvass Committee, it is altogether fitting that individual pledges be made. The pledge cards will be in the pews and the ushers will receive these and bring them to the chancel and communion table or altar. As has been the custom for thousands of years, the act of dedication of one's promises, in a moment of deep reverence and significance, can be moving to all those who participate. A prayer of dedication and thanksgiving to the Lord may be a source of deeper commitment and relationship to Him and the whole cause represented by the Man of Nazareth.

VI. CHURCH OFFICE FINANCIAL RECORDS

Every responsible church will keep a careful record of pledges made and receipts week by week. Each denomination will provide guidance as to the type of card and record to be retained. The Finance Committee, composed of men who are competent in the field of record-keeping, will devise the proper program in terms of the needs of the individual church.

The financial records should be accurate and, whatever system is used, should enable any individual who contributes to the church to have a prompt and accurate report of his or her contribution. These annual records should be carefully kept and stored for at least ten years.

VII. MONTHLY REPORT TO THE OFFICIAL BOARD

The church treasurer will prepare a monthly statement to the Official Board showing the financial situation of the church.

The following report happens to be a twelve-month report, but it includes the significant items in a good report. First, the treasurer presents his comments. Second, there is a clear indication of the numerical items to be considered. Being able to number the item can lead to very clear and helpful discussion or the raising of any questions. The simplified statement shows also the special funds and the endowment fund spelled out in the clearest kind of simple detail. Such a report should be presented each month to the Official Board.

CHRIST CHURCH

TREASURER'S COMMENTS ON DECEMBER 1968
FINANCIAL STATEMENT

General Fund income in 1968 exceeded expenses by $6,045, as shown on line 14. Total income was $1,043 less than the budget figure, but expenses underran by $7,088, mainly in the Administration and Maintenance group, with salary and wage savings accounting for almost $5,700. Pledges for 1968 came very close to the objective, although some had not been fully paid at year's end. Further payments can be expected and they will be credited to income in 1969. Plate offerings were disappointing, but income from other sources exceeded our expectations.

Our cash position is always strong at the end of the year because of advance payments on next year's pledges—see line 21. Accordingly, we have invested $30,000 of General Fund cash in 4 per cent certificates of deposit maturing in the spring of 1969.

Turning to page 2, it will be noted that the Endowment Fund benefited by some $40,000 in gifts and legacies, plus investment earnings. The market value of the fund is more than $57,000 greater than it was a year ago.

The mortgage principal was reduced by $27,000 during 1968 and by the end of 1969 it will not exceed $40,750, on the basis of regular payments provided for in the 1969 budget. The level could, of course, be reduced further if funds for supplemental payments became available.

William O. Peterson
Treasurer

January 28, 1969

ject to year-end audit)

CHRIST CHURCH

A CONDENSED FINANCIAL STATEMENT FOR DECEMBER 1968
GENERAL FUND

	12 months this year		
OME STATEMENT	Actual	Budget	Over-run (a)
Pledge Income	242,597	246,562	(3,965)
Plate Offering	8,742	12,000	(3,258)
Income - Real Estate	10,900	10,000	900
Other Income	17,280	12,000	5,280
Total Income	279,519	280,562	(1,043)
Leadership	39,367	41,090	(1,723)
Christian Education	18,642	18,240	402
Music	25,312	25,300	12
Administration and Maintenance	106,649	113,787	(7,138)
Benevolences	49,409	48,000	1,409
Debt Service	29,119	29,169	(50)
Denominational Assessment	4,976	4,976	0
Total Expense	273,474	280,562	(7,088)
Net Income	6,045	0	6,045

LANCE SHEET	This Month	Dec. 31, 1967
Cash	71,856	72,195
Pledges receivable-current year:		
16,690 less 12,964 reserve	3,726 (b)	4,816
Advances	888	266
Other assets	0	13,742
Total assets	76,470	91,019

20. Accounts payable	647	12,321
21. Contributions applicable to next year	48,241	49,895
22. Deferred pledge income	0	0
23. Suspense credits	18,304	25,570
24. Other liabilities	833	833
25. Accumulated surpluss	8,445	2,400
26. Total liabilities	76,470	91,019

PLEDGES

27. Budget objectives	259,539	276,700
28. Actual to date (less cancellations)	259,287	258,828
29. Less 5% reserve (line 16)	12,964	12,942
30. Less amount taken up as income (line 1)	242,597	241,070
31. Balance carried in suspense credits (line 23)	3,726	4,816

APPROVED OVER-BUDGET ITEMS: None

William O. Peterson
Treasurer

(a) Under-runs are shown in parentheses.
(b) Balance of pledges receivable is stated after actual collections, rather than after deducting amount taken up as income. (Open pledges applicable to prior years are bv 100% reserves.)

(Subject to year-end audit)
December 31, 1968

OTHER FINANCIAL DATA

SPECIAL FUNDS	This Month	Dec. 31, 1
Cash:		
Deacon's Fund	4,326	2,154
Church School Benevolences	1,826	2,002
Sermon Publications	1,405	1,717
Music - Sermon Recordings	314	314
Chapels' Fund	12,219	9,842
Reserve Fund	28,684	25,767
Program Development Fund	285	193
Memorials	8,344	7,139
Other	2,639	599
	60,037	49,727

ENDOWMENT FUND

Cash:	10,318	16,914
Securities (Market Value 12/31/68 - 303,120)	267,989	206,018
	278,307	222,932

The increase since 12/31/67 consists of:
    a. Dividends, interest, etc.   15,325
    b. Gifts and legacies   40,050
                                   55,375

SERY SCHOOL FUNDS

Cash	3,059	1,996

.NT FUNDS

Assets
Cash	15,933 *	19,761
Plant Assets	2,314,805	2,311,985
	2,330,738	2,331,746

Liabilities
Mortgage Payable	65,750	92,750
Unexpended Contributions	15,933	19,761
Net Investment in Plant	2,249,055	2,219,235
	2,330,738	2,331,746

cludes 15,173 for memorials and other special purposes.

VIII. THE ANNUAL AUDIT

Each year the Official Board should appoint an auditor to prepare a complete audit of the church books. It should be reported to the congregation that the books are audited. The Official Board may not distribute the audit to all of its members, but certainly the Finance Committee should study it and present it to the Official Board for approval.

Any recommendations made by the auditor should receive careful attention, and where needed, proper action.

The congregation should be informed that the audit has been made and the complete audit should be made available to any interested parishioners.

The treasurer and any members of the staff who have relationship to any of the financial operations should be instructed to make available to the auditor all records pertaining to the finances of the church. The auditor is usually selected on the recommendation of the Finance Committee and approved by the Official Board. The auditor is usually engaged for a specified fee, which fee would also be approved by the Official Board on recommendation of the Finance Committee. The annual fee for the auditing of the books will, of course, be included in the annual budget each year.

IX. Principles of Budget Control

Once the annual budget is set and allocations are made for the various departments of activities of the church, it should be understood that no change in the budget in the way of increase for any particular item will be made without the study of the committee in charge of that activity and the approval of the Official Board.

One individual should be authorized to approve payment for any item within the scope of the particular department. Usually the ordering of any supplies or materials by any department will be reported to the treasurer, assistant treasurer or whoever is authorized to prepare the checks for payment. No check should be prepared and sent without the approval in writing of the individual who did the ordering or made the purchase. Usually just an initialing of the bill with the date of approval, is sufficient to give authorization for payment.

Records of all bills and payments should be kept in order for the review of the auditor.

The Finance Committee, in preparing its monthly statement for the Official Board, will be sensitive to any areas where there seems to be an overexpenditure. In instances where there is no expenditure of an item allocated in the budget, the Official Board will seek to find out why. Consultation with individuals who are in charge of the various budgetary departments of the church should be informed if there are any unusual over- or under-budgetary expenditures so that adjustments may be made in the ensuing course of the church year.

X. Special Gifts and Memorials

On occasion it may be that a special gift which has not been pledged and which is not a part of the church budget may be received by the church. Devoted parishioners may remember the church in their wills and provide special legacies.

In other instances there may be special gifts that are provided for specific memorials to be established in the church. This may involve a particular item such as the provision of a stained-glass window or some special piece of furnishing.

In each instance the church office and particular individual in charge of the financial records, under the oversight of the Finance Committee, will see that a careful record is made of all such gifts, and that the proper allocation in terms of the stipulation of the donor shall be made.

It may be highly desirable to have a special book in which memorial gifts and remembrances are recorded. Such a book may be properly exhibited in a special cabinet or location of the church, or may be made available for the congregation to see from time to time on special occasions.

Definite rules should be established by the Official Board with regard to the receiving of any special gifts. The integrity of the fabric and furnishings of the church should be retained, and it should be established by the Official Board that no gift of furnishings will be received without the approval of the Building and Memorials Committee.

The establishment of a Memorials Committee may be highly desirable. Such a committee should have on it representatives of the Official Board, desirably a representative of the architect, if not the architect himself, and other selected individuals who may know the congregation and may be effective in suggesting specific memorials to specific individuals in the parish.

The pastor as ex-officio member of the Memorials Committee can be extremely helpful, both in suggesting to the committee individuals who may be helpful in the provision of special gifts and memorials, and in counseling such individuals.

It is altogether proper when a major gift is given either for endowment or for a special memorial that the congregation be informed. In the case where an item such as a window in the sanctuary is given, there might be a brief but dignified dedication at the appointed hour of worship.

8

The Music Department

I. THE MUSIC COMMITTEE

I have never been able to agree completely with Hartzell Spence, who wrote in his book, *One Foot in Heaven,* "Choir singers are a peculiar breed, a 'cross,' as father used to say, 'between the devil's grandmother and a mountain wildcat.'" While this department of the church deals with creative and often highly sensitive people, it is one that has a significant place in the ministry of worship and demands the finest of supervision and the highest of support.

The key to this supervision and support is the Music Committee. It should be a standing committee of the Official Board and be responsible for the oversight of the ministry of music in the church, and should make regular monthly reports to the Official Board.

The Music Committee should be composed not alone of board members, but of certain representatives of the congregation who may have aptitude, skill, or training in the field of music.

Organization and Functions of "Council of Music"

One church, rather than calling it a committee, named the group the Council of Music.

STATEMENT ON THE COUNCIL OF MUSIC
CHRIST CHURCH

The Council of Music of Christ Church came into existence in September, 1960, charged with the supervision of the entire music program of the church, responsible to the Official Board for its activities.

The council is made up of the following: three members from the Official Board, one being the chairman; three representatives from the Women's Association, six members from the congregation at large, the president and secretary of the Chancel Choir, and the ministers of the church and members of the music staff as ex-officio members.

The work of the council is administered by the chairman, the minister of the church and the minister of music.

At present the council meets regularly in January, May and September, although any additional meetings may be called by the chairman or the Official Board as the need might arise.

Minutes are kept of each meeting by the secretary of the Chancel Choir, and are in turn prepared into a report for the Official Board.

The Council of Music does not determine the detailed musical program for the church, since this program must be flexible and should be determined by the minister of the church together with the minister of music.

The work of the Ministry of Music consists of two parts— education and worship—both seeking to fulfill the purpose of its existence, to glorify God. To accomplish this, the staff of the Music Department is given the responsibility:

(1) Of either teaching its seven choirs, from ages four through adult, or arranging and supervising lay leadership to help in the fulfillment of this responsibility.

(2) Of coordinating the music of the Church School with that of the choir program, including study of the music curriculum and leadership in this phase of the Church School program.

(3) Of the preparation of the four older choirs for leadership in regular worship, as well as for all choirs in additional services of music on special occasions.

(4) Of coordinating the entire program of music for the church, including participation in music for the Women's Association, Men's Club, Youth Fellowship, as well as community projects, such as World Day of Prayer, Reformation Festival, and other programs.

(5) Of planning for and participating in weddings and funerals.

(6) Of counseling with those closely associated with the music program, visiting those who are ill, and becoming acquainted with those who are new to the church family.

Prime Purposes of Music Committee

From my experience and observation I would say that the prime purpose of the Music Committee is to oversee the whole musical program of the church, and to assist the organist and choirmaster as required. If there is both an organist and a choirmaster, such individuals should be invited to the Music Committee meetings. Opportunity should be given to them to report to the committee any of their problems and needs, and they should be assured of the sympathetic support and assistance of the Music Committee. Changes in the budget regarding the Music Department, if any, should be approved by this committee and appropriate recommendations made to the Official Board for final approval.

II. THE ORGANIST AND CHOIRMASTER—JOB
    DESCRIPTIONS

In most of our churches the position of organist and choirmaster is centered in one individual. However, so that there may be guidance for churches having both an organist and a choirmaster, the following job descriptions may be helpful as guides:

JOB DESCRIPTION FOR DIRECTOR OF MUSIC

CHRIST CHURCH

1. Be responsible for the organization, operation and direction of an effective multiple choir program, reaching all ages of children from first grade through eighth grade, youth choir of high school age, and adult choir.

2. Be responsible for future development of a choir school program for children of grade-school age.

3. Work with the minister of Spiritual Life Committee of the Official Board in planning and carrying out the music program of the church.

4. Meet regularly at least once a month with the senior minister in planning and coordinating the music for all worship services—Sundays and other occasions.
5. Act as adviser for organizations in the church desiring special assistance with music activities.
6. Be responsible for all rehearsals pertaining to the choirs of the church.
7. Arrange for supplying vocal or instrumental selections, in consultation with the ministers, for each church worship service during the summer period when the choirs are on vacation.
8. Make quarterly reports to the Spiritual Life Committee, to be presented to the Official Board by said committee, on the work of the various choirs, their needs and future plans.
9. Be responsible for all attendance records, for all vestments, and for the care of all music. This responsibility may be carried out by committees within the choirs, appointed by the director. The supervision of such committees shall be the responsibility of the director.
10. On those Sundays when the children's choir participates in the Sunday morning worship services, clear the dates in consultation with the ministers.
11. Be responsible for the selection of all music—instrumental, solos, duets, trios, quartets and choirs. Care should be taken to make these selections with reference to the days of the Christian and civil year, and after consultation with the minister.
12. Consult with the minister and Spiritual Life Committee of the Official Board before scheduling any participation of any choir group in secular engagements.
13. Select, after consultation with the minister, and purchase all choral music that is to become a part of the church music library.
14. Meet with the Spiritual Life Committee at the director's discretion or at the invitation of the committee.

JOB DESCRIPTION FOR ORGANIST
CHRIST CHURCH

DUTIES:

1. Be responsible for cooperating with the ministers, the Official Board, and the director of music to provide and promote an appropriate, enriching musical program for the church.

2. Have full responsibility of providing organ music, including the provision of a suitable substitute organist when necessary, for all regular Sunday church worship services and other established services.

3. Play the organ, or provide for a suitable substitute, at the regular weekly choir rehearsal of the Westminster and Chancel Choirs, and accompany any and all Christ Church choirs singing for the worship service.

4. Furnish the organ music as required for weddings and wedding rehearsals in the sanctuary, and piano music for such in the chapel in accordance with the regulations for weddings established by the Official Board. Fees collected by the church for such services shall be paid to the organist.

5. Consult with the ministers and director of music as necessary to assure a satisfactory musical program and to provide opportunity for all concerned to contribute constructively to the entire worship experience.

6. Cooperate with the Spiritual Life Committee of the Official Board in the church's music program, and meet with the Spiritual Life Committee at the invitation of the chairman.

7. Be the chief staff consultant to the Spiritual Life Committee in all matters having to do with the repairing, remodeling, and upkeep of the organ.

8. Make decisions concerning the use of the organ for requests or occasions not covered in the foregoing. The organist will consult with the Spiritual Life Committee of the Official Board on all unusual requests. The organist shall be permitted to use the church organ for practice and for teaching any time not in conflict with other scheduled church activities.

III. Care of Organ

The organ is a highly specialized instrument, and a contract should be arranged through the Music Committee with the approval of the Official Board for the year-round maintenance of the organ. The contract should specify monthly, or certainly seasonal, checks on the organ, with the understanding that the company in charge would tune it and make recommendations for repairs that are required.

It should be emphasized that the organ of the local church is in charge of the organist. No one should play the organ without his approval and/or supervision. Occasions will arise when guest organists will be requested for funerals or weddings. The Music Committee and the Official Board should firmly uphold the organist in terms of the use of the organ for such occasions. It is my judgment, from long experience, that the organist should have complete authority over the use of the organ in the church to which he has been called. Exceptional circumstances will always occur. But if the Music Committee and the Official Board will agree on a ruling that the organist should play not only for the recognized worship services but for weddings and funerals without exception, it is highly desirable.

IV. Soloists and Multiple Choirs

One of the most effective instruments of spiritual education is through a vital and inspiring musical program in the local church. Congregations that have a high percentage of young people and children in the parish will be vastly enriched by developing a multiple choir program.

The Music Committee, with the guidance of the choirmaster, will determine what soloists are required, what their payment shall be and their responsibilities for attendance at both regular and special services throughout the year. A simple letter of contract can take care of all items that will be involved in their attendance and number of occasions when they will be excused. This contract, developed by the Music Committee, should have the approval of the Official Board.

Where multiple choirs can be developed for the enrichment of the total and educational and inspirational program of the church, the Music Committee, again, must be the primary instrument for planning the strategy and support of the program. One church developed a series of goals for a multiple choir ministry. The objectives were established as follows:

GOALS FOR THE CHOIR SCHOOL
CHRIST CHURCH

The teaching of:

1. The basic Christian truths—
   Spiritual values must be built in each chorister. Through the use of hymns and anthems containing the thoughts fundamental to our Christian faith, each child may soon have as a part of him a vital and growing faith.
2. The art of worship and the practice of reverence—
   We must experience worship in order to comprehend it.

To this end the choirs will participate in worship services of the church that they may grow into a knowledge
of, and joy in, the worship of Almighty God.

3. The appreciation of beauty—
   Music is one of the mediums through which the beauty
   of God and the marvels of His creation are expressed.
   Developing an appreciation of this medium develops an
   appreciation for all the arts.

4. Correct and vocal habits—
   Children do not need to be taught voice-building; they
   only need guidance in avoiding faulty vocal habits. The
   child who spends fourteen years in the choir school program will know only the right way to use his voice.

5. The great music of Christianity—
   Through the choir program the children will learn music
   which may be called "great." They, as well as older
   people, will come to appreciate music of the highest
   nobility.

6. Cooperative endeavor—
   In order to have a choir sing beautifully, each individual
   must learn to cooperate with the group, to merge his
   personality with the whole ensemble. In so doing the
   individual personality and voice will steadily grow. This
   is possibly one of the greatest values from the program—
   the sense of cooperative participation in "the good, the
   true, the beautiful."

7. Self-discipline—
   Our aim is self-discipline rather than an enforced discipline. Through the exercise of self-control, needed to
   establish the mood of reverence through a service of
   worship, there will come a discipline for the child over
   himself that will be invaluable in the building of character.

In this particular church the choirs were outlined as follows, giving
definite dates and hours of rehearsal:

SCHOOL OF CHOIRS

FOR CHRIST CHURCH

Group   *Rehearsal*

CHERUB IV CHOIR

4 year olds . . . . Wednesday, 9:25 to 10 A.M.

CHERUB V CHOIR

5 year olds .... Wednesday, 4 to 4:30 P.M.
Activities period (optional), 4:30 to 5:15 P.M.

CAROL CHOIR

1st, 2nd and 3rd grades ...... Wednesday, 4:30 to 5:15 P.M.
Activities period (optional), 4 to 4:30 P.M.

CANTUS CHOIR

4th, 5th and 6th grades .... Thursday, 4 to 5:15 P.M.
(Combined rehearsal of both sections.)
a. 9:30 section sings for the first church school worship.
b. 11 section sings for the second school worship.

CARILLON CHOIR

7th, 8th and 9th grades .... Sunday, 7 to 8 P.M.
(W.F. meeting precedes rehearsal)

CHAPEL CHOIR

10th, 11th and 12th grades .... Sunday, 5:30 to 6:30 P.M.
(W.F. meeting follows rehearsal)

CLOISTER BELL CHOIRS I AND II

Junior high and high school .... Tuesday, 4 to 5:30 P.M.

CHANCEL CHOIR

Adults .... Thursday, 8 to 10 P.M.

COVENANTER MALE CHOIR

Men .... Second and fourth Thursdays,
5:30—dinner (optional)
6 to 7:15—Rehearsal

It is desirable that a leaflet be prepared during the summer to be sent to all potential participants in the choir program, showing the choir programs throughout the church year. Ingenuity can be used in photographs, line drawings and other appealing visual representations, which may be done simply on a mimeograph, to make the whole program arresting to those who are possible participants.

I have seen leaflets of choral programs in local churches that range from a very simple folder which outlines what is most important— the time of the choir rehearsal, the hours when the choir will be expected to sing at both regular and special services, and the individual's name and telephone number who should be called for additional information or for enrollment. Other leaflets have been filled with line drawings and photographs, provided such are within the music budget.

Each parish will develop its own program and the type of information that will give all individuals, from small children to adults, an essential understanding of the program of the various choirs of the local church.

V. THE CHOIR GUILDS

Choirs for pre-school and school children should each have a Choir Guild. The guild should involve the mothers of the children who participate. There should be a chairman and a vice-chairman. The program of the guild is essentially to assist the director of the choir in maintaining order at rehearsal, caring for the choir robes, assisting the children when they participate in a worship service in being properly robed, guiding them in their participation in the processional, and providing such hospitality as may be required at the rehearsal hour.

It is my judgment that the adult and/or Chancel Choir should have an organization. The Official Board, through its Music Committee, may very properly recognize the senior choir annually, in terms of a dinner or some kind of formal recognition.

An organization within the senior or Chancel Choir not only can be helpful on significant occasions such as an annual recognition occasion with the cooperation of the Music Committee and the Official Board, but it may be an instrument to provide other occasions throughout the church year when a deepening fellowship may be developed among the members of the Chancel Choir.

If there are multiple choirs in the church, and mothers guilds have been established to assist in the educational and supervisory program, it is a fine thing to recognize all members of the guilds at a worship service in the early fall. This can be done on an occasion when one or more of the choirs participate in the church service. Guild members' names should appear on the Sunday Bulletin and an appropriate, simple service of dedication should be made.

VI. SUMMER CHOIRS

Most of our Protestant churches adjourn the regular senior or Chancel Choir for the months of July and August. Here is an occasion when certain members of the parish may be engaged in a new experience—leading in the singing of hymns during the worship service. It is advisable to have one or more of the senior soloists to be a part of the summer service. In many churches, that individual will sing the Offertory solo or anthem at the appropriate time in the liturgy.

Many people love to sing, but cannot give their time to regular rehearsals, and feel they do not have the skills to participate in a regular choir. But a summer choir that may rehearse an hour before the worship service, may enlist the interest of many fine people and give them a sense of participation in the worship service which they would not have as members of the worshiping congregation.

If a summer choir is formed, the choir guild should appoint one individual to be present to assist in the proper robing of those who participate. The choirmaster will give his time and enthusiasm to the project. It is helpful to announce the formation of the choir a month or so before the first rehearsal, and members of the Music Committee should make special effort to tell people about this program, which might enrich their personal lives.

VII. HYMNS AND CONGREGATIONAL SINGING

Hymn-singing in the normal Protestant worship service provides one of the significant occasions for the participation of all worshipers. There are several principles with regard to the selection of hymns that are important.

a. The minister and organist or choirmaster should agree on the hymns to be sung each Sunday morning.

b. Variety should be planned, with hymns that are familiar and those that are not so familiar to the local congregation.

c. Hymn-singing may be a form of education, giving the congregation a sense of participation in forms of music other than those with which they have been familiar. A good idea is to select a "hymn of the month"—one with which the congregation is not familiar. They will sing that hymn for four Sundays, until all have a familiarity with it.

d. In many instances it is wise to print in the Sunday Bulletin the background of a particular hymn. Who was the author of the words? Who was the composer of the music? Are there other items of information that may enrich the meaning of both the words and the music of that particular hymn?

e. Some congregations have found it helpful to offer a survey on "What is my favorite hymn?" A simple mimeographed questionnaire may be given out at the worship service of the morning, asking for the worshipers to nominate their favorite hymns in order. The result of such a survey will indicate hymns of particular meaning to the congregation and will be helpful to those selecting the hymns for divine worship.

The choral and musical program of the church is an instrument of great teaching value. The wise Music Committee and Official Board, together with the pastor of the church, will devise ways to make this instrument one of high meaning to children and adults.

9

Publicity and
Public Relations

1. THE PUBLIC RELATIONS COMMITTEE

A permanent Public Relations Committee should be composed of key members of the Official Board. This committee should draw into its membership individuals in the church who are in the field of public relations and specialized fields of communication. The committee's report should be on the monthly agenda.

The size of the committee will be determined by the program of the local church and by the degree of involvement the particular parish desires in the local community.

2. LOCAL FACILITIES

Within every community there are many facilities that may be used to let the community know of special events occurring in the local church.

The Public Relations Committee should make contact with the local newspaper editor and ask about policies regarding church publicity. Operation within the guidelines he provides can be helpful to the church. Special advertisements may be placed. Special news articles should be sent to the religious editor or the city desk, in terms of the ground rules outlined.

Most local television and radio stations welcome announcements of special events in the local church. The Public Relations Committee should decide the individual responsible for sending announcements to these agencies of the press, radio and television. Announcements should be prepared in writing and sent several days ahead of the appointed time for announcement. Depending upon the local community, it may be advisable to have an individual of the Public Relations Committee telephone the announcer or editor, asking that attention be given to the scheduled event.

3. PASTORAL LETTERS

As the spiritual leader of the church, it is good, from time to time, for the pastor to send a pastoral letter to all members of the parish. If there is no regular bulletin sent to the parishioners, or a church magazine, the sending of a letter from the pastor to all the people may be of significance. The letter may be sent at a time of high spiritual meaning in the church year, such as the beginning of Advent or the beginning of Lent. A letter at occasions such as these will call parishioners to worship and to a deeper rededication.

There may be other occasions when it is appropriate for the pastor to send a letter to all members of the parish calling their attention to a particular need or cause.

Denominational causes and emergencies involving the commitment of a denomination should have priority, and, with the approval of the Official Board, a pastoral letter that conveys such emergency need may be particularly helpful.

4. BULLETIN BOARDS AND SIGNS

Where it is appropriate, the local church should place signs that will help travelers or individuals who are new in the community to find the church.

Bulletin boards should be of the highest simplicity. The name of the church, the denomination, the pastor should be identified. Someone should be charged with changing the bulletin board from Sunday to Sunday. No out-of-date announcement should be left on the board.

A number of denominations prepare signs, weatherproof and of a dignified nature, which can be purchased at modest cost and put at strategic corners indicating the direction of the church. Approval for the placement of the signs should be sought from local authorities. It may be of value, in a small community, to join with the Council of Churches in placing a sign or board at the entrance of the city, inviting travelers to worship at the church of their choice. Each church should have a proper indication as to denomination, and information as to hours of worship, in the clearest way. Signs and bulletin boards should have letters large and clear, not alone for pedestrians passing by, but for those driving in cars.

In cooperation with other churches in the community, it may be advantageous to cooperate with "the Welcome Wagon" or other groups welcoming people to the community, presenting a leaflet that will invite newcomers to worship, and give the specific location of churches in the area.

5. Letterheads, Postcards and Other Types
   of Correspondence Material

The basic letterhead of the church should state the name of the church, its address, town, state and zip code number. It is highly important that the telephone number appear on every type of business letterhead.

The name of the pastor or pastors should appear. It may be advisable to include the name of the director of Christian Education and the organist and choirmaster. This one type of letterhead may then be used by several departments.

Many pastors I have known have used a postcard-size card to be used for long-hand notes which they wish to send to parishioners at occasions when a more businesslike letter is not suitable. The postcard size requires a minimal of writing and may be sent in an envelope or as an open card.

Every church office should have an adequate supply of mimeograph paper with the proper letterhead printed on it. If it is needed in the local parish, social stationery should be always on hand.

A number of churches have found that it may be helpful, and in some instances profitable, to an organization within the church to prepare special stationery or Christmas cards, showing the altar or an attractive view of the church, which will be made available to the parishioners. In all instances where material of this type is ordered, the Public Relations Committee of the church should be consulted. Substantial savings can be made in large orders, adequate for several seasons.

In the ordering of any material for the church, the budgetary item should be considered. Consultation with the printer in the selection of the type and quality of paper and the design of the printing should be developed carefully. The printer should always provide a proof for final approval.

6. CHURCH PUBLICATIONS

Every parish will profit by the proper use of publications to communicate with members.

a. The Sunday Bulletin

There are several items to be observed in the design of the Sunday Bulletin. Among them I would list these:

1) Dignity.
2) Simplicity.
3) Creativity.
4) Information about parish activities, presented in the clearest possible fashion.
5) The Order of Service should be printed in such type face that the parishioner can read it at a glance. Small print and italics should be minimized.

A number of churches have constructively combined a message from the minister with the Sunday Bulletin, including the worship service, together with other announcements. A copy is mailed to each member in the middle of the week, prior to the Sunday service.

b. A Church Magazine

The Public Relations Committee, with the approval of the Finance Committee and the Official Board, will decide whether it is desirable to publish a parish magazine once a month, for nine or ten months of the year. If the decision is that a publication would assist the overall ministry of the church, the following points should be considered:

1) The publication should be informative, telling the story of parish activities. It is desirable to have a representative from each major organization of the church supply announcements concerning its programs and activities.
2) Photographs add to the appeal of any publication.
3) The periodical should be an instrument to convey to all

members of the parish information regarding specific members. One section of the publication should be devoted to births, baptisms, marriages and deaths. Items that have proved desirable are brief biographical sketches of the church's officers and leaders of its several departments.

4) An editorial by the pastor is in order. This can be deadly, or it can be one of the most delightful features of the magazine. One church publishes a monthly magazine widely sought by pastors throughout the country, primarily because of the pastor's incisive and pertinent editorials.

5) The periodical should be designed with the counsel of a printing and/or public relations designer. Visual appeal is highly important.
Variety in the style of type and format should be considered.

6) Consideration might be given to the use of advertising to defray the cost of publication. Some churches ask for a special contribution for the magazine. Others include it as a part of their annual budget. Each parish should determine the most effective way to handle the publication and distribution of the magazine at a minimum of cost and effort.

c. *The Annual Directory*

Many churches have found it helpful to publish an annual directory in the fall. The directory may be mimeographed at the least possible cost or be printed, with photographs, if the budget permits. In any event, it should include the following:

1) The church staff, names, addresses and telephone numbers.

2) The Official Board, names, addresses and telephone numbers.

3) All permanent committees of the Official Board, names, addresses and telephone numbers.

4) All church members, names, addresses and telephone numbers. If, in a particular parish, there is to be a division between local and out-of-town members, these should be listed in two separate categories. It is desirable, where there is husband and wife, that the wife's name be printed

in brackets following the family name, as: Mr. and Mrs.
John W. Abron [Dorothy].

5) A brief schedule of church events throughout the church
year should be included:

    Hours of Sunday Worship
    Communion dates
    Special services, such as Lent and Christmas
    Annual meeting of the congregation
    Any other regular annual meetings

6) Certain annual directories may helpfully include material regarding various organizations of the church. What
is their purpose? When do they meet? Who are the
officers? Where are the regular and special meetings held?
How does one make contact if there is a desire to participate in any of the meetings or programs? It may be helpful, if there is an extensive amount of material regarding
the church organizations, for a brief index to appear at the
front or back of the directory.

7) If such an annual directory is prepared, it should be
mailed to each family or member. A covering note or
letter from either the pastor or the Public Relations Committee of the Official Board should accompany the mailing. The note should request that the directory be kept
near the telephone and be used to contact church members.

8) Every church in our fast-moving society loses contact
with some of its members. The annual directory should
include names of individuals for whom addresses have
been lost, and request members who may have such information to provide it to the church office for "the lost
sheep."

9) Some churches have published a "supplement" to the
membership address and telephone directory. The supplement may go into greater detail, listing all standing
committees of the board, together with the responsibilities
of each committee. All officers of every organization may
also be listed. The advantage of having a supplement must
be determined by each individual congregation. Such a
supplement can be most useful to the leaders throughout
the church, whereas the information of a more specialized

nature which it contains may not be so desirable for the membership as a whole.

d. Annual Reports

Many congregations have found it useful to prepare for the annual meeting of the congregation materials that will show the work of the church throughout the preceding year. Reports from all organizations should be included. The desirability of such a document is evident. The material is made available for all members attending. They can read the reports quickly, thus eliminating a tedious reading aloud of every detail.

Included in the annual report may profitably be:

1) A brief introductory statement by the pastor.
2) The stated clerk's or secretary's report on the membership of the church, gains and losses.
3) The treasurer's report showing income and expenditures for the preceding year.
4) If there are assistant or associate ministers, written reports of activity for the year.
5) A full report by the minister of music.
6) The Christian Education director's report on the Church School. This should include departmental superintendents and all officers of the Church School; a statistical report of the number of pupils and attendance. Any pertinent material regarding the Christian Education trends or needs and recommendations should be included.
7) If the church has an endowment fund, a report on this, separate from that showing current income and expenses.
8) Reports from all organizations of the church, such as Couples' Club, Women's Association, Men's Clubs, and others. Financial statements should be included.

In view of the fact that this annual report may have only limited attention or appeal to the total membership, it is wise to print it as inexpensively as possible. Mimeographing the reports on 9×11 sheets, perhaps using different colors of mimeograph paper, has proved effective.

All key leaders who are to make reports should be notified of the deadline date. One individual should be in charge of the compiling, editing and preparing of the annual report. This individual will remind officers or appointees when they are remiss in sending in their material, and may also serve in an editorial capacity, seeing that the material submitted is clear to the reader and with a minimum of errors in spelling and punctuation.

Following the annual meeting it is desirable to have extra copies of the annual report available in the narthex and the church office or on literature tables for those who were unable to receive a copy at the annual meeting.

e. Sermons

The publication of the pastor's sermons and suitable distribution of them can be an effective instrumentality in widening the orbit of the church's influence.

If the Official Board decides that the regular publication of sermons is in order, it is proper to appoint a Sermon Publication Committee. The committee should be related to and report regularly to the Official Board, although the membership may be made up of representative members of the church who are regular in their attendance at worship. The committee should meet periodically, review the sermons recently preached, and decide on those for publication.

If the decision is to put the sermons in mimeographed form and simply make them available on the literature tables, the church office may handle such printing and easy distribution.

It may be the wiser course to print one sermon a month for ten months of the church year, and mail such sermons to the entire membership of the church. Some Sermon Publication Committees will see that sermons are distributed beyond the bounds of the church. One committee regularly placed sermons in the hospitals of the area. Others were sent to students away at school, to members serving in the armed forces, and to others such as chaplains in the armed services and on college campuses. Sermons printed in leaflet form, on 3 × 5 inch sheets, are extremely convenient. They may be easily mailed or placed in a man's pocket or a lady's purse.

The method for the payment of publication should be determined. Some churches find that an annual letter inviting the membership to share in the cost of the printing and distribution of the sermons provides sufficient funds. Other churches find it desirable to include the cost for the publication in the annual budget. From my experience, an invitation for church members to "subscribe" annually is not desirable.

Ideally, the sermon publication leaflet should include the

name of the chairman of Sermon Publication Committee, with the address where he may be reached.

f. Departmental Publications and Notices

The Christian Education Department may find its program enhanced and its communication to all children enriched by a periodic bulletin informing students of anticipated and planned programs, and also containing any items of particular interest. Certainly from time to time throughout the church year the director of Christian Education must inform students and their parents of the calendar of the church school. All such material should be planned on the basis that it should be brief, clear, state the facts, and be of interest. It cannot be said too often that our church members receive a wide variety of mail. Reading time is limited, so the more succinct bulletins or notices are, the more likely they are to receive attention and response.

The Music Committee is another department that may wish to prepare special bulletins and notices and other leaflets regarding its program. I have long felt that it is desirable to provide each participant in any program or activity of the church with an annual calendar of the events of that department or division. If such are prepared at staff conference in the spring or summer, or early fall, and distributed before the beginning of the program, any change that is made will require that a notice be sent to all involved.

g. Special Leaflets and Brochures

During the church year it may be appropriate to prepare special leaflets and brochures. One such occasion is the Lenten season. After the careful planning and programing of worship services during Lent, it may be helpful to prepare a modest leaflet, approximately 3×5 inches, that can be carried easily in the pocket and easily mailed, describing the hours of special services, as well as regular ones, for this holy season.

Christmas is another occasion when a special brochure may be printed—"Christmas and the New Year at Christ Church."

Other special leaflets may be those that are made available to strangers and newcomers to the community. Leaflets of this type should be as brief as possible, but with full informative material. Such leaflets may have to do with:

The history of the church

The inconography of the windows
The memorials in the church
Other items of interest

Denominational publication houses and bookstores of various types increasingly are making available a wide variety of leaflets that may be helpful in the development of individual spiritual life. The selection of such materials and the method of their distribution and availability is a matter that should receive the careful attention of the pastor and possibly a Spiritual Life Committee or a specially appointed Literature Committee.

Every organization of the church that engages in the preparation and distribution of any kind of leaflet, brochure or special letter should be informed that the Public Relations Committee is always available for consultation. The wise chairman of every department and activity of the church will be free from "any sense of pride of authorship" and will welcome revisions and suggestions made by the chairman of the Public Relations Committee, or perhaps one individual of that committee who may be appointed to assist any one of the church departments.

10

The Maintenance of
Christian Education

There are basically four important elements for effective control in maintaining an adequate standard of Christian Education in the church. They are as follows, and will be described in turn: (1) The Christian Education Committee; (2) Recruitment and Training of Teachers; (3) Records That Are Meaningful; (4) Teaching Materials.

1. THE CHRISTIAN EDUCATION COMMITTEE

The Christian Education Committee, appointed by the Official Board, shall be responsible to it, and should make regular reports, as each of the standing committees is called upon to do.

The duties of this and of all committees should be carefully outlined. A suggested outline for the Christian Education Committee follows:

a. The Christian Education Committee is in charge of the oversight and coordination of the church's program of Christian growth and nurture.

(1) *Duties:* To plan and supervise the work of the Sunday Church School.

(2) To plan and supervise the youth organizations of the church (not choral groups unless requested).

(3) To coordinate the work of the Scout Committees (Boy Scouts of America and Girl Scouts of America) and supervise the God and Country Award work.

(4) To plan and supervise the adult study groups, the vacation church school, the camp and conference programs and the recruiting and training of leadership.

(5) To give aid and counsel in the educational activities of all organizations of the church.

(6) To provide materials for missionary education, stewardship, social education and action, and the nature and purpose of the church.

(7) To have concern for the spiritual growth of the membership (in both personal and family life).

(8) To assist the pastor in arranging for communicant classes.

b. The committee is directly responsible to the church's assistant in Christian Education. (The pastor is an ex-officio member of the committee, without vote.)

This committee may also be charged with the finding of a director of Christian Education, when such a vacancy occurs in the staff. (An outline of a job description for director has been detailed elsewhere in this volume. See pages 100-102.)

2. RECRUITMENT AND TRAINING OF TEACHERS

The effectiveness of any religious education program will be determined by the leadership of the director and the quality of the teachers and their spirit of dedication. The matter of recruitment is a task for the whole church. Utilization should be made of the church magazine, the Sunday Bulletin and by individual enlistment of the most capable individuals in the church for particular teaching offices. A service in the early fall, dedicating all leaders and teachers in the Christian Education Department at divine worship is most appropriate. At this time a special prayer for the whole educational aspect of the church will be made. The names of all teachers will appear in the bulletin, and the Lord's blessing will be invoked upon them and their work.

Utilization should be made of opportunities for training sessions. Usually this is done cooperatively with several churches. All teachers should be urged to attend.

One church has devised its own teacher training program, developing quarterly seminars, at which time, in addition to special lectures and group meetings, there are specialized departmental gatherings. An outline of the material covered at such a meeting is as follows:

CHURCH SCHOOL FALL SEMINAR
CHRIST CHURCH   September 9, 19___

PRIMARY DEPARTMENT

CURRICULUM—Christian Faith and Life—Teacher's quarterly magazine is *Opening Doors.* The reading book for the October–December quarter is *People of the Promise,* and will be distributed September 20. These books should be kept in classrooms for use during the quarter and then may be taken home.

MEMORIZATION PROGRAM *(To be completed by November 15)*
    1st Grade—The Lord's Prayer
    2nd Grade—Selected Graces
    3rd Grade—100th Psalm (King James Version)

SPECIAL ACTIVITIES
    1st Grade—Old Testament Coloring Book (one per student)
    2nd Grade—Stained-Glass Windows (one per class)
    3rd Grade—Worship the Lord Murals (one per class)

AUDIO-VISUAL PROGRAM—On the second Sunday of each month special films (which have been selected to supplement the curriculum) will be shown: Noah and the Ark, Joseph in Egypt, The First Noel, Baby Moses, Ten Commandments, Joshua, the General, Call of Samuel, and David and Saul. Additional filmstrips, records, maps, etc., are available on request from the Audio-Visual Library (third floor).

MUSIC—Hymns sung in worship services will be taught by Mrs. Jones (assistant to Mr. Davis) in Carol and Children's Choirs.

CHURCH VISITATIONS—Primary children will visit the main sanctuary for the first part of the worship service on November 19, February 18 and at such other times as indicated in the department schedule. Pews will be reserved in the front of the church. Recession will take place during the singing of the "middle hymn."

STORIES (take-home pieces)—Commencing in October, *Stories,* the bi-weekly magazine for primary children, will be distributed to 1st, 2nd and 3rd graders as "take-home" pieces.

SUPPLIES—Each room is supplied with crayons, pencils, scissors, construction paper, etc. Extra supplies may be obtained from Room 105. *Please replace all paste jar tops,* and other supplies after each class session.

TEACHING PICTURES—Each classroom is provdied with a complete set of teaching pictures and are to be used as suggested in *Opening Doors.*

CHAPEL SERVICES—Generally the superintendents will conduct the worship services in the Martin Luther Chapel. These services are patterned after regular worship services with some modifications. Teachers are requested to sit with their students during the chapel service.

TEACHER-TRAINING PROGRAM—In addition to the fall seminar, quarterly departmental meetings will be held. Also, teachers will benefit greatly from the Old Testament Prophets' Lectures, Quarterly Pre-Views, which include demonstration classes and presentation of quarterly materials by professional instructors, and other programs to be announced.

The familiarization of each teacher with the quarterly program ahead and with the materials and resources available will assist in developing an effective program.

At the beginning of the Church School year each teacher should be made acquainted with the materials needed for an effective teaching experience. It may be desirable to present each teacher with a mimeographed "manual." Such a manual will outline the room numbers of the classes, the names of all teachers, their addresses and telephone numbers. Ideally, there should be a substitute teacher for each class. Such names also will appear in the manual. A calendar for the Church School year should be included. Also, the teacher-training program should be outlined—the time, the place, the subject.

The budget for the Church School year, and any information concerning benevolent expenditures should be included.

A statement of aims of Christian Education and other materials that will raise the sense of commitment to the teachers are appropriate. Information should be included regarding the Church Library and any special books or materials available to assist the teachers in their program.

The teachers should be exposed to the finest and most practical methods of teaching. One Christian Education program included in its annual manual the following section:

WHAT MAKES A GOOD TEACHER

1. Friendliness
2. Preparation
3. Her own conduct—deportment
4. Promptness—arrival ahead of time for classes
5. Alertness to techniques of seating, lighting, moving about
6. Rapport with pupils
7. Good relationship with other teachers
8. Sensible division and use of time
9. Use of a variety of materials
10. Recognition of accomplishment
11. Living witness to a healthy personal faith
12. Depth of worship responsiveness

THE WISE TEACHER . . . .

. . . . . understands the characteristics of each maturity level.
. . . . . establishes a close working relationship with parents.
. . . . . lets boys and girls know she is their friend.
. . . . . knows what to overlook.
. . . . . builds confidence and self-respect by words of praise and appreciation.
. . . . . is consistent in what she expects in the way of behavior.
. . . . . gives a classroom a "lived-in look."
. . . . . watches temperature, fresh air, lighting, physical comfort.
. . . . . trusts children in small things.
. . . . . provides periods of rest and activity.
. . . . . is concerned about each child's physical health, emotional needs, and social adjustment.

Teachers in the Church School need the same characteristics as those in public or private schools, PLUS a radiant faith that is catching, and a willingness to learn more day by day from the greatest of all teachers, Jesus Christ.

3. Records That Are Meaningful

A properly prepared registration card can be helpful, not alone for the immediate information it provides, but for permanent information regarding the enrollee as the following suggested form will indicate:

CHRIST CHURCH SCHOOL

REGISTRATION FORM

New registration ☐   Date ....
Previous enrollment ☐

Name .... Nickname ....
     (last)   (first)   (middle)

Address ....

Date of birth .... Public school grade ....

Baptism: Yes .... No .... When and where ....

Father's name .... Church affiliation ....

Mother's name .... Church affiliation ....

Department .... Teacher ....

Session: ☐ 9:30 A.M.   ☐ 11:00 A.M. ....
                                                 Registrar

Church School processing:

☐ P. E. card   ☐ Family card   ☐ Cradle Roll
☐ Junior Hi Club   ☐ Youth fellowship   ☐ Pledge card

A carefully prepared permanent record is invaluable. A suggested form follows:

Name _____ Address _____ Telephone _____

Father's name _____ Occupation _____ Member of what church _____

Mother's name _____ Occupation _____ Member of what church _____

Date of birth _____ Baptized _____ Enrolled in Church School _____

Attended Communicant's Class _____ Joined church _____

Year	School	School Grade	Ch. Sch. Grade	Church Teacher	School	Attendance Sun. Pres.	Special Activities and Other Information
			Crd. Roll				
			Toddlers				
			Nurs.				
			Kind. 1				
			Kind. 2				
			Prim. 1				
			Prim. 2				
			Prim. 3				
			Junior 4				
			Junior 5				
			Junior 6				
			Jr. Hi 7				
			Jr. Hi 8				
			Y Chap. 9				
			Y Chap. 10				
			Y. Chap. 11				
			Y Chap. 12				

233

4. TEACHING MATERIALS

The Christian Education Committee, on recommendation of the director of Christian Education, will survey and approve the curriculum materials to be used by the teachers in the Church School and in the total educational program. Such materials will be available at the appointed time of the class meetings.

The importance of providing additional teaching materials that may enrich the presentation of the teacher cannot be overemphasized. Many churches find it desirable to have a place in the church where additional materials to be used in teaching may be available for instructors.

If the church decides to have a church library, careful consideration should be given to the types of literature available in the local library. The church should not compete with institutions that have resources and a staff beyond that which can be provided by one local congregation. The teachers should be informed of special material available in the library or the "teaching closet" of the church. Maps, adequate and clean blackboards and any other equipment of this kind desired by the teacher should be provided.

Audio-visual aids can be effective tools in teaching. The educational leadership in each local congregation should survey the sources of effective audio-visual material. Denominational boards of Christian Education have departments that prepare and provide materials of this nature. Many local churches are developing audio-visual materials which are kept on hand and made available to the Christian Education Department, much as the Music Department acquires music and catalogues it for use in the ministry of music.

One church, in developing its audio-visual library, prepared a brochure available to all teachers and leaders in the educational program. The catalogue listed each item, slides, motion pictures or filmstrips. Other materials can be included in such a brochure—disc recordings, tape recordings, charts, posters, photographs and special maps. Symbols can be used, such as, b/w for black and white, and C for color. The symbols on audio-visual materials were broken down as follows:

N—Nursery (up to 3 years)	JH—Junior High (12–14)	YA—Young Adults (24–40)
K—Kindergarten (4–5)	SH—Senior High (15–17)	A—Adult (over 40)
PRI—Primary (6–8)	YP—Young People (18–23)	PAR—Parent
J—Junior (9–11)		L/T—Leaders/Teachers

Each item should be identified by a code number. The aim and synopsis of the material should be identified clearly and briefly. The running time should be indicated in terms of minutes. Also, there should be indication whether there is available a script or a guide which the teacher may use as the various frames of the material are shown.

The introduction to this audio-visual teaching material catalogue could well have a foreword such as the following presentation:

FOREWORD

The weight of evidence indicates that when the proper audio-visual materials are correctly used, the aims and purposes of the church are more effectively accomplished. Research has proved that approximately 50 per cent more is learned with the use of audio-visuals, and in certain specific subjects, up to 85 per cent. Since the church has so little time with each individual—only an hour or two a week in many cases—the teacher should remember that audio-visuals make for more rapid and meaningful learning, for longer and more accurate retention.

There are some basic factors in the proper use of audio-visuals which should be borne in mind. These are:

1. Determining the purpose; what is to be accomplished by its use?
2. Selecting the type of audio-visual to best assist in the achievement of the purpose, then deciding the specific material to be used.
3. Reserving the audio-visual materials for the date desired.
4. Preparing for its use; preview; study of leader's guide, if available; integrating it with other instructional material. Is it to be used to introduce subject or summarize it? Will it prompt discussion?
5. Preparing the room for audio-visual use.
6. Preparing the group by statement of purpose; discussion prior to its use; questioning the group to sharpen observation.
7. Following through to see that purpose is achieved.

Just as there are these things to be thoughtfully considered prior to and following the use of audio-visuals, there are some pitfalls to be avoided:

1. Audio-visuals are NOT INTENDED as ENTERTAINMENT.
2. They are NOT "baby sitters" to keep children quiet.
3. They are NOT SUBSTITUTES for a teacher NOR for good teaching.

4. Failure to preview the audio-visual can result in embarrassment, presentation of unsuitable or undesirable material, or loss of opportune learning experience.
5. Failure to allow sufficient time for discussion and follow-through can minimize the effectiveness of the audio-visual's use. If necessary, use only a part of material that is too long.
6. Faulty preparation and use of equipment can cause situations which negate the value of the audio-visual as a supplemental tool in teaching.

It is hoped that this catalogue will assist those involved in Christian education, and those who lead the various church organizations, to a better knowledge of the audio-visual materials available for their use. To this end and to the greater fulfillment of Christian principles under the spiritual guidance of the Living Lord, this work is dedicated.

The creative Educational Committee in the local church will constantly be seeking and providing to teachers and leaders materials that will assist the overall task of informing men and women and boys and girls of the heritage and the tasks and the hopes that make up the Church of Jesus Christ.

11

The Individual
Church Member

1. THE OUTREACH PROGRAM OF THE CHURCH

The local church will be attentive to new individuals who move into the community and a letter of welcome to them is appropriate. The following is a sample:

CHRIST CHURCH

(Letter of welcome sent to those who are newly arrived in town. Names obtained from credit bureau or other agencies.)

Mr. and Mrs. . . . .
Address . . . .
Address . . . .

Dear Mr. and Mrs. . . . . :

Word has reached us that you have recently moved to Central City. The officers and members of Christ Church most heartily welcome you and your family. We trust that you will be very happy here. Our church desires to help you make your transition into this community one that will be most fulfilling for each member of your family.

We cordially invite you to attend our services of worship held each Sunday at 9:30 and 11 o'clock. At 9:30 a.m. there is a complete Church School, including nursery through adult classes. At 11 a.m. the Church School includes a nursery group through grade 9. In addition, there are many other activities to serve all interests.

If there is any service that we can render you or yours, please call on us.

Cordially yours,

Allen Jones
Minister

AJ:jh
Enc.

P.S. If you are already a member of another local church, please accept this letter as a sincere expression of welcome to our community.

Such individuals should be called on by the pastor or one of the church officers or a member of the Outreach or Evangelistic Committee of the church.

Strangers visiting the church for a worship service should be greeted with cordiality and introduced to as wide a number of parishioners as possible. Many churches find it desirable to have a coffee hour following the worship service. Here is provided an occasion for the mingling of church members and strangers.

A greeting may most fittingly be sent to those who attend church for the first time. A possible note along this line is as follows:

CHRIST CHURCH

(To people attending worship services in Christ Church for the first time.)

Mr. and Mrs. . . . .
Address . . . .
Address . . . .

Dear Mr. and Mrs. . . . . :

I am happy to note that you were in attendance at church on Sunday, April 25, and that you signed a visitor card. I trust you felt the friendly Christian spirit that is present in our church fellowship.

We strongly believe that every Christian should have a church home near home, and hope we can be of help to you. Be assured this church stands ready to serve you in any possible way.

The minister and the whole church staff are here to make your church relationship meaningful. A member of our Board of Deacons will be calling you soon. Do come and worship with us again, and feel that this is your church home.

Sincerely,

John J. Lee

JJL/mg

Contacting New Members
Moving into Community

The names of new members moving into a community may be obtained from a number of sources. It may be desirable for the pastor to contact the local bank, real estate agencies, and the local Welcome Wagon agent, to gain their cooperation in giving the names of new people who move into the community. According to the policy of the local utilities companies, here again may be a source of names of people moving into the area. Individuals should receive a greeting from the local church.

A modest leaflet describing the work and activities of the church may be very appropriate. Such a leaflet should include the following:

a. Name and address of the church and the telephone number.
b. The name of the pastor and other key members of the staff, and where they may be reached and at what hours.
c. The hours of the worship services.
d. The Church School, its hours and program.
e. Organizations of the church should be included. The name of the organization, age limits, if any, where the group meets, when, the name of the key officer to be contacted, together with address and telephone number, must be included.
f. The choirs of the church may be listed. Here again, the individual to be contacted should be given, together with address and telephone number.

g. Occasions for the Sacrament of the Lord's Supper should be included.

h. A brief editorial or word of greeting from the pastor is in order.

If the church has developed an Outreach Committee, the committee should meet regularly, and names should be assigned. The committee members should be trained in how to make an effective call. Information should be supplied to all members so that they know the program of the church and can answer any questions from those on whom they call.

The committee should report back, and a careful record should be kept in the church office of calls made on prospective members. Any information that may be obtained concerning the individual or family called upon can prove invaluable for the future.

2. Inviting and Receiving New Members

Nothing can replace the personal influence of a call in the home of a prospective member, by the pastor or an officer of the church. Some larger congregations may precede the personal call in the home with a letter of invitation to join the church. The letter should be carefully phrased and should provide the occasion when the individual is to meet with the officers of the church, if that is the custom, and also the date when the church membership reception will be held.

Some churches find it helpful to prepare, in either printed or mimeographed form, a statement regarding any particular requirements of church membership.

Most churches receive individuals on their confession or reaffirmation of faith, or by letter of transfer. The enclosed material with the invitation, should make all of these details clear, and should indicate that the pastor of the church will write for the letter of transfer, if that is desirable.

Each new member should fill out an information card so that the church records may be accurate. One such form is as follows:

CONFIDENTIAL INFORMATION FOR THE CHURCH RECORDS

Name (in full) . . . .
                              (Wife—give maiden name)

Address . . . . Telephone . . . .

Business Connection ....

Business Address .... Telephone ....

Date of Birth .... Married ...... Single ......
       Month   Day   Year

Parents' Names in Full (if under 21) ....

....

Parents' Church Affiliation ....

HOW RECEIVED

Have you been Baptized? Yes .... No .....

Do you come

a. By Confession of Faith ...., or

b. By Reaffirmation of Faith ...., or

c. By Certificate ....

If you come by (b) or (c), what is the name of the church with which
you were formerly connected, and its address:

    Name ....

    Address ....

    Shall we send for your letter? Yes ...., No .....

Have you previously engaged in some form of service in churches and
Sunday Schools? If so, please specify ....

....

Members of the family who are not members of this church:

Name .... Age ....

Name .... Age ....

At the same time that the new member fills out this basic information, there should also be provided another form that asks about interests and skills of the new church member which may be utilized in the congregational life. One such form, to be used for adaptation for each local church, follows:

ENLISTMENT FOR SERVICE

To be a Christian is to serve according to our abilities and talents. Please check the things which interest you.

Radio Station ....□
Teaching ....□
Pianist ....□
Women's Organization ....□
Sewing Guild ....□
Church World Service ....□
Choir (name voice part) ....□
Westminster Fellowship ....□
Business and Professional Young Adults ....□
Mariners (Married Couples) ....□
Faith at Work Groups ....□
Girl Scouts ....□
Volunteer Office Help; Secretarial; Clerical ......□
Visiting ....□
Ushering ....□
Helping with Church Dinners ....□
Church Newspaper ....□
Helping with Nursery ....□
Children's Church ....□
Junior Church ....□
Helping in Friday Night School ....□
Men's Missionary Society ....□
Women's Prayer Groups (Friday Afternoon) .....□
Church School Class ....□
Others I Am Interested in ....□
....
....

3. INTEGRATING THE NEW MEMBER INTO THE CHURCH LIFE

A Certificate of Church Membership should be given to each individual who is received into membership of the church. Most denominations provide suitable certificates which may be obtained through church bookstores or other avenues of distribution. In some instances the local church may wish to prepare its own certificate of membership.

The Service Book or the Book of Common Order of the denomination will be followed in receiving new members in a public ceremony, into the fellowship of the church. Every effort should be made to inform the entire congregation of the names and addresses of the new members. This may be circulated not alone through the Sunday Bulletin, but the church magazine, and in some instances by a special letter that will be sent to neighbors of the new member in the area where the residence is established. Such a letter might suggest that the new member be called upon and welcomed by fellow parishioners who live in the neighborhood.

A number of churches have found it desirable to provide the new member with materials regarding the history of the church denominationally and also of the local congregation.

If the new member has indicated certain interests in various organizations or voluntary services that might be rendered for the church at the time of reception into membership, one member of the staff should see that this information is passed on to the proper individual. For instance, if the new member has indicated interest in singing in the choir, the notification should be given to the choirmaster or director of music, who will immediately follow up, calling on the new member and inviting participation in that program. It has been wisely observed that every human being is sensitive and every human being wants to feel the sense of acceptance. No possibility should be overlooked to make the new member acquainted with the church, with its people, with its program, and with those individuals who may share similar interests, backgrounds and skills.

4. THE PASTORAL RELATIONSHIP TO EACH MEMBER

The minister, as spiritual leader of the church, will do all in his power to achieve a friendly personal relationship with each member of the "flock." This is done by regular pastoral calling. Where a congregation is of such size that one pastor alone cannot call at the homes of members on an annual basis, other ways must be found to develop the sense of the pastoral interest in each individual. This may be done in part by notes sent to individuals in the church on their birthdays, and on other occasions of significance and meaning in their lives.

Special groupings within the church membership should have special attention, such as students away at college, members of the church serving in the armed services, and out-of-town members.

Young parents who have brought their children to the church for baptism should have particular attention from the pastor and director of Christian Education. The child should be enrolled in the Cradle Roll. A birthday greeting should be sent, and material that may be helpful to young mothers and fathers as they establish their family may suitably be sent from time to time.

Most of our churches sing the hymn, "Blest Be the Tie That Binds." That beautiful hymn suggests that we share each other's woes and bear each other's burdens, and in the fellowship of Christ, love and support each other. Any way that the total congregation may be made aware of the illnesses, the tragedies and the joys of the individual member will be helpful in fulfilling this supportive pastoral function. The church magazine and Sunday Bulletin should carry notices of baptisms, weddings, deaths, illnesses. A church may be deeply enriched by the formation of prayer groups that regularly meet for meditation and prayer, and for special prayers of individuals in the parish who have special needs.

One congregation, in connection with its annual yearbook, published the entire membership of the church in terms of the street numbers. Any individual whose address was, for example, 180 Ashland Avenue, could readily note that the Herr family lived at 168 Ashland, the Greens at 167, and the Davis family lived at 183.

5. The Older Church Member

The "senior citizens" of the local church require special concern from the pastor, the Official Board, and the congregation. The effective church will develop a file of older members and those who are shut-ins.

Particular attention should be given in the program planning of the church for special activities for men and for women who are in the retired and "senior citizen" period. Here can be a reservoir of wisdom and usefulness to the church. Many people in this category can give voluntary service to the church office in its mailings and other required duties that can benefit the staff and also be a source of satisfaction to those who participate. One church has made a survey of the skills and backgrounds of retired men, and has enlisted their agreement to consult with any young people in the particular fields that have been theirs, who desire counsel and guidance as they develop their careers.

Many local churches have found it an instrumentality of help to organize senior men and senior women's programs. Lectures, service projects, varied tours and study programs can make up the agenda for the year.

Some older people cannot drive automobiles or are without them. The thoughtful parish administrator may consider the organization of car pools. Individuals will volunteer to bring to the church service or special activities older individuals who otherwise might not be able to attend and participate.

Individuals who are semi-invalids should receive continuous loving attention. A special committee may suitably be organized and authorized to give continuous attention to shut-ins. Calling on such individuals with regularity, remembering their birthdays, mailing them the Sunday Bulletin from the church, and from time to time bringing them flowers from the church altar, constitute one of the gentle and fulfilling ministries of the thoughtful parish which serves in Christ's name.

Special recognition of the older members who have served the church for many years may be appropriate. The annual meeting of the church provides an occasion to give particular recognition to those members of the parish who have been longest in its membership.

6. THE SICK AND HOSPITALIZED MEMBER

When the church member faces illness or serious hospitalization, the pastoral "heart of the church" should be there. Repeated announcement should be made that the pastor desires to have the entire membership be helpful to him in giving information regarding people who are ill or hospitalized. The thoughtful pastor, in his call, will know "how long to stay and what to say." Reading matter with a high spiritual content may be appropriately left at the bedside.

The Altar Guild should be informed of members who are ill, and should regularly distribute the altar flowers to those who are in the hospital or ill at home. The pastor or an appointed member of the staff should be responsible for giving to the chairman of the Altar Guild or Flower Committee each Sunday the names of individuals who properly should receive flowers from the church. Many congregations include with the flowers a card that expresses the concern of the whole congregation. Such a card may be extremely simple, saying,

"These flowers are from the sanctuary of your Church. They were on the Communion Table when the hymns were sung, the prayers offered and the sermon was preached. May they convey to you the message of your fellow church members that you were missed, that our love is with you, and our confidence that God's Grace is upholding you."

In instances where the parish has a sizable membership it may be desirable to form a group of individuals who will assist the pastor in calling on the ill and hospitalized. Such individuals should receive careful training and instruction. Often the healing process for people who are desperately ill can be furthered by "staying away." No visit or counsel should be offered without assurance that the patient may be benefited. The family, doctor, and nurse should be consulted before any visit.

7. CONGREGATIONAL PROGRAMS

Special programs and activities for each group and for special interests can be as varied as the needs of the men and women and boys and girls that make up the parish. A list of such can go on almost to infinity. A number of areas that should be considered by a thoughtful pastor and the Official Board are the following:

a. The men's club
b. The women's association
c. "Senior citizens'" activities
d. Church volunteers
e. Couples' club
f. Annual congregational meetings
g. The church fair
h. Drama
i. Special lectures
j. Evangelistic services
k. Youth conferences
l. Summer camps
m. Officers' retreats
n. Prayer groups
o. Conventions and conferences
p. Recreational and cultural programs
q. Youth programs
r. Activities for college students
s. Scouting
t. Contact with military personnel
u. Social service programs
v. The physically handicapped
w. Special worship services
x. Nursery school
y. World missions

A quarter of a century ago, Dorothy Canfield wrote about "Hillsboro People." In her portrayal she pictured Mrs. Brownell breaking her leg. This meant something definite to all of the community, because some action had to be taken. Miss Canfield pointed out that the oldest daughter, who was of a sickly nature, wouldn't get the care she needed if somebody didn't step up to help out. There was a bright son in the family who would have to leave school just when he was about to win a scholarship for college. There was many a crisis in human lives which called forth, not just sympathy, but some active response and participation. She went on to say, "In other words, we are not only the characters in our unwritten dramas, but also part authors. Something of the outcome depends on us." Effective congregational programs, clubs, groups, service activities, should be marked by this spirit.

Basic Principles for Congregational Programs

To provide detailed suggestions and blueprints for each possible congregational program and activity could well involve a number of volumes. However, there are certain basic principles regarding any and all congregational programs that are established to enrich the fellowship, educational emphasis, spiritual deepening, or service outreach of the individual church.

a. It should prove that the proposed activity or program is in keeping with the overall objective of the church. A study should be made and the report of the survey conveyed to the Official Board with appropriate recommendations. Such surveys in all probability will come through the instrumentality of the pastor, and usually in connection with an already established standing or special committee.

b. Every organization and every activity of the church should have the approval of the Official Board. Regular reports should be made to the Official Board through an appointed representative or through an overseeing committee of the board. At the annual meeting a full report should be prepared and presented for the congregation as a whole.

c. Every activity and program within the congregation that has had Official Board approval should have the enthusiastic assistance of the staff in helping the leadership in making the activity or program effective.

d. The special programs and congregational activities should be reviewed annually at a retreat of officers and staff to evaluate their effectiveness. It is understood that suggestions and recommendations will be in order and thoughtfully received from the Official Board as to how programs and activities may be improved.

e. The Public Relations Committee of the church should be sensitive to assist all of the church organizations and special activities in achieving the maximum influence in terms of the particular purpose for which they were intended.

f. The Finance Committee of the Official Board, in like manner, will serve as consultant and cooperate with the treasurer of each organization and any activity that involves the receipt and expenditure of funds.

g. Many a wisely administered church will appoint one individual from the Official Board to be "consultant, adviser, friend" to the individual organizations and clubs within the congregational life.

h. The wise pastor and the sensitive Official Board will seek to involve the maximum number of individuals in the church in the participation in its educational fellowship and service life as well as in its worship. This will involve a spirit of openness and creativity, a spirit that will never forsake the primary aim of the church to serve the cause of Jesus Christ and to enrich the lives of men and women and children through His spirit and teaching. But it will also recognize in His name and spirit that new occasions teach new duties, and that fresh problems require new ways of answering them.

Any and every church will fulfill its mission for Jesus Christ if, with its leadership, it looks at Him, engages in prayer, is sensitive to the needs of its people, seeing them through His eyes and His heart, and uses as its guidelines those virtues which Paul called the greatest of all: "Faith, Hope, and Love."

Index

A

Administrative Assistant duties, 102
Administrator, duties of, 75
Agenda for meetings, 41ff
Annual budget, 180ff
Annual directory, 221
Annual inspection, 108
Annual reports, 223
Annual staff conference, 89
Appreciation for gifts, 192
Architect, 175
Assistant Minister job description, 97
Audio-visual aids, 234ff
Audit, annual, 203

B

Baptisms, 136f
Board room, 163
Brochures, special, 225
Budget, annual, 180ff
Budget, control, 204
  preparation, 183
Building committee, 174
Building projects, 173ff
Bulletin Boards and signs, 218
Business Manager, duties, 74, 103
Bylaws, 4ff

C

Canvassers for Every Member Canvass, 187ff
Capital fund raising, 176
Chapel, 168

Check list for public worship, 159ff
Choir robes, care of, 113
Choir rooms, 164
Choir school, 211
Choirs, multiple, 211ff
Christian Education Committee, 227
Church office equipment, 116
Classrooms, 168
Committees, 15, 25, 28ff
  efficient functioning, 49
  responsibilities of, 30ff
Communion ware, care of, 114
Congregational programs, 246
Correspondence, handling of, 117
Correspondence material, 219

D

Dedication, new building, 177
Dedication of pledges, 199
Director of Christian Education, duties, 100f
Director of Music, duties, 100
Directory, annual, 221

E

Education in stewardship, 196ff
Equipment, care of, 110f
Evaluation Study and reports, 60f
Evangelism, 33
Every Member Canvass, 185ff
Executive Committee, 2

F

Files, for the church office, 118
  for the pastor, 115
Finance Committee, 180ff
Financial reports, 40, 184
Fire equipment, 170
First aid equipment, 167
Funds, handling of, 183
Funerals, 140ff

G

Groundbreaking ceremony, 177
Grounds Committee, 107f
Guilds, for choirs, 214

H

Heating system, care of, 111
Holidays, 94
Holy Communion, 147f
Hospitality Committee, 51ff
Hospitalization, 78
Hospitalized church members, 245
House and Grounds Committee, 107
Housekeeper and kitchen personnel, 105
Hymns and congregational singing, 215

I

Installation of officers, 17
Insurance, types of, 110
Interview of staff personnel, 76, 81
Inventory and appraisal, 108

J

Job description, organist and choirmaster, 208

K

Kitchen, care of, 112

L

Letterheads, 219
Literature racks and tables, 165
Long range planning, 59
Lord's Supper, 147f

M

Machine room, 126
Magazine for local church, 220
Mail, handling of, 117
Maintenance Committee, 152f
Marriages, 128ff
Meetings, preparation for, 35
  agenda for, 41
  conduct of, 37
Membership records, 119
Memorials, care of, 171
Memorials Committee, 204
Minister, as administrator, 1
Minutes of meetings, 45
Music Committee, 206
Music Council, 207

N

Newcomer, welcome of, 160
Newcomers to the community, 239
New members, reception of, 240
New members and stewardship, 197
Newspapers, used, for public relations, 217
Nominating Committee, 11

O

Office hours and other details, 95
Office and study of pastor, 114f
Officers, how to select, 11ff
Official Board, duties of, 12
Older church members, 244
Ordination of officers, 17
Organ, authority for use of, 211
Organ, care and maintenance of, 111, 210
Organist, choirmaster, 100
Organist, job description of, 209
Organizational charts, 20ff

P

Parlor, 164
Pastoral letters, 218
Pastors, duties of, 74f
Personnel Committee, 65, 80f
Personnel policies, 77f
Pledge history records, 122ff
Primary Department, 229

Principles for congregational programs, 249
Projectors, use of, 163
Property, care of, 108f
rules concerning, 171
Proportionate giving, 195
Public Relations Committee, 217
Publication of the pastor's sermons, 224
Publications of the local church, 220

R

Reception of new members, 240
Records, Christian Education, 231ff
Records, financial, 200
Records of new members, 241
References for employees, 75f
Reports, pastoral, 37f
financial, 40
Restroom facilities, 166
Retreats, 63f
Review of staff work, 82

S

Safety equipment, 170
Salaries, 78
Sanctuary preparation for worship, 127
Schedule, weekly, 95
Seasonal publicity, 225
Senior Minister, job description, 96f
Sermons, publication of, 224
Sextons, 104
Sick and ill, 245
Signs, demonstrational, 218
Soloists, 211
Special gifts, care of, 171
Special leaflets, 225
Staff, determining need for, 67f
duties of, 72f, 92
introduction of, 79
supervision of, 83
Staff, annual conference, 88
in relation to Official Board, 27
meetings, worship, etc., 84
Stage and its equipment, 162

Stained glass windows, 113
Statement, monthly, 200
Stewardship education, 194
Summer choirs, 214
Supervision of staff, 83
Supplies for church office, 124
Supply closet, 126
Symbolism of the sanctuary, 160

T

Teacher, a good one, 231
Teachers, recruitment of, 228
Teachers, training of, 228
Telephones, rules governing, 125
Treasurer, bylaws concerning, 9
Treasurer and financial statements, 200f

U

Ushers and ushering, 154f

V

Vacations, 78
Ventilation, 152
Vestments, care of, 114
Vision in planning, 55ff
Volunteer workers, 104f

W

Weddings, 128ff
check list, 135f
fees, 135
regulations, 133ff
Welcoming newcomers to the community, 237
Woodwork, care of, 112
Work schedule, 90
Worship, check list, 159f
preparation for, 127

Y

Youth rooms, 168